Date Due

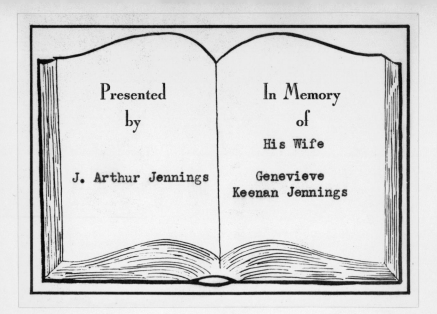

Presented
by

J. Arthur Jennings

In Memory
of
His Wife

Genevieve
Keenan Jennings

Music

IN YOUR LIFE

Music
IN YOUR LIFE

THE LIVES OF THE GREAT COMPOSERS

BY DELOS SMITH

HARPER & BROTHERS PUBLISHERS NEW YORK

42113

MUSIC IN YOUR LIFE

FIRST EDITION

H-G

Library of Congress catalog card number: 57-10253

For Jeannette Reynes Smith

Contents

Acknowledgments

The author gratefully acknowledges his indebtedness to Woman's Day magazine, which first published these "lives," and particularly to Donald Parker Hanson, its publisher, and Mabel Hill Souvaine, its editor, who initiated the project and encouraged its completion.

Introduction

In reporting the pageantry of musical geniuses across five centuries, which is the content of this book, I had what no objective reporter should have: a point of view. This was the notion that each one of these geniuses was a human being before he was a genius, remained a human being despite his genius, and never, even in his flights of genius, rose above his humanity. When stated that baldly it sounds like something no one could argue with. It is basic enough to be commonplace. Yet, while not unique, it is by no means the usual point of view of musical geniuses among musicians and musical people.

The usual point of view is that the essence of musical genius is superhuman and, therefore, the genius is both apart from and infinitely above human beings; so let everyone become prostrate, utter sounds of rhapsodic praise, and refrain, please, from looking into, under, or behind the godhead. One must deplore that. Aside from being silly, it makes music a cult and people who enjoy music cultists. The fact is that music is the most accessible of all the arts. It requires only functioning ears and a receptive mood.

Perhaps we'll never really understand the nature of musical genius. But we'll never so much as approach understanding unless we make a point of having a close, hard look at the human beings in whom genius resided. No matter what musical genius is, it is a human phenomenon fabricated exclusively from human materials. Human phenomona should never strike human beings as weird, strange, superhuman, and inexplicable, although, of course, they do.

The methods applied in these studies of the forty-six geniuses who created the overwhelming bulk of the music in your life and mine are reportorial. It couldn't have been otherwise. I am a reporter by trade. I have dug out all the facts, I have sorted them, I have arranged them in the order of their relative importance and significance, so that I might say to you as an honest reporter, here is the man as he was, here is what he did and what was done to him. Make of it what you will. As for me, I neither prove nor disprove, blame nor defend, glorify nor defame.

My attitude has been as objective as I could make it. Many people say pure objectivity is impossible. However that may be, it is the highest ideal of my trade and I have never ceased striving earnestly to achieve it. But that is not to claim I haven't subjectivity in me. Although it is a private matter, I don't mind saying that if music were taken from my life, the loss would be grievous and, perhaps, insupportable. Privately, I believe the forty-six geniuses described in this book are among the greatest human beings who ever existed. Indeed, it is my private belief that Wolfgang Amadeus Mozart was the greatest of all human beings. It pains me exquisitely to have to report to you, in my professional capacity, that he was something of a nincompoop.

Taken together, these forty-six lives make up the known history of music. Before Palestrina were the Dark Ages; he is the first giant who comes striding down to us out of the unknowable past. He and the giants who followed were the telling forces in the evolving, shaping, and channeling of the musical art from Palestrina's time to our own. To be sure, this book is no technical history because it was not written for technicians, musicologists, or musicians except to the extent they are interested in the musical giants as human beings. Within these covers not one fugue is dissected and there is not one gasp over the appearance of an inharmonic chord in bar 73. I have refrained from musicianly shoptalk and double talk. The effectiveness of the art of music is not in how music is made but in how it strikes you, the listener, after it is made. The fact is the "laws" and "rules" are so far from governing that all it has ever taken to shatter them has been a little genius.

Music

IN YOUR LIFE

1

Palestrina

T HE very first giant in the history of music was Giovanni Pierluigi of the town of Palestrina, 25 miles from Rome. His was one of the really great musical minds of all time—comparable to those of Bach, Mozart, and Beethoven—and its influence reaches down to the present day.

When he was born, well over four hundred years ago, such arts as painting and sculpture were in the full flower of the Italian Renaissance. Michelangelo was fifty years old, Leonardo da Vinci had been dead but six years, and Raphael only five. But music was just emerging from its dark ages and was being preserved in printed, and therefore inheritable, form for the first time. We can assume, however, that a genius like Palestrina's must have culminated centuries of musical evolution.

He was born—this progenitor of our modern music—probably in 1525, but maybe in 1524. The Pierluigis were ordinary and unmusical people. Even then, Palestrina, their home town, was quite obscure. Some of his ancestors evidently were living there in the very ancient days when Rome ruled the world. Portraits of him present classic Roman features. He was one of the four sons of Sante Pierluigi and his wife, Palma. There was no reason to suspect he might turn out differently from his parents. Indeed, it is remarkable how very much like them he always was except in the one particular that gave him immortality.

Near the house where he was born was the cathedral of St. Agapit, familiar to him from his earliest days. His parents were noted for piety as well as for industry, and so was he. In those days, the solemn choir singing in churches and the frivolous singing and lute playing in the noble courts were just about all the music there was. The latter wasn't accessible to people like the Pierluigis.

He was still quite young when he became a member of St. Agapit's choir. Clearly, he made an extraordinary impression. When he was nine or ten, the bishop of Palestrina, Andrea Cardinal della Valle, became archpriest of the Roman basilica, St. Maria Maggiore. The cardinal valued music. He took the boy to Rome with him and put him into the basilica's famous choir and choir school.

About ten years later, Palestrina returned home, a music master. He became organist, assistant choir leader, and singing teacher of St. Agapit's. The appointment was for life, and the youth settled into the post as though he intended keeping it that long.

Father and Mother Pierluigi owned two houses and several vineyards, and Father was handy at turning small but profitable, deals. They were most aware of the comforts afforded by worldly goods, and they looked around for a wife for him, one who would bring a proper dowry. Lucrezia Gori was the choice. Her dowry consisted of a few fields, a vineyard, pots, pans, mattresses and other housewares, cash, and a donkey.

Thus fortified, he began his career of model husband and, in due course, of excellent father. When he wasn't busy with his church duties, which included composing music to accompany the Mass and other services, he was busy with the vineyard, the donkey, and petty real-estate trading. We can see he wasn't dreaming great dreams, or even dreaming, for he did not consider himself merely an obscure church musician in an obscure town. In his mind, he served God, and the town of Palestrina was the world.

In 1551, the reigning Pope died. His successor was the bishop of Palestrina, Cardinal del Monte, who ascended the papal throne as Julius III. He knew the quality and promise of the musician back home in St. Agapit's and lost little time in appointing him head of the Julian Choir of Rome's mother church, St. Peter's. This choir had been founded by Julius II in 1513 and by now was one of the most celebrated musical organizations in the world. Thus an obscure musician in his middle twenties was catapulted overnight into prominence.

He took it in calm and calculated stride. To him, it was a better job but with the drawback that he had to move, with his wife and their two babies, Rodolfo and Angelo, to Rome. Yet, he was practical to the core. He composed a Mass in honor of his all-powerful patron and had it published, at his own expense, with four earlier Masses, all lavishly dedicated to Julius.

The Pope showed his pleasure and appreciation by appointing Palestrina to the Pontifical Choir, a stupendous honor. Belonging to it was like belonging to a musical House of Lords. Membership was supposed to be limited to thirty-two—a member had to die for a new one to be appointed. By tradition, the choir could pass on the Pope's appointee.

Julius simply overrode these restrictions. The choir's secretary entered into the record, with manifest resentment, that the new member —this unknown youth—had been admitted "by order of our Lord, the Pope, without examination and without the assent of the singers." But the new member, who gave up the tedious duties of master of the Julian Choir, had every right to feel he was set for life. Six months later he was expelled.

By then, the Pope was Paul IV, who found it shocking that there were married men in the Pontifical Choir—Palestrina and two others. He was shocked that several members had not only composed madrigals about love and life—the madrigal was the popular song of the day—but had also published them with the notation that their composers belonged to the Pontifical Choir. Palestrina had offended here, too.

We can imagine the harshness of the blow. Nevertheless, Palestrina was preoccupied with a matter of much greater importance to him —the composition of the work posterity has always considered his masterpiece. Marcellus II had reigned for only three weeks after the death of Julius. An aged and godly man, he had made a very deep impression on Palestrina. The result was **Missa Papae Marcelli (Mass for Pope Marcellus)**, to this day a model of liturgical music.

With his habitual efficiency, he was taking care of his practical troubles. He wrangled a pension from the Vatican to compensate for his forced "retirement" and soon was in charge of the music at the basilica of St. John Lateran, among the more important of Rome's many churches. He bought the wine used for sacramental purposes at wholesale and sold it to the priests at retail prices. He took Rodolfo into the choir, since it meant free board and free education. But he was methodically composing, day in and day out, piling up the Masses and motets, the hymns, offertories, lamentations, the litanies, psalms, magnificats, and sacred songs.

There was never a time when he lacked important friends. But we must not think he was a toady. An entry in the chapter books of St. John's, dated August 3, 1560, shows he wasn't. It recorded that the "director of the choir has gone off without notice, taking his son with him, because he would not abide by the recent decree of his superior authority that nothing more than 25 julios a month be allowed for the boys' victuals." Musicians, then, were not supposed to question "superior authority." To walk out on it was unthinkable. Another case in point—Guglielmo Gonzaga, Duke of Mantua, was an amateur composer who sent manuscripts to his friend for criticism. No true courtier ever criticized a duke, even on invitation. Palestrina did.

About this time—he was thirty-five years old—people began to call him "The Prince of Music." It was an age of princes—princes ruled the world, and he was beginning to rule music. To his contemporaries, the power of his devotional music was undeniable. The eminent musicologist, the late Sir Donald Tovey, said he was "God-intoxicated."

While being God-intoxicated, he was on intimate terms with some of the worldly noblemen of the day. One friend and patron was Ippolito Cardinal d'Este, of the enormously wealthy, princely family, who created the Villa d'Este at Tivoli, one of the most beautiful palaces in the world.

But life among the worldly was not for Palestrina. In 1569, in the introductory remarks to a book of his motets, he spoke critically of composers "who devote their gifts to light and vain ideas." As for himself, he was "mature" now, and "whatever gifts I possess, although they may be of little account, will in future always be devoted to something more dignified and serious, worthy of a Christian being."

The following year, when he was forty-five, he returned to the service of the Church, again as master of St. Peter's Julian Choir, and that post he held for the remainder of his life. By then, titles meant little to him. He could have had just about any musical post, church or private.

In his family, he was the senior member and, therefore, the master. As a religious man, he expected immortality in heaven through his devotion to God. And he seemed to know full well his music was going to make him immortal on earth, provided he could get it transmitted to posterity. But he also expected immortality from descendants who would carry on his name.

He was tenderly watchful over his three sons. Rodolfo now was entering manhood. Angelo wasn't far behind. They had been carefully educated in the classics, in languages, in theology, and above all, in music; and their musical talent warmed their father's heart. Iginio was still a boy—he was undergoing education which eventually was to bring him a doctorate in law as well as high competence as a musician.

For all its brilliance, the Renaissance was not a happy time for people. There almost always was a petty war raging somewhere on the Italian peninsula, and periodically waves of pestilence and famine killed many thousands. In 1572, Rodolfo, then about twenty-two and without issue, died in an epidemic.

Palestrina turned to Angelo, who was about nineteen. He decreed that Angelo must be married at once and selected the bride—a girl of good family and with enough of a dowry to be worthy of the son of the master of the Julian Choir, naturally. In less than a year, Angelo was a father, but of a daughter. In a little less than two years, Angelo was dead, victim of another epidemic. His second child was born afterward, and this one was a son.

We have no way of knowing what comfort this infant was to his grandfather. We do know that, for the first time, Palestrina wasn't composing, and we can believe he was having difficulty bearing up. His wife, Lucrezia—his wife now for twenty-eight years—must have supported him as he supported her. But five years later, when a new epidemic swept through Rome, Lucrezia died. To this last blow, his first reaction was to plan his retirement from the world by entering the priesthood. In the midst of his preparations he met an attractive widow. She was forty-two; he was fifty-six. In her he seemed to find the promise of the peaceful domesticity he had known with Lucrezia. They were married in February of 1581. Lucrezia had died in July, 1580.

The bride's late husband had left her an extensive retail business in furs and hides. He began operating it, and most successfully, but as a kind of side line, for he was composing again. The profits he invested shrewdly in real estate. The profits from these deals he used to publish his music.

Music publishing then was extremely costly and, because there was no possibility of profit, music was published only at the composer's expense. Many composers of the time didn't bother unless they had wealthy patrons to stand the cost. Palestrina consistently bothered throughout his career. It seems clear he was bidding for our notice, since we are his posterity. Thanks to his foresight, we have available to us almost 100 of his Masses, over 250 of his motets, more than 150 of his madrigals, 41 hymns, 66 offertories, and a miscellany of other works.

His last years were devoted to business, composing, and publishing —and to the personal affairs of his remaining son, Iginio, who was only nineteen when his father found a well-dowried bride for him. In time, Iginio fathered eight children. Only two sons survived childhood. One became a priest; the other married and fathered one son, who became a priest. Since Angelo's son had died in childhood, the composer was defeated along this road to immortality. He was defeated in the main along the musical road as well, because posterity has given him the name of his home town and has largely forgotten that his name was Pierluigi.

Palestrina died in 1594 and was buried in St. Peter's. On his coffin was engraved: "Prince of Music." Ninety-one years later, Johann Sebastian Bach was born. One hundred sixty-two years later came Mozart, and one hundred seventy-six years later, Beethoven. But his successor in the line of musical giants, Claudio Monteverdi, was already living and twenty-seven years old.

Counterpoint, which is the art of combining melodies into music fabric—existed before Palestrina's day. He perfected it to the point where others have been unable to add anything substantial, and he developed structure and form. His experiments pointed the way for many innovations of latter-day composers. From any scholarly point of view, he was the father of the "father of modern music"—Bach.

Palestrina's music belongs to its own century, and sounds quaint to a superficial twentieth-century ear. Also, it is liturgical, built around sacred concepts and themes. That also discourages performance in public concert halls. Finally, most of it was composed for voices without instrumental accompaniment, which isn't popular today.

2

Monteverdi

CLAUDIO MONTEVERDI'S music speaks to us with directness and immediacy, as though he had been living and striving during a recent yesterday. But that yesterday was a long time ago. The word "modern" must be made to cover more than three centuries to call him the first modern composer. Yet, certainly, he was the first user of modern harmony, the first composer of music dramas, the genius who presided over the infancy of opera. It's startling to hear him anticipating such a latter-day revolutionist as Richard Wagner and even some of the innovators of our own time.

He was music's first identifiable revolutionist—a man of daring and imaginative originality. He endowed music with humanistic qualities, or perhaps we should say he clothed human emotion in musical dress. At any rate, we know to whom "Divino Claudio" was speaking. It was to us, very personally.

Cremona, a town in north Italy, which was the birthplace of the greatest violin makers—Amati, Guarneri, and Stradivari—also gave rise to this superb musician, who was born there in May of 1567. On which day in May is now unknown.

His mother's name is thought to have been Maddalena; otherwise she and everything about her are forgotten. We do know he was the eldest of five children, and his father, Baldassare, was a physician and a man with considerable means and broadness of mind and spirit.

Baldassare saw to it that Claudio was well educated—in letters, in philosophy, in science, and especially in music, since music seemed his native bent. The boy published his first compositions when he was fifteen. Pedants now point to their errors, yet no one can prove that persons such as he ever make errors in truth, even when young. One thing is certain—these boyhood compositions display a mastery in the manipulation of forms which many learned graybeards never achieve.

When he was twenty-two or thereabouts, he journeyed the forty-

7

some miles to Mantua and became a viol player in the splendid court
of the reigning duke, Vincenzo Gonzaga. There, for more than twenty
years, he maintained himself as a moral man, and with much difficulty
and sorrow, in the midst of such calculated moral rot as the world has
seldom known.

This Vincenzo was the son of Duke Guglielmo, who had been
a patron of Palestrina. Vincenzo was a wastrel and a sensualist, so
notorious that, centuries later, when Giuseppe Verdi's librettist
needed an archtype of sensualist in his opera, **Rigoletto,** he chose
"The Duke of Mantua."

In Vincenzo's day the Italian Renaissance had passed the point
of perfect ripeness. Now it was overripe, and the duke was not un-
typical of the elite of the age. He was civilized to exquisite fineness.
His tastes in music, in art, in literature were informed and dis-
criminating. But pleasure was his only interest.

He evidently was quick to recognize the genius of the young musician who was composing madrigals of pure and unique beauty for
his court, and for a while Monteverdi appears to have been a member
of the duke's inner circle. After a time he seemed not to like the
musician, while still liking the musician's music very much. This was
inevitable. As the duke got to know the young man well, he had to
find out he was more than pure of heart—he was incorruptible.

Such a young man was not the kind of intimate Vincenzo found
entertaining and upon whom he bestowed generous favors. For one
thing, Monteverdi was interested in only one woman. For another,
he was keenly interested in working. Either attitude would have bored
Vincenzo to the point of pain.

The musician was disapproving of his patron and so very clever that
he could express himself insultingly to the ducal person without ever
seeming to be other than a respectful vassal. Vincenzo, being clever
himself, could read clearly what his musician had said between the
lines. So he piled work upon him but gave him no more in recognition and money than he was compelled to give.

Four times in twelve years the top job in his musical establishment
—*maestro di musica*—became vacant. Three times he passed over
Monteverdi in favor of a time-serving nonentity. The fourth time he
gave Monteverdi the job. He might have lost him if he hadn't. By
now, Monteverdi was going back to his father's home in Cremona
and staying for weeks at a time when he could endure no more of the
duke and his ways.

Meanwhile, he had married the one woman in his life. She was
Claudia Cattaneo, a singer, and daughter of another of the duke's
musicians. Their first son, Francesco, was born in 1600; their second,

Massimiliano, in 1604. According to legend, perfect conjugal love blessed this Claudio and Claudia. But it was short-lived. She died in 1607, twelve years after they married. Although Monteverdi survived her for thirty-six years, he never married again.

Claudia was in frail health for a long time. During the last year of her life, Monteverdi was at work on **Orfeo**, the first opera composed by a professional and also the first composed by a genius. Opera had had a secluded beginning in a nobleman's palace in Florence in 1597. In February, 1607, **Orfeo** was performed by the ducal singers and musicians for the court at Mantua.

Claudia's death came on September 10, in the home of her doctor father-in-law in Cremona. Fourteen days later, a peremptory command was sent to Monteverdi to return to Mantua at once and get to work. The duke's eldest son and heir, Francesco, was getting married the following year; the festivities were to go on for many months. The court had been delighted with **Orfeo**, and the duke and Francesco wanted more operas like it.

Monteverdi probably was glad to have work to do, since it could deaden his grief. He composed an opera, **Arianna**, and an opera ballet, **Il Ballo delle Ingrate**. For the role of Arianna, he selected Caterina Martinelli, who was not quite eighteen and who, for five years, had been living in his home and receiving musical instruction. Monteverdi regarded her as a daughter—he called her his Caterinuccia. While **Arianna** was in rehearsal she came down with smallpox, and died on March 9, 1608. This was only six months after he lost Claudia. The double blows were just about all he could bear. Yet he had also to bear the insensate harassments of Vincenzo and Francesco, who were striving to make the wedding festivities the Gonzaga masterpiece in prolonged and extravagant pleasure seeking.

We can imagine the burdens of a composer who also was *maestro di musica* and so responsible for every detail of innumerable and all but continuous musical performances. In June he retreated again to Cremona. There seems no doubt he was exhausted and ill. But he also was embittered. A number of his letters have survived, and from them we can see how adroit he was in insulting the duke by indirection.

During this visit to Cremona he wrote the ducal treasurer: "I have received a letter from Your Honor from which I gather that His Highness commands me to hold myself in readiness to return to Mantua as soon as possible in order to tire myself out once again with exacting tasks. At least he so commands. . . ." He detailed how the duke had shortchanged him over the years, and then said, "I am fully aware that His Highness easily alters his intentions."

He got his father, the aging Baldassare, to write the duke's long-suffering wife and ask her to "beg your illustrious consort" for his son's release from service.

Whether he was waging a campaign or not, we don't know, but Vincenzo signed a decree in January, 1609, which settled a not ungenerous annual sum on Monteverdi for life. But the composer still had trouble getting money from the ducal treasury, which was flat broke.

Nevertheless, there was no further trouble for well over two years —until February, 1612, when Vincenzo died. Francesco succeeded, he who admired Monteverdian operas. One of his first acts as sovereign was to dismiss the *maestro di musica*. We have to assume he was only trying to show Monteverdi who was the duke—that he wanted to discipline him rather than get rid of him—because within weeks he was trying to get him back.

Monteverdi made the most of this. After more than twenty years of service, he had only "twenty-five scudi" to show for it, he said. (The scudo was worth something less than a dollar.) This bitterness he spread far and wide.

Francesco made some conciliatory overtures. He ordered a revival of **Arianna**. Then smallpox intervened and killed both Francesco and his son and heir. Ferdinando, his brother, became duke but he was too busy for a while with the tangled affairs of the duchy to seek out the family's dismissed maestro.

At this juncture, the *maestro di cappella* of the church of St. Mark in Venice died. This was one of the very best musical posts in all Italy. The pay was high, the tenure was for life. What's more, the maestro got a free residence. Without having made application or so much as raising a hand, Monteverdi was elected to the post—such was his fame. He was forty-six years old.

Through all the thirty years of his service, the republic of Venice never ceased being delighted with him—nor he with it. Note the flexibility of the man. He, the revolutionist, who had changed and was changing the entire mechanism of musical composition, restored the traditional polyphonic church style of Palestrina at St. Mark's, where it had fallen into decay. This was what his employers wanted of him, so he gave it to them.

In his spare time he was furthering his revolution in harmony and advancing opera as music drama by composing operas for various princely courts, including that at Mantua. Ferdinando had been after him to give up his republic employ and return to that of a prince. This gave Monteverdi the chance to exercise his irony and sarcasm, yet the Gonzagas persisted.

Monteverdi composed the opera ballet, **Tirsi e Clori,** and four full operas for their court before 1627, the year of doom for the house. Ferdinando died in 1626. His brother-successor, the last of the male line, died the following year. A war over the succession broke out. In 1630, Mantua was sacked and burned. Lost in this carnage were many Monteverdi manuscripts, including that of **Arianna** (of which only a fragment, the famous **Lament,** has survived), and all the late Mantuan operas.

His Venetian years were as serene as circumstances permitted. His elder son, Francesco, studied law but gave it up in 1620 and became a friar. The younger, Massimiliano, was graduated from Bologna University in 1626 as a doctor of medicine, like his grandfather. When he began practicing in Mantua, some of the other doctors trumped up a charge against him with the Inquisition and he was thrown into prison. His loving father, after much suffering, got the charge dismissed.

This was followed by the burning of Mantua and the disappearance of many Mantuan friends. The same year the plague broke out in Venice, and before it ended sixteen months later, forty thousand persons died. This appalling piling of horrors may have caused Monteverdi to take the step he now took—which was to become a priest. It may be he would have taken the step when Claudia died if he hadn't been the father of two small children. But now he was Reverendo Monteverdi—"Divino Claudio."

He was sixty-five years old. For a while he composed only sacred music, while plunging more deeply into the musical chores at St. Mark's. But opera still was close to his heart, and soon there were more services he could do for it. Since its birth it had been the toy of princes. It became the property of people in general in 1637, when the first opera house was opened in Venice. For the first time anyone who could buy a ticket could hear and see music drama.

Such a turn had to excite the old priest. He began composing operas again. The first one of his old age was produced in 1639. Two years later he had two more ready, and the following year, 1642, when he was seventy-five years old, he composed the fourth, **The Coronation of Poppea.** It was produced that fall. A little over a year later, on November 29, 1643, he died. In that year the birth of Alessandro Scarlatti was seventeen years away.

Only four of Monteverdi's sixteen operas survive, of which **The Coronation of Poppea and Orfeo** are considered the finest musically although neither can stand up as opera today. Madigrals and sacred works survive in abundance; also arias and other fragments from the lost operas.

3

The Scarlattis

THERE were two musical giants whose names were Scarlatti, Alessandro and his son Domenico. Anyone who wants to believe creative genius is inheritable may point to them—until he is asked to account for Domenico having been the only genius among Alessandro's ten children, and for Alessandro having had seven brothers and sisters not one of whom was a genius.

Alessandro was born in Palermo, Sicily, May 2, 1660. Of his family we know nothing except that his father was a musician by trade. Alessandro was a musician by inner compulsion.

To us his childhood is a blank. We encounter him first in Rome when he was in his late teens, being driven along by his insatiable desire to "make" music in the most literal sense—to create music out of his own inner substances, whatever they were.

Musicians in his day served princes or nobles, in which case they were known only to the princely or noble court. Or musicians served the Church, and in that case personal humility, including a large degree of anonymity, was required of them. Or musicians could serve the public generally, although this was something quite new.

Alessandro served courts and the Church to the extent needed to establish and advance himself. His eyes were on the larger public. He knew how to genuflect to a king or a queen, a prince or a cardinal; he licked exalted boots with a fine skill. But it was a matter of form—the accepted thing. Exalted people were useful. From our distance in time, he appears to have had no use for the humility, anonymity, or seclusion which had been the lot of composers before him.

Rather, his urge was to create music conspicuously. So he made himself the first popular composer, the first to cater to popular tastes. After his start in Rome, where he acquired a wife and became the father of three sons and two daughters before he was twenty-four, he took charge of the Royal Opera in Naples, where he spent the rest of his life (save for occasional leaves and one extended period elsewhere) laying the musical foundations for the opera we know today.

Soon after Alessandro's arrival in Naples, his sixth child, Domenico, was born, on October 26, 1685. This was a standout year in music, by the way; in addition to Domenico, it saw the birth of Johann Sebastian Bach and George Frideric Handel. As in the case of Alessandro's childhood, no record whatever survives of Domenico's. Yet we can have an idea of what it was like.

There was a small home—composers couldn't support large ones. It was crowded by a mother and her six children to whom another and another and another, up to a total of ten, were added at suitable intervals. In this small, crowded home Alessandro was working like a veritable fury, composing operas, arguing with librettists, receiving singers and players, instructing pupils in various instruments, particularly the harpsichord, of which he was a master. All the children who came out of this home were musicians. It would be a wonder only if they hadn't been.

Sometime in his very early teens Domenico began composing. When he was seventeen he was appointed organist of the Royal Chapel in Naples. But the most impressive testimonial we know about came from Alessandro himself. It was written in 1705 by which time Alessandro had made himself one of the most famous if not the most famous musician in Italy—the year in which he was able to boast of having composed 88 operas in 23 years, and in recognition had acquired the noble title "cavaliere." (Incidentally, the end was not in sight; he was going to compose 114 plus a mass of other vocal music, particularly chamber cantatas.)

Domenico was not yet twenty when he presented himself to Prince Ferdinand of the house of Medici, which then reigned over Florence and Tuscany, with a letter of introduction from his father. "Royal Highness," Alessandro wrote, "my son, Domenico, brings himself humbly with my heart to the feet of your Royal Highness in observation of his and my debt of profound consideration and most humble obedience. . . . This son of mine is an eagle whose wings are grown."

Eagle though he was, he was the most self-effacing—and the sweetest —of eagles. Surviving documents attest to that, and also agree on the somberness both of his mien and his habitual dress. The eighteenth-century English musical historian, Charles Burney, gives an account of him as a young man, in describing the experiences of Thomas Roseingrave, an Irish musician, while visiting in Venice.

Roseingrave was invited to a musical party in the palace of a nobleman, along with a number of other musicians. He was invited to play the harpsichord for the company and felt he played quite well, which was confirmed by warm applause. A little later "a grave young man dressed in black and in a black wig, who had stood in one corner of the room, very quiet and attentive while Roseingrave played, was asked to play."

Burney continued: "When he began to play Rosy said he thought ten hundred devils had been at the instrument. He never had heard such passages of execution and effect before. The performance so far surpassed his own, and every degree of perfection to which he thought it possible he should ever arrive, that if he had been in sight of any instrument with which to have done the deed, he should have cut off his own fingers."

Around this time the young man was making his choice of whether to be a public and most conspicuous musician like his father or a private, secluded musician very much unlike his father. It wasn't a choice made in its entirety in an hour or a day, but one evidently made by degrees, slowly, and most probably, with pain. But what the choice was going to be was inevitable all along. Father was aggressively outgoing; son was passively inturning.

Until he was thirty-four he was father's pawn and was moved this way and that. For some ten years he was around Rome benefiting from being the brilliant son of the even more brilliant Alessandro, who was affectionate and proud in his regard for his prodigy, but also quite proprietary. Thanks to Alessandro, Domenico had a high musical post in the Church, was a private composer and performer for an exiled queen, a cardinal, and assorted nobles.

During these Roman years he was also making moves in Father's direction—he composed fourteen operas. But twelve were for private performance and only two intended for public opera houses. At the age of thirty-four, he gave this up and abandoned his posts in order to accept service as chapelmaster to John V, king of Portugal. To understand what this meant, we must keep in mind that Italy then was the music center of the world and Lisbon, in Portugal, was a musical limbo. Since he spent the rest of his life in limbo, musically speaking and from obvious preference, we can hardly believe it meant nothing.

We may believe Alessandro was disappointed. Yet, so far as we can tell there was no real estrangement between father and son. Domenico returned to Italy to visit his family in 1724, which was the year before Alessandro's death, on October 24, 1725, at the age of sixty-six. Domenico returned to Italy only once again, to marry Maria Catalina Gentili in 1728. We have to assume this marriage was by arrangement, since he hadn't been around to be attracted by the girl or to court her. She was only sixteen and by now he was forty-two.

From the start of his duties in Lisbon he had been the music teacher of the king's daughter, Maria Barbara. She had been only eight when his instruction began, an intelligent and charming child, no doubt, since history remembers her as an intelligent and charming woman. At the time of his marriage, she was seventeen and only a few months away from her politically motivated marriage to the crown prince of Spain. After her marriage, she asked her father for his chapelmaster, and got him.

No matter how devoted, in a paternal kind of way, he may or may not have been to the young princess, following her into Spain was as complete a renunciation of the conspicuous world of music as he could have accomplished. It was a sharp step down from the distinction of being a reigning king's chapelmaster; it was a far retreat into the seclusion of very private musician. And he remained the princess' private musician for twenty-eight years, that is, until he died.

And also, we have every right to believe, her close and private friend. By her own bent and through his tutelage she had become a first-rate musician. Music was both her passion and consolation throughout her tedious and troublesome life. Musically she was the most fortunate of royal personages—to have had a major musical genius at her beck and call from the age of eight onward; and also to have had the capacity to appreciate his merits fully.

Since private friendships of royalty are always cloaked, the records are scant. What records there are indicate she made no demands and couldn't do enough for him; they make it rather clear that he insisted upon obscurity for himself, with her indulgence. During all the years of his service, he took little if any part in the musical activities of the royal court. He had nothing to do, evidently, with the official music; he was not displayed in the various royal palaces for the benefit of courtiers and ambassadors as an exhibit of superior royal tastes.

He played the harpsichord for the princess—and for her husband, too, since the prince's love of music was also intense. And that, we can believe, was all that was required of him, although, to be sure, its value was a great deal since there can be no doubt that he was one of the greatest masters of the harpsichord who ever lived. So far as we know, this surpassing virtuoso never once in the whole course of his life played his instrument for a paying audience.

Domenico was getting along in years when he went to Spain with his princess, and he hadn't yet composed one thing which would have given him a greater distinction in our eyes than that of being one of the ten children of Alessandro. His composing is shrouded in almost as much mystery as is the private man. His fame to us and his place in the hierarchy of composers rests upon his 555 sonatas for the harpsichord. Their composition began about this time, and it seems apparent that they came into being under stimulation from the princess.

She was a master of the instrument, and so he would have wanted to provide such a patroness with music to play which would delight her. Since she was a musical sophisticate, with very exacting tastes, to please her would have put him on his mettle. We can imagine from their content that many of these sonatas were originally improvisations —free flows of fancy as he played for her. Realizing that, it is not hard to imagine the princess insisting that he get these free flows onto paper so she could play them herself.

Most of them were published during his lifetime, in volumes issued periodically. We have no possibility of ever knowing but we may wonder what the princess had to do with their being published. The composer wrote a short preface to the first volume. It sounds real and sincere. "Reader," he wrote, "whether you be dilettante or professor, in these compositions do not expect any profound learning, but rather an ingenious jesting with art, to accommodate you to the mastery of the harpsichord. Neither consideration of interest nor visions of ambition, but only obedience moved me to publish them."

Maria Barbara was crown princess for twenty years before she became queen of Spain. During that time her power to do things in a royal way was limited by the fact that her father-in-law, Philip V, was thoroughly dominated by his second wife, who had no love for Philip's eldest son and heir and, so, no love for the son's wife. We guess Maria Barbara tried to finesse a Spanish title for her musician and failed.

We guess that because her father bestowed a Portuguese knighthood upon him, which gave him the title of "Don," nine years after he had left the royal service, John V could have had no reason of his own or any pertaining to the Portuguese state for elevating an Italian musician living in Spain. Indeed, his decree said he was acting for "certain particular reasons presented to me," and those reasons were probably Maria Barbara's which she had presented herself.

The court of Philip V was very musical. The king found music indispensable. It boasted, among other facilities, a large and highly polished opera company which was dominated by Italians—and Italians who were friendly toward Domenico. Amazingly, this son of Alessandro, who had made such a name in opera, had nothing to do with it. Surely these Italians would have felt themselves honored by the opportunity of staging an opera by Domenico. They never had the opportunity. Domenico now completely shunned the field which had been his father's.

Philip V died in 1746. Maria Barbara's husband became king, as Ferdinand VI. Now there was no question of her ability to get for her musician anything she wanted or, rather, anything he wanted. The new court was even more musical than the old one. Foreign ambassadors complained there was so much music, music was becoming something to endure rather than enjoy. Yet Domenico continued to compose only privately, in the main harpsichord sonatas for the private enjoyment of the queen and king. His withdrawal and obscurity remained undisturbed.

He was sixty-one years old now, and he had eleven years more to live. We find in the few documents a letter of his to a Spanish grandee of the ducal level in which the tone is familiar and intimate. His social position, obviously, was of the best. And it is evident that Maria Barbara had seen to it that he was always well cared for financially. His home was spacious and richly furnished.

The sixteen-year-old bride he acquired when he was forty-two died eleven years later, leaving five children. A few years later he married a Spaniard, Anastasia Maxarti Ximenes, and by her he became the father of four more. The mother of the first wife had come into his home and remained even after the second wife came in. From this we can believe that the sweet amiability on which everyone remarked in the young man remained in the older man—and served him well.

He died in Madrid on July 23, 1757. Maria Barbara and Ferdinand, to honor his "fair memory," ordered royal pensions for his five minor children although his own will showed he had been a man of no little means. Maria Barbara survived him by only thirteen months and he was in her will as "my music master who has followed me with great diligence and devotion." One striking fact remains: all ten of Alessandro's children were musicians. Not one of Domenico's nine was a musician. That couldn't have happened very well on its own.

Of Alessandro's 114 operas, only 36 survive more or less complete and none is in the standard repertoire. But he was one of the major inventors of the musical language we know today; he was one of the "fathers" of the "classical" music of Bach, Mozart, Haydn, and others from which stemmed the "romantic" music of the nineteenth-century composers. This is his importance. More specifically, he was the formulator of the foundations of opera, dramatically as well as musically.

Domenico invented keyboard techniques and created a complete conception of keyboard music which made possible the piano music of Mozart, Beethoven, and their successors. But his harpsichord sonatas are most enchanting, since they have just about every shade of human emotion in them, from the most somber to the gayest. Their humor seems limitless in inventiveness; their imaginativeness invites the listener to endless fancies and fantasies.

4

Handel

HANDEL was a man to respect. The Princess of Wales, when she saw his face darkening, whispered excitedly to her ladies, "Hush! Hush! Handel's in a passion." He even tamed operatic sopranos, an endeavor reserved for the bravest of the brave.

He was big and muscular. His mind was quick, his tongue sharp. And his smile, according to a person who knew him well, was "like the sun bursting out of a black cloud. There was a sudden flash of intelligence, wit, and good humor."

This flash broke through the veil of his singular concentration on music. Few great composers were quite as one-track minded as he; yet none lived so completely in the competitive hurly-burly of the world. From early childhood to blind old age, he was music's man.

He had a few cronies with whom he liked to eat, drink, and crack jokes. But he never married; probably because there was never a real love in his life. The only personal emotion he expressed was over his mother; yet, in manhood, he showed no wish to have her near him.

Work was his endless preoccupation. He relished it more than food, and he was very fond of food. It was nothing for him to compose an opera or an oratorio in a couple of weeks; nothing to compose through the day, the night, the following day.

He composed almost as much as Bach and Beethoven together. And he was such a practiced performer that the keys of his harpsichord eventually had hollows in them like spoons. The most enduring picture of him is of a big man walking the crowded streets of London, talking to himself. He was on intimate terms with kings and the nobility; he was the most famous musician alive. But to kings and fame and almost everyone and everything he was completely oblivious.

He was born Georg Friedrich Händel, in Halle, in German Saxony. He died an Englishman with an anglicized name, George Frideric

Handel, and he sleeps now among the English immortals in West-minster Abbey.

There wasn't a shred of musical talent in the Händel family until February 23, 1685. On that day Georg Händel, a sixty-three-year-old barber-surgeon, and his second wife, Dorothea, thirty-five and daughter of a Lutheran pastor, became parents of one of music's surpassing masters. Less than a month later and less than a hundred miles away, Johann Sebastian Bach came into the world. But Bach was born into a family of musicians. Handel's family was hostile toward music. His old father, hard and practical, considered it a frivolity.

Somehow the small child learned something about music. At the age of seven or eight, he impressed the reigning duke, his father's employer, who said such a boy should certainly have music lessons. His father didn't think it politic to ignore this advice. So from Fried-rich Wilhelm Zachau, a church organist, young Handel learned to play the organ, the harpsichord, the violin, the oboe, and to compose.

The child's fame spread. The Electress Sophia of Berlin wanted him trained by the best masters of Italy at her expense. But his father said no—his son was going to be a lawyer, because the law was solid and respectable. When the time came, the obedient son became a law student. For two years he struggled between his father's wishes and his own nature. There could have been no doubt as to which was going to win. While a student, he got a job playing a fiddle in the Hamburg opera orchestra and composed his first two operas. They were staged with considerable success. And he fought a duel. Fortu-nately, the opponent's sword broke on Handel's coat button. He was all of nineteen!

When he was twenty-one, he went off to Italy and soon became the dearly beloved of the musical Italians, who called him "The Saxon." Not only was the big, straight blond charming; he was an astounding musician. At a masked ball, Domenico Scarlatti went into a room where a masquerader was playing the harpsichord. He listened but a minute before exclaiming, "It is either the devil or the Saxon!" Among Handel's admirers were Germans who wanted to capture him for the musical German kings and Englishmen who wanted him for the greater glory of England.

After four years in Italy, he went to Hanover and became music director in the court of the elector, Georg Ludwig, but asked at once for a leave of absence and went on to London. There he was received by Queen Anne and was made much of by the nobility. In two weeks he composed an opera that was a hit. The stimulating excitement of big-city living was to his liking. Unhappily, he had a boss in Hanover. Reluctantly as well as belatedly, he returned to him.

As soon as he could, which was a year later, he asked for another leave. It was granted—on condition that his visit to England would be of reasonable length this time. This second visit began in 1712, when he was twenty-seven. It lasted until April 14, 1759, when he died in his London house, aged seventy-four.

It was clear from the start he was abandoning His Hanoverian Majesty. Queen Anne encouraged him. She wasn't above spiting her distant and despised kinsman, Georg Ludwig, by depriving him of a prized musician. Handel was quite at home in London by 1714. But in that year the queen died and was succeeded by none other than Georg Ludwig!

Handel was understandably nervous. However, the new king of England, George I, wasn't irked. He loved music too much. Anne had given Handel a pension of £200. George added £200. His daughter-in-law, Caroline, Princess of Wales and afterward queen of George II, made it £600, in return for music lessons for her daughters. Many lords also were generous patrons.

With this secure financial backing, Handel could have taken up luxurious quarters in an ivory tower and composed only when and what his genius demanded. But he didn't. His spirit was restless. It demanded excitement; it craved activity.

Having a one-track musical mind, he couldn't have found excitement except through music. This being so, he had to find it in Italian opera. Other musical forms stirred up no excitement in his day, no matter how much they might elevate their special audiences. But Italian opera was in the public eye; profligate society patronized it. Operatic audiences were vociferous to the point of riot, fickle as the wind. Operatic composers could make—and lose—fortunes.

Italian opera by then had become a sickly and empty thing. It was full of high-flown gesticulations and posturings, of fancy and meaningless warblings, with music interspersed through nonsense. From our viewpoint, it is sad that Handel devoted the best part of his creative life to it—without making an effort to reform and improve it. He found it sick; he left it sicker.

He was no artistic idealist, and anything but a reformer. Christoph Willibald Gluck was going to reform opera in the next generation. Handel not only composed forty-one operas; he staged many of them with his own money. Some were put together with such haste it is hard to believe they came from a master's hand. All this labor added hardly at all to his enduring reputation. We hear only a string of excerpted arias and a few adaptations for symphony orchestra, including the **Largo** from **Xerxes.**

But Handel had his fun. He made several small fortunes, lost them. His will disposed of more than £20,000, which, by today's values, would amount to several hundred thousand dollars. However, money wasn't important to him. His four-story house on Brook Street, Hanover Square, where he lived for thirty-four years, was plainly and sparsely furnished. He never kept a carriage. His clothes were of good quality, without frills. About all he spent sizable sums for were fine foods and wines, charities, and paintings. During his lifetime, he owned several Rembrandts.

His excitement came from rival composers and managers, from audiences and singers, and from enemies in society who mocked his guttural, accented English and caricatured him as a hog playing the organ. He was the king's man, and George I was unpopular. In 1727, George II came to the throne. His oldest son, Prince Frederick, was a pinhead. Father and son were open enemies. The son, to be hateful to his father, organized an "Opera of the Nobility" for the purpose of ruining his father's composer.

Frederick's friends gave parties the nights Handel's operas opened, to keep society away. Hoodlums were hired to hoot his singers and threaten his patrons. But he was by no means helpless. When one opera failed, he stayed up nights composing its successor. He imported the fanciest singers from Italy. Some were unbelievably difficult; but by cajolery, flattery, and even violence, he had them all singing their hearts out.

One wildcat soprano was in his powerful arms and on the way to an open window when she had a second thought and promised to be a good girl and sing his music the way he had written it. He even dared to have two such wildcats in his company and to compose operas in which both had leading parts.

Londoners became rabid fans of one singer or the other. The instant either opened her mouth, she was drowned out by catcalls from the partisans of her rival. One night the two women locked in battle on the stage, with much clawing, hair pulling, and shrieking, to the delight of the audience and, probably, of Handel, conducting from his harpsichord.

This went on for over twenty years. Toward the end, his trouble was his own bullheadedness. The public was tired of it all. Neither he nor any one of his enemies was making money. He experimented some with oratorios, but he kept right on composing and staging operas.

He was fifty-six when he was forced to give them up. He was broke and weighted with debt. He had had two serious bouts of illness, brought on by overwork, and his health was none too secure. On August 22, 1741, he retired into his house with a compilation from the Bible that had been put together for him by one Charles Jennens.

Until September 14 he never left the house, hardly got up from his table. He was setting the compilation to music. His servant brought food that often went untouched. He was in the throes of composing **Messiah**, which is to music what Michelangelo's *Last Judgment* is to painting.

Handel had been invited to Ireland, and arrived in Dublin on November 18, with **Messiah** in his baggage. It was sung for the first time the next spring, in Neal's Musick Hall. At its first London performance, George II was so overwhelmed by the first bars of the **Hallelujah Chorus**, he got to his feet and stood for all of it.

Messiah is an oratorio, and oratorio is an operatic form. It is less sharply dramatic, nothing is acted out, the singers just stand and sing; but it has principal parts for soloists and chorus, and an orchestral foundation. Handel now was concentrating on this form, turning out oratorios almost at the same rate he had turned out operas.

There were twenty, plus thirteen serenatas, masques, odes, and pastorals, all of which are singing entertainments for the theater that closely resemble oratorios. Some were failures on first singings; others were successful. There were troubles, too, especially with the clergy over the introduction of sacred themes into the theater; and trouble from his old enemies.

But slowly these difficulties vanished. All performances were to packed houses. (The English have doted on oratorios to this day, particularly on those of Handel.) He was now a portly old gentleman, a character even in that age of characters. No one laughed any more because he still spoke English with a German accent. His walking excursions through the streets were attended with pride and affection. He busied himself with the affairs of his favorite charities, the Foundling Hospital, of which he was a governor, and the "Society for the Support of Decayed Musicians and their Families."

His sight began failing when he was sixty-six, in 1751. There was an operation. Two years later he was almost blind. Bach, too, was blind at the last, but he lived in blindness only a matter of months. Handel had some six years to live. He was of good heart, and still composed, dictating to a secretary. He still played the organ and harpsichord in public, and these concerts were packed with reverent audiences. And he conducted his oratorios, especially **Messiah**, from the organ.

On April 6, 1759, he fainted and was put to bed. He knew he was dying and summoned his friends. Good Friday was to be on April 13.

He hoped for death on that day, but lived until the morning of April 14.

Three thousand Londoners went, unasked, to his funeral in Westminster Abbey. From that day to this, he has never ceased to be to the British "the Greatest English Composer." In point of fact, his name will be forever honored in the world commonwealth of music.

5

Bach

BACH, the German word for brook, was the name of several score related musicians, most of them christened John, who flourished for more than two centuries. In some of the small German towns where they plied their trade the word "bach" came to mean musician.

When we say Bach, we mean Johann Sebastian Bach, in whom the family's means of livelihood culminated in a genius of monumental proportions. He is no brook, exclaimed Beethoven, he is the sea! . . . Music owes to this Bach almost as much as Christianity owes to Christ, said Schumann. This Bach filled Mozart with joy. Mendelssohn with reverence, Wagner with respect.

He died over two hundred years ago, on July 28, 1750, but only physically. Now more than ever he is the musician's musician, still influencing, at times dominating, the art. He has been called the father of harmony and the father of counterpoint. Actually, he is the father of music as we know it. He is also the creator of music ranging from the sublimely happy to the profoundly sad. Musically, he is the creator of matchless grandeur—of mighty rainbows of sound. His variety is endless, and despite the efforts of cultural snobs to make a cult of him, he belongs to anyone who listens and hears.

During his lifetime, people thought he played the organ much better than most and was disturbingly stubborn in his insistence on the rights of music. Nevertheless, he seemed to be just one more of the musical drudges who plugged away for churches and towns or as musical servants for kings and noblemen.

Since he was unique, we know he was not one more of anything. But he was a drudge. From childhood to death, he worked as hard as any laborer, with little more security and not a great deal more recognition. He lived out his sixty-five years within a radius of a few hundred miles of his birthplace, the ancient town of Eisenach, in a storied German countryside that knew Martin Luther and was to be the setting of Wagner's opera **Tannhäuser**.

His was a simple life. Loving God with an uncomplicated depth of pure spirituality, he trusted Him without a murmur and saw to it that his own ways were upright. His art, which now is spoken of with reverence, was to him a way to earn a living for himself and a large family. By two wives, he was the father of twenty children, of whom ten died in infancy or childhood.

He was thrown upon the world young, his mother and his father, Johann Ambrosius Bach, violin and viola player, having died before he was ten. An older brother, Johann Christoph Bach, musician in the town of Ohrdruf, took him in and took over his musical education. Probably thinking he wasn't ready for the music of the celebrated composers of the day, brother-teacher forbade him access to it. So the youngster slipped out the music through the lattice of a locked cabinet and copied it by moonlight, night after night, for six months.

This is an oft-told tale and a useful one. It points up the insatiable curiosity and inexhaustible capacity for work that were basic in his genius. All his life he was to make copies of other composers' music of all countries and times. He absorbed everything, and then made everything his own by extending and perfecting until the originals were hardly recognizable.

His sweet soprano voice earned him an education in a religious school. When his voice broke, he maintained himself there by playing the violin and viola. Meanwhile, he was absorbing the techniques of organ playing, which were to earn him, when he had extended them far beyond the capacities of teachers or contemporaries, the little fame he enjoyed.

By eighteen, he was organist of a church in Arnstadt, where he was also required to train the boys' choir. The boys gave him trouble. The authorities wanted to restrain him musically. And he was preoccupied with learning. He was accustomed to walking for days, and on a lean stomach, to get to distant churches where famous musicians presided at the organ. Offering his cousin, Johann Ernst Bach, as substitute organist he got a one-month leave to go to Lübeck to hear Dietrich Buxtehude.

He stayed three months instead of one. When he returned, he was in real trouble. All the long-simmering, official complaints had come to a boil. First, why had he stayed away so long? Second, what was the idea of the "surprising variations" and "irrelevant ornaments" in his organ playing? Third, why didn't he do better with the boys' choir? And fourth, what about the "stranger maiden" who had been heard singing in the organ loft while he practiced?

About this time a church in Mühlhausen asked him to become its organist. He accepted and married (in 1707) the "stranger maiden," who was his cousin, Maria Barbara, daughter of Johann Michael Bach, an organist, too. They spent a year in Mühlhausen and then moved on to Weimar, where he became court organist to the autocratic and stiff-necked Duke of Sachsen-Weimar. Nine years later, young Prince Leopold of Anhalt-Cöthen, who was very musical and knew a musical genius when he heard one, offered him the post of court *Kapellmeister*.

But he had to get his release from the duke, who was not in the least disposed to grant it. Bach insisted, and the duke had him imprisoned for his impudence. Coolly, he turned his enforced seclusion to composing. In less than a month the duke bowed to superior obstinacy.

Bach's new master, who was only twenty-three—nine years younger than he—treated him as a friend. Whenever he traveled, his *Kapellmeister* had to be along. In the summer of 1720 they went to Karlsbad. While they were away, Maria Barbara sickened suddenly and died.

We can surmise Bach's shock and grief. He was now the father of four living children. The eldest, a girl, was only twelve. Wilhelm Friedemann and Carl Philipp Emanuel, both destined to become famous musicians, were ten and six, respectively. Johann Gottfried Bernhard, the youngest, was only five. Three other children had died in infancy.

Seventeen months later he married Anna Magdalena Wilcken, a singer in the prince's court. She was twenty years old, and he was almost thirty-seven. She was to be his wife the remainder of his life, to bear him thirteen children, to outlive him by only ten years, to live her last days on charity, and to go to a pauper's grave. Three of her seven daughters and three of her six sons survived infancy and childhood. One son was mentally retarded. But another was Johann Christian Bach, who was to become music master to the queen of George III of England and to have a sizable place in music history as "the English Bach."

Anna Magdalena and Johann Sebastian loved each other deeply. The evidence is scanty, but conclusive. One bit is this: He had endless music copying to do. We know she helped him, because many of his manuscripts are in her handwriting. Over the years it became more and more like his. In some examples the two handwritings are all but indistinguishable.

Another bit is in the music book he made for her, to speed her clavier practice. In it were copied, in his hand, the wedding poems he had written for her, such as:

> Your servant, sweetest maiden Bride.
> Joy be with you this morning.

To see you in your flowery crown
And wedding-day adorning
Would fill with joy the sternest soul.
What wonder, as I meet you,
That my fond heart and loving lips
O'erflow with song to greet you?

In 1721 the prince had also married. His bride didn't like music and was jealous of the time he gave to it. The result was a slow change in the atmosphere at Cöthen, which had been so congenial. And so, in 1723, Johann Sebastian moved to Leipzig to become cantor of the Thomas School. This was to be his place until his death, twenty-seven years later.

The school was for the boys who made up the choirs in the four town churches. The cantor trained these choirs and supervised the music of the two principal churches, St. Thomas and St. Nicholas. He was also required to compose cantatas for all the Sundays and feast days of the church year. In addition, he kept check on the church organs and taught some Latin.

All this kept him very busy, and he was poorly paid. His children were being born, and more than half of them were dying, which was not unusual in those days. Since he was industrious, his family knew no want. But it knew no great prosperity either. Within the family circle there evidently were happiness and close ties.

In one of his very few personal letters that have survived, there is this description: "The children of my second marriage are still small, the eldest, a boy, being six years old. But they are all born musicians, and I can assure you that I can already form an ensemble both *vocaliter* and *instrumentaliter*, particularly since my present wife sings a good, clear soprano, and my eldest daughter, too, joins in not badly."

He was picked on by the authorities, who didn't like this or didn't like that—the innovations in his music, how he dealt with the choirboys, his responses when they presumed to correct him. There were years of tension with the school rector. Bach didn't hesitate to go over the rector's head to the town council. Getting no satisfaction, he went over the council's head, and finally appealed to the king-elector. That personage, obscure in his own day and forgotten now, gave him the title of "court composer." It was the peak of his official recognition.

In Bach's old age, Frederick the Great of Prussia was kind to him, and this, to him, was his crowning glory. Carl Philipp Emanuel, having grown up, was now in the king's service—and whatever else history has to say of that sovereign, he knew and loved music.

Flute in hand, Frederick was among his musicians one evening when word was brought to him that Carl Philipp Emanuel's father had arrived to visit his son. Excitedly, the king got to his feet. "Old Bach is here!" he cried. He showed the old man his magnificent instruments, invited him to play on the newly developed piano, of which he had no small number, and gave him a musical theme to improvise on.

When the old man returned to Leipzig, he wrote a set of playful and delightful variations on the royal theme and sent them to Frederick with a fulsome dedication. How the monarch responded to what Bach called a "musical offering" is not known; but he knew old Bach was not just another Bach. There were others who shared this opinion —his few pupils, a few musicians.

The summer he was sixty-four, his sight failed rapidly. There was an operation—then total blindness. The following summer, his sight returned suddenly, but about ten days later he had an apoplectic stroke, lingered for some days, unconscious, and died. With his sons ended the long line of Bach musicians. Nature needed some two hundred years to produce its towering giant; after him there was little left.

Johann Sebastian thought he would be forgotten. The style had changed—he saw his works as old-fashioned. And he was forgotten for many decades, save for a few musicians. Johann Philipp Kirnberger, one of his pupils, made a shrine of his portrait. A Leipzig merchant, a few years after Bach's death, spotted the portrait and made a disparaging remark. The next instant the enraged Kirnberger had him by the collar and was pushing and booting him toward the door, shrieking, "Out, dog!"

Thirty-nine years after Bach's death, Mozart—who, as a child prodigy, had delighted the English Bach, Johann Christian—visited Leipzig, and the Thomas School boys sang for him one of Johann Sebastian's motets, none of which had been published. In the words of a witness, "Mozart sat up, startled. A few measures more and he called out, 'What is this?' And now his whole soul seemed to be in his ears."

In 1792, a young pianist, Ludwig van Beethoven, arrived in Vienna and caused a sensation in musical circles by his playing of the **Well-Tempered Clavier's** preludes and fugues by a little-known and long-dead composer, one J. S. Bach. In 1829, Mendelssohn conducted Bach's **St. Matthew Passion** in Berlin. This was its first performance since the composer himself had conducted the work in St. Thomas Church in Leipzig a century before.

The belated appreciation and recognition of Bach can be dated from that event. In 1850, a society was formed to publish all his surviving works. Only a minute percentage of the total had been published while he was alive. A hundred years later, his manuscripts were scattered, fragmented, and many were lost.

The society needed forty-nine years to do the job. It revealed what was to be expected. While he was at Weimar and before, he had composed mainly for the organ—he had been an organist then. During his Cöthen years, while he was *Kapellmeister* for a lively young prince, he composed much of his worldly music, for orchestra and for solo instruments, especially the clavier or harpsichord, at which he was a master performer, and the violin. The organ music had been from religious inspiration; he had been employed by churches. In his Leipzig years there was a return to this inspiration, as his job was to compose for and direct Lutheran church music. There can be no question of his profound religious feeling. Still, it is worth reiterating that music was his business. It belies the character of the man to suppose he went through life as a mystic or a zealot. He was of serious mien, yet he knew how to play and to appreciate frivolity, within limits. In short, he was human.

6

Gluck

Music's most conspicuous reformer was Christoph Willibald Gluck. The zeal for reformation came upon him late in life and was rather fitful. He was anything but strait-laced, musically or personally. But if it hadn't been for him, opera, as we now know it, might not be.

No great musician had a more obscure ancestry. He came from the mysterious shadows of forests, this cynically wise man of the world who was at home in any society in any country, who was a better politician than technical musician, who knew how to manipulate even royalty and nobility, who usually was the master of any situation or setting.

His father and his father's father were foresters and huntsmen in the service of landed lords. His father—shrewd, forceful, and close to nature—rose to the status of superior servant. Aside from this, we know nothing of his paternal background. About his mother and her ancestry we know nothing whatever.

Even the date and place of his birth were in dispute for a long time. Now we know he was born on July 2, 1714, in Erasbach, a village in a German forest not far from Nürnberg. He left his first clear trail at twenty-two, when he appeared as a chamber musician in the Vienna establishment of Prince Lobkowitz, his father's lord. His specialty was the bowed string instruments, although he also played the clavier and the organ and had an excellent singing voice. But his skills were not profound, since his education, musically and generally, had been sketchy.

He was one of many servants around the palace. But this musician was no flunky. He was a man of independence and spirit, animated by a fast, alert mind efficiently harnessed to reservoirs of ambition, imagination, and keen awareness of the values of the world. Within a year, he found it to his interest to switch his service to another lord who was changing his residence from Vienna to Milan in Italy, where a young man of humble position and little money could learn to be a composer of opera.

Opera was one way for a young man to advance himself in the world. It was the chief musical fare of the masses and of nobility and royalty. But such opera! There was little plot, no drama, no effort to illuminate character and motivation with music and poetry. The singers engaged in a species of high-flown conversation, at times chanting, at times singing. When they sang, it was with such a hodge-podge of trills and high-pitched shrills and gurgles the ear scarcely could credit what it heard. To compound incredulity, men frequently appeared in women's roles.

Opera was up this blind alley, some hundred thirty years after its birth in Florence. The year was 1737. The births of Mozart and Beethoven were nineteen and thirty-three years in the future. And here was Gluck acquiring his first competent music teacher.

This Milanese maestro thought his new pupil slow and dull. But he was easygoing and so persevered, since the young man was doggedly determined. More than three years passed, and then the pupil composed an opera. It was carefully tailored to prevailing fashion. However, connoisseurs judged it to be below standard.

Whether it was or was not, the public liked it, which was enough for the composer, who began turning out operas as though he were on a treadmill. All were box-office successes—Gluck's chief consideration then and always. He liked money; he knew how to make it and how to hang onto it. After money, he liked good food and good wine. Only then came women.

But he liked people, and even though he lent no money, he lent a sympathetic ear to just about anyone. This people found flattering, and it enabled him to manipulate them into doing the things which were useful to him. His was a warming countenance, enlivened with sharp and merry eyes. Energy bubbled out of him as from an inexhaustible spring—energy for play as well as for work.

Never once during this period, it must be noted, was Gluck showing even an inclination to rescue opera from artistic debasement and intellectual swamps. He was advancing himself with the wealthy princelings who had favors to bestow and who exercised influence which could be useful. Yet he never fawned or toadied, he never sold himself short. The lords could take the impression from him that he was something of a lord himself, although, to be sure, a lesser lord than they.

After three years of composing Italian operas in Italy and a brief period in London, where he knew Handel, he was off to fields which

seemed to have more for him. Those were the capitals of the German
principalities, where Italian music masters were in much demand. This
one had an advantage over the others. He was a German—a German
Italian.

His chief occupation for the next few years was conducting for a
traveling Italian opera company and promoting his own prestige and
fame. He did comparatively little composing, but whenever he came
upon plans to celebrate a royal wedding—or the birth of a crown
prince or the return of a queen to society after a confinement—he
composed an opera especially for the occasion and managed to get
it inserted as a core of the celebration.

Soon the noble and wealthy families were competing for the
privilege of receiving him. One of these families was that of Joseph
Pergin, a wealthy banker and merchant of Vienna. Gluck lost little
time in making love to Pergin's only child, Marianne. Pergin objected,
but he died shortly afterward. Marianne was his heir, and when
Gluck married her, he became a wealthy man.

He now was thirty-six years old. Evidently, he had arrived at the
goals he had set for himself, because he gave signs of settling down,
there in Vienna, to idle if fashionable living. For the moment, there
were no more worlds to conquer.

He still composed the same kind of empty and meaningless operas,
however, and he still was interested in acquiring wealthier and more
influential patrons—by now, this was ingrained in him. He used these
friends as the ascending rungs of a ladder and on them climbed to
the position of musical director in the court of Emperor Francis I
and his wife, Maria Theresa. Among his duties was giving singing
lessons to the imperial children, who included Marie Antoinette,
future queen of France. She, too, was going to serve him.

We are now in the year of 1761. Our composer is forty-seven
years old, living securely and serenely at the top of a world of
intrigue, amiably disposed to all sides, managing to keep one foot
in all camps. He has wangled a papal decoration, which bestowed a
knighthood but which no noble nor nobility supporter accepted as a
patent of nobility. Nevertheless, Gluck now was styling himself as
a noble, calling himself *von* Gluck and getting away with it.

But up to this point he had shown very little, if any, musical genius.
It is all very well for people living now and knowing all about his
genius to go over what he had composed up to this time and say of
this or that fragment, "*Ah! A stroke of genius!*" But the truth is, if
Gluck hadn't changed his musical ways in 1761, only a few scholars
poring over dusty manuscripts would ever have heard of him.

Immortality came to him by way of an obscure and somewhat disreputable Italian poet, Ranieri Calzabigi, who was also forty-seven and plying his trade in Vienna. He was on the ragged edge because the only profitable outlet for Italian poets was librettos for Italian operas. A poet who called himself Metastasio blanketed the field, and Calzabigi couldn't bring himself to write Metastasio's kind of high-flown nonsense.

Calzabigi, who dreamed of overthrowing Metastasio and all the man stood for, constructed an operatic libretto that was the very opposite of the Metastasio model. It told a story. It was a very simple story. Furthermore, it was a very dramatic story. Even more sensational, and despite the characters being gods and demigods, it was an intensely human story—Greek gods as the Greeks created them were perhaps more human than human beings.

This libretto Gluck set to music. The music was welded to both human character and human motivation; operatic music was given emotional and dramatic tasks to perform; music and poetry and drama were blended into one overwhelming force. The opera is **Orfeo ed Euridice.** It was first produced in 1762 in the Austrian court theater and remains healthily alive to this day. It is the oldest opera in the living repertoire. All other operas of its time and before are dead theatrically, although a few are disinterred now and then.

With the first performance of **Orfeo**, the operatic school of Metastasio and his imitators was dead, although it took some time for it to lie down and be still. Even Gluck did not realize this at first. After **Orfeo** he set another insipid libretto by Metastasio. Indeed, he worked with librettos of the Metastasio kind until Calzabigi interested him in another of his. This opera, produced late in 1767, was **Alceste.**

Meanwhile, **Orfeo** was making its way, always gathering force. The first critics were hostile. But the operatic public understood its human values right from the start. The public—before the critics and certainly before the singers and other makers of opera—knew that a revolution had been accomplished. Although he was not among the first to know it, Gluck was not among the last.

The score of **Alceste** was published two years after its first performance and one year before the birth of Beethoven. This is of interest because of a dedicatory preface which showed that by now, at least, Gluck had thought out the revolution quite carefully. He said that, when he composed **Alceste**, "I resolved to divest it entirely of all those abuses, introduced either by mistaken vanity of singers or by the too-great complaisance of composers, which have so long disfigured Italian opera and made of the most splendid and most beautiful of spectacles the most ridiculous and wearisome."

It could, of course, become a question of who really reformed opera, Gluck or Calzabigi? Yet it is readily answered. Poetry is not opera until music is affixed to it. Calzabigi's retelling of the legend of Orpheus couldn't have survived without Gluck's music.

Calzabigi and Gluck collaborated on a third opera, **Paris and Helen,** before the poet got into an amorous scrape that so shocked Empress Maria Theresa he had to make tracks from Vienna.

Gluck and his Marianne stepped up their high scale of living one more notch by moving into a splendid, if smallish, Viennese palace —smallish as palaces in Vienna went in those days. They were congenial, enjoying people and life together. The one shadow over their happiness was their childlessness. Both were lovers of children. This shadow they finally dispelled by adopting Gluck's ten-year-old niece, also named Marianne. At fifty-five, he was a father at last, and how he relished it! Wherever he traveled, his daughter went with him. He was cultivating her native singing voice, and he enjoyed nothing more than having her show off to his friends.

By now, another of his singing pupils, Marie Antoinette, had been married to the heir to the throne of France, and she was exercising much influence in Paris. She was happy to further his ambitions to become a composer of French opera (in addition to Italian and German), and in 1774 the Paris Opera produced his **Iphigénie en Aulide** with much success. He Frenchified **Orfeo ed Euridice,** purifying its melodic lines and transposing the part of Orfeo down from contralto (it was composed for a male contralto) to tenor. He also made a French version of **Alceste** in 1776.

While he was staging it in Paris, word reached him from Vienna that his daughter was dead of smallpox. She was seventeen—he was sixty-two. Even Gluck, who was too much of a natural noble to vulgarize his heart by parading it, couldn't conceal the effect. But he drew the curtain very quickly.

For some time he and his wife continued to divide their time between Paris and Vienna. They whirled through the gay, thoughtless living of the noble and the wealthy of both capitals. But he wasn't thoughtless—he was groping with the future of his operatic revolution, which he hadn't been able to advance after **Alceste** and which he failed to advance in his last two operas, staged in Paris in 1779.

That year he had a series of apoplectic strokes. He recovered but he was warned that it was time for him to give up everything strenuous. Thereafter he lived mainly in his Vienna palace, occupied his thoughts with German epic poetry (in addition to the ever-changing ins and outs of high society) and composed only a **De Profundis** for chorus and orchestra. He met the youthful Mozart and was enough impressed to invite him to dinner, but he was not going to live long enough to know that Mozart advanced his revolution to stupendous heights.

The dinner table Gluck still adored, but for some years, because of his occasional and minor strokes, the doctors had been telling him that rich food and rich drink were poisons for him. Marianne was more impressed than he was. She saw to it that he kept to his diet.

But she was absent from the table for a few minutes on November 15, 1787. Liqueurs had been served to the two guests. One didn't drink his, and old Gluck kept eying it, his mouth watering. Finally, he couldn't stand it, and down went the drink. A few hours later he had a massive apoplectic stroke which killed him. He was seventy-three years old.

7

Haydn

JOSEPH HAYDN left home when he was six years old. Thereafter, he received, in his words, "more cuffs than gingerbread." From eight to seventeen, he was a dormitory-living choirboy, disciplined with a whip and usually hungry. At seventeen, he was turned out into the streets of Vienna to fend for himself.

From this cruel childhood emerged a man to whom life was a pleasant duty and for whom life required the utmost in work, tact, and humility. The child had known little kindness. The man was prodigiously kind. Of parental love, the child had little. The man, before he was middle-aged, was calling adults "my children" and giving others so much parental love that they were soon calling him "Papa Haydn."

His driving force was optimism, and he was almost always cheerful and happy. His only failures in human relationships were with women. The woman he married he didn't love, nor did she love him. She was barren; so he was never really a papa. Of this wife he spoke the only unkind words known to have crossed his lips.

The making of the mistreated child into the serene and sublime artist was a slow, slow process. He was born with a singing voice and a sense of time. Nevertheless, he gave no early signs of any natural endowment of a high order. He was never outstanding as a performer. If he had died before he was fifty, most of us would never have heard of him.

He arrived at the full estate of genius in his old age. At sixty-seven, he lamented, "Oh, God! How much yet remains to be done in this splendid art, even by a man like myself!" And again: "I have only just learned, in my old age, how to use the wind instruments. Now that I do understand them, I must leave the world."

As he looked back over his life, it all looked good. "I am something made out of nothing," he said. But he insisted he had had little to do with the making. Nor had his parents. And, as he said, he never had "proper teachers." Who did the making, then? Haydn hadn't the slightest doubt. "God gave me a talent," he said, "and I thank Him for it."

He loved God. The Eternal Father loved him. From boyhood to old age, his simplicity was childlike. Told his Masses were too gay, he said, "When I think of God, my heart is so full of joy the notes fly from me as from a spindle." His whole life shows that the loveless child discovered that God is love. It is just as evident that music was father and mother to him, and wife too. Witness the child, quite on his own, devoting sixteen hours a day to music—and the man doing the same. One of his manuscripts tells us graphically about this. He noted on its margin: "Written while asleep."

Matthias Haydn and his wife, Maria, were good people, according to their time and station. Both were peasants on the feudal estate of the Counts of Harrach in southern Austria, bordering on Hungary. Matthias had learned the trade of wheelwright. Maria was a cook in the castle kitchens before he married her. The great Joseph Haydn was the second of their twelve children, born in their thatched-roof hovel in the village of Rohrau on March 31, 1732. In that year Bach was flourishing in Leipzig, Handel in London. Mozart's birth was twenty-four years in the future; Beethoven's, thirty-eight years.

Matthias and Maria liked to sing. Their little son soon was adding his voice, true and clear, to theirs. One day Johann Matthias Franck, choirmaster and schoolmaster at Hainburg, ten miles away, came to visit. He was related to Matthias Haydn by marriage. Responsible for a church choir, Franck was always on the lookout for boy sopranos. Young Joseph's voice could be very useful to him, and he persuaded Matthias and Maria to give him up—for the child's own good, of course. Franck promised to take him into his own home and teach him music. If he knew music, he said, he might become a priest when he grew up.

What parents aren't ambitious for their children? Yet Maria was reluctant; she feared if she let the little one leave, it would be forever. It was, just about. His returns were few and brief. Long after she and Matthias were dead, "the great Haydn" came back to see a monument the current Count Harrach had erected in his honor. Now sixty-three, Haydn kissed the threshold of the house where he was born.

He remembered the filth of the Franck home and the cuffings he got from Franck and his slatternly wife. But he bore them no malice. "I shall always be grateful to that man for keeping me so hard at work," he said.

There came to Hainburg Georg Reutter, imperial court composer and choirmaster for St. Stephen's Cathedral, Vienna, on the hunt for boy singers. The Haydn boy qualified and was accepted. To his parents, it was a magnificent opportunity—which it was, in a loveless, practical way. Music had a huge part in Austrian Catholic ritual at the time; St. Stephen's was the most important cathedral in the empire, and Vienna one of the most musical if not *the* most musical city in the world.

And so Haydn became a St. Stephen's choirboy at the age of eight. Reutter was a learned musician and composer; he was also set against warmth and sympathy. The choirboys were flogged often and thoroughly. They were half starved, too, since Reutter diverted state funds allotted for their care to his own luxurious living. Haydn said he had only two lessons from him in nine years. Eventually, when his voice broke, Reutter turned him out, in his poor clothes and without a penny.

Haydn sang and played in the streets, composed little pieces for street musicians, found a few pupils, at pittances. His voice returned —tenor—and he sang in churches and in rich men's homes. He played the violin and harpsichord for something to eat or a few pennies. Each day, or almost every day, he found time to study and learn.

Then he managed to become the flunky of Niccolo Porpora, singing teacher and composer of much fame in his time, now a crabbed old man existing on past glory and a small group of pupils. Haydn gladly cleaned his shoes, brushed his clothes, accompanied the pupils at the clavier, and suffered his cuffs and kicks, all to be near enough the man to learn what he knew about music.

After ten years of this kind of living, Count Ferdinand Maximilian von Morzin hired him as private orchestra conductor and composer. About this time Haydn decided he ought to be married. Two of his pupils were Theresa and Maria Anna Keller, daughters of a hairdresser. He thought Theresa, the younger, would do. But she entered a convent. Their father said, why not the other? Why not, indeed? Haydn evidently thought, and so they were married. He was twenty-eight; she, thirty-two.

They soon separated, but now and then, over many years, made efforts to pretend they were a normal married couple. She was sloppy, bigoted, jealous, and a spendthrift. Moreover, she was unmusical. On the other hand, he was not without sin, including the kind best designed to rouse her jealousy. At any rate, he supported her for forty years, until her death at seventy-two.

For Count Morzin's orchestra he composed the first of his 104 symphonies. One of the count's guests who heard its first playing was Prince Paul Anton Eszterházy. Morzin was living beyond his means. The piper caught up and compelled him to disband his orchestra. The prince snapped up its conductor. This was on May 1, 1761—the beginning of an association that was to last until Haydn's death, and weave a peasant-genius' life with that of a princely house in unbreakable intimacy.

The Eszterházys were (and are) an ancient, noble family. Then they were enormously rich. Prince Paul died within a year and was succeeded by his brother, Nicholas, who at once set out to earn his appellation, "the Magnificent." Addicted to display and luxury, he rebuilt the family hunting lodge, Eszterháza, into another Versailles.

He loved music, knew music, was a skilled musician, and wanted plenty of music. Eszterháza had concert rooms for music of various proportions, a private opera house, and a marionette theater. To operate these facilities, the prince maintained a large orchestra made up of the best players he could find and a shifting troupe of opera singers. As a matter of routine there were two opera performances and two full orchestra concerts weekly, plus daily performances of one kind or another in the prince's private chambers. When there were guests, this schedule was greatly increased.

Haydn was in charge of all this for almost thirty years—until 1790, when Nicholas died. It was hard work, but Haydn loved work, and he was well paid. In musical matters he had his own way. "My Prince was always satisfied with my work," he said when it was all over. "Not only did I have the encouragement of constant approval but as conductor of an orchestra I could make experiments, observe what produced an effect and what weakened it, and was thus in a position to improve, to alter, make additions or omissions, and be as bold as I pleased. I was cut off from the world. There was no one to confuse or torment me."

During these years he slowly approached the high genius level from which he entered musical history as the perfecter of the sonata form and thus the father of the symphony and the string quartet. He composed some 90 of his symphonies, almost all of his 77 string quartets, 17 of his 19 operas (not counting 4 marionette operas surviving from the unknown number he composed for the prince's puppet theater), 5 of his 12 Masses, and a vast body of music for voice, piano, and violin.

Nicholas rarely permitted him to leave the place. He couldn't go to the world, but the world came to him. In 1781, the Spanish envoy came out from Vienna to present the royal compliments of Charles III and a gold snuffbox. Ferdinand IV of Naples invited him to visit. Frederick William II of Prussia sent him a diamond ring.

Publishers demanded scores. Foreign orchestras sent commissions. He was outgrowing his restricted surroundings, becoming too big artistically to be confined. By 1790, he realized it, and wrote to a Vienna friend, "I am doomed to stay at home [at Eszterháza]. It is indeed sad to be a slave."

Within months, however, the confinement vanished. Prince Nicholas died, leaving him a generous pension. Prince Anton, the successor, disbanded the musical establishment, but retained Haydn on the payroll as family *Kapellmeister* on indefinite leave.

Now fifty-eight, Haydn went to Vienna, bubbling with pleasurable anticipations like a schoolboy. At last he could see more of Mozart, whom he had met some nine years before and seen only occasionally since, and satisfy his curiosity about the big world outside the Eszterházy circle.

Mozart he esteemed above all other musicians; he loved him, thought him the greatest composer who had ever lived. Mozart loved him, too, and called him "Papa." These two struck sparks off each other. Each wrote his greatest works after they had talked and played music together. During this period, they enjoyed their longest, most intimate association—which was broken by the arrival of a stranger.

This was Johann Peter Salomon, musician, musical go-getter, and London impresario. He offered Haydn fat fees if he would accompany him to London, compose some new symphonies, and conduct their performances. No one resisted Salomon's charms for long. Haydn didn't try—he liked the man and he liked the prospect of adventure. At their farewell, Mozart burst into tears and said he'd never see his old friend again. He was right—but it was he who died the following year.

Haydn arrived in London on January 1, 1791, stayed for eighteen months, and had a wonderful time. He was a guest in great and noble homes; his concerts played to packed houses. The University at Oxford made him a Doctor of Music, and he found time to make love to an attractive widow.

Returning to Vienna in June, 1792, he found an impatient youth of twenty-two, named Ludwig van Beethoven, demanding lessons in composition. Amiably, Haydn took him on, although now, in his old age, he was preoccupied with a miraculous burst of creativity. He had composed and conducted six of his finest symphonies in London; and he was much too kind to have been an effective teacher of such a whirlwind as this young man. Beethoven soon sought out other and tougher teachers. Haydn called him "the Grand Mogul," and Beethoven said he had learned "nothing from Haydn."

In 1794, Haydn went back to London for another triumphal round of concerts, at which he conducted his last six symphonies, and more fun in high society. George III addressed him respectfully as "Doctor Haydn." Queen Charlotte offered him apartments in Windsor Castle if he'd stay in England for good. But a new prince now headed the house of Eszterházy, and he sent word to the family *Kapellmeister* to return and revive the family music.

His duties involved very little work. A younger man was hired as his assistant and did most of it. And so Haydn busied himself with a new libretto he had brought back to Vienna. This was for an oratorio based on Milton's *Paradise Lost*. The libretto, it was said, had been prepared for Handel. Haydn tackled it slowly and carefully, because "I want to write a work which will give permanent fame to my name in the world." This was **The Creation**, which was performed for the first time in April, 1798.

Working even more slowly, he composed the oratorio **The Seasons**, completing it in 1800. This just about finished him as a creator. He lived nine more years, growing more and more feeble, but receiving visiting dignitaries and musicians, accepting honors and presents with frank pleasure.

In March, 1808, in observance of his seventy-sixth birthday, a performance of **The Creation** was given in the Hall of Vienna University, attended by the great and near-great. At the passage "There Was Light," the audience rose in an ovation. Trembling, Haydn pointed upward, and quavered, "Not from me—from there, above, comes everything."

He was tiring fast. They carried him out before the performance was over. At the door, the bearers put down the chair for a moment. Up rushed Beethoven, now thirty-eight years old. He knelt and kissed the old man's hands and brow. It was Haydn's farewell to the world, as it turned out. He died the following spring, on May 31, 1809, aged seventy-seven.

8

Mozart

WHEN Wolfgang Amadeus Mozart and his sister Marianne were very young children no one could have measured factually who had the more native musical ability, he or she. All her life this sister of his was permeated with profound musicality. No one bothered in that age to blow on female sparks of genius. She had babies and in the other particulars contented herself with a woman's role.

Her usefulness now is to point up the seeming biological affinities of Leopold Mozart and his wife, Anna Maria. They were parents of seven children. Only the fourth, Marianne, or "Nannerl," and the seventh, Wolfgang Amadeus, survived infancy or early childhood. There were two completed trials, so to speak—and two geniuses. Think about that and it will confound your imagination.

Leopold was the only musician among his children's utterly undistinguished ancestry. He was a music servant of the prince-archbishop of Salzburg, Austria. Nannerl was musical in her cradle. Father found it relaxing to mingle music instruction with routine baby care. He was pleased with so much infant musicality, of course, but he didn't let it excite him very much.

Nannerl was born on June 30, 1751, and over four years later, on January 27, 1756, came Wolfgang Amadeus. He also was musical in his cradle. Even the first signs excited Leopold extraordinarily. As the signs increased and enlarged, much as Nannerl's signs had, he began devoting all his thoughts and almost all his time to cultivating and advancing the genius of his son. His daughter then became incidental.

When Wolfgang Amadeus entered this life, Leopold was being charmed by as satisfying a daughter as a man possibly could have. She grew into a woman who was much more than her father's daughter. She was his very good friend. To the newly arrived Wolfgang Amadeus, however, the most conspicuous explanation for all

42

the love in which Leopold enveloped Nannerl was her responsiveness to anything and everything he showed her about the keyboard of a clavier and about music.

Wolfgang Amadeus got to the clavier the instant his baby legs were capable of taking him to it. He was self-driven in a relentless, even a cruel way. No aspect of music gave him pause. He was exploiting precocity as though precocity was an exchangeable coin. To Leopold the highest single value of life was music. Here was his babe seeking his loving approval by humiliating him as musician and artist. Leopold was mightily stirred. After much soul searching he concluded that his obligation to music required him to launch this prodigy at once into the big music world.

He took the boy and his sister first to the music-loving court in Munich. Wolfgang Amadeus was not quite six, so Nannerl was over ten. That same year he took them to the court in Vienna. The following year they went all the way to France and England. It wasn't too long before Nannerl was left at home. In the eleven years from the time Wolfgang Amadeus was six until he was seventeen, he and his father were away from Salzburg a total of seven years. This was the glorious unfolding of the "Mozart miracle" which took place in just about every town in Western Europe which had any claim to being a music center.

It was going to have many a weird side issue, such as avaricious parents beating, cajoling, starving, and threatening thousands upon thousands of children in the hope of forging "another Mozart." There's no telling how many outspoken enemies of music resulted although Ludwig van Beethoven was one of these kids and Carl Maria von Weber was another. But all these parents were laboring with faulty information. Wolfgang Amadeus was never forced except by himself. Leopold regarded him with awe, even with reverence.

The first musically knowing witnesses of the "Mozart miracle" thought there were two miracles. Nannerl impressed them as much as her brother did. But Nannerl never pushed at any time in her life. These witnesses and the witnesses who succeeded them were struck by the boy's urgent passion for Leopold's approval. He often told the strangers who questioned him, seeking his "secret": "Next to God, Papa comes first." Another continuing aspect of the child which was repeatedly noted was the eagerness with which he gave love to all and especially to Papa, in the hope of receiving love. He asked all manner of people—plaintively, as though he was tortured with hellish doubts—"Do you *really* love me?"

This child was subjected to all kinds of tests by the most learned musicians of the time. They had him play the clavier through a handkerchief spread on the keyboard and discovered it made not the slightest difference. They gave him themes to improvise with and were staggered by the variety and depth and spontaneity of his improvisations. They asked him to compose and often got back, sometimes within hours, music that would have given an adult a lasting reputation. Sitting between the knees of Johann Sebastian Bach's youngest son, Johann Christian, the child played the piano alternately and on equal terms with that mature master musician. But listen to the account of a contemporary, Friedrich Melchoir Grimm, who was a philosopher, a journalist, and man of the world:

"The most unbelievable of all is his [the child's] profound knowledge of harmony and its intricate ways, so that the Prince of Brunswick, truest judge in these matters, has said that many a superior kapellmeister would die without ever having learned what this nine-year-old boy already knows. We have seen him for an hour and a half under the impact storm of musicians from whose brows the perspiration ran down in streams, and who had all the trouble in the world to withdraw creditably from this struggle with a boy who left the battlefield without the least sign of fatigue."

Somewhere along in his teens this most pleasing and loving child began turning into an unloving, unpleasing man. Here is a proper place to recall a remark by Richard Wagner, who had as much talent for being right as he had for being obnoxious. Wolfgang Amadeus, said Wagner, was "music's genius of *light* and *love*." The individual steps from child to man are barely perceptible but they lead inexorably from a child who forever sought love to a man who did not seek love but rather repelled it while creating music of ineffable beauties and great truths which is shot through and through with *light* and *love*.

Inspiration—whatever "inspiration" is—came to him from no outside person or force or thing. The most delicate flower, the most beautiful woman, the most awesome landscape touched him very little if at all. He would hardly lift his eyes to look because he was absorbed in pouring himself onto paper as music. He was a fragile-looking little man whose greatest concern often seemed to be with the appearance of his hair. He was somewhat foppish in his excess of frills. He could appear gay and warm and at times he would delight in rough play, in practical jokes, and in pornography. But all who knew him well learned quite soon that all this was an overlay and beneath it was a pitiless indifference to the feelings and rights of others.

Only Nannerl and Papa Haydn endured in his affections. Papa Leopold was thrown out. Very sad documents are Leopold's letters to Nannerl in which he speaks of the genius whom he fostered so lovingly and painstakingly, as "your brother." Mozart's own letters show us a tightly self-contained man with the desire to see all people at their worst. His mind produced no leavening out of compassion or mercy.

Yet this same mind created music that is both a glorification and a justification of the human race. Speaking of The Magic Flute, George Bernard Shaw said it contained the only music ever composed which wouldn't be out of place in the mouth of God. The human heart and the human character have no more loving exemplifications in all art than in The Marriage of Figaro and Don Giovanni. "Slow" movements of some of the symphonies, piano concertos, and string quartets and quintets are irradiated with so much compassionate understanding that they seem to justify the theological concept that Love is what God is.

Wolfgang Amadeus is the only genius of music who spread-eagles the art. If you ask, which are the greatest symphonies, three of his have to be included (Nos. 39, 40, and 41). The greatest operas? Two of his are Everests in the operatic Himalaya (Figaro and Giovanni). Music for piano or violin? Chamber music? Songs? Liturgical music? Music for oboe, for harp, for flute, for clarinet, for bassoon or barrel organ? In all these and in everything musical, he is an unsurpassed master. All this the genius accomplished in a little less than the thirty-six years which were his span from birth to a pauper's grave.

The story of the man is readily and briefly told. Leopold capsuled it when he said his son as a child was prodigiously adult and as a man was prodigiously childish. His first biographer, Friedrich Schlichtegroll, who consulted Nannerl and others who knew him well, gave detail. "For just as this rare being early became a man so far as art was concerned, he always remained—as the impartial observer must say of him—in almost all other matters a child. He never learned to rule himself. For domestic order, for sensible management of money, for moderation and wise choice in pleasures, he had no feeling. He always needed a guiding hand, a guardian, to take care of domestic affairs for him."

His life as a man was what it had been as a child, that of a professional musician, but without Leopold's sensible management. He composed to order, he gave concerts when and where he could (he was among the first of the piano virtuosos and could have been, if he had wished, a violin virtuoso, too), taught when he had pupils, sought in vain the highest appointments in the musical establishments of kings, princes, and bishops. When he was twenty-six he was finagled into marrying Constanze Weber, a cousin of Carl Maria von

Weber, by her unscrupulous mother. Constanze was a flibbertigibbet, no less childish than he. In ten years she bore him six children and produced no end of harassments, without having a glimmer of his true merit as a creative artist. On at least one occasion she carelessly gave him evidence that she had made a cuckold of him. But he placed no great value on it. Probably he had never expected anything better.

He attracted no long-term personally devoted friends such as those who were always attached to the irascible Beethoven. There were many persons who were most aware of his genius. A few found themselves able to go all the way with the man. They have earned the gratitude of posterity because they lent him money and repaired as best they could the damage he constantly inflicted upon himself. Others are immortal in infamy because they were human enough to respond in kind to backbiting and to damaging intrigues. There was a court official who had the misfortune of losing his temper and applying his kicking foot to the Mozartian person. But Antonio Salieri, who for over fifty years was *Hofkapellmeister* to the Austrian emperor, did even less to earn a black remembrance. He merely protected his job against a would-be underminer with superior intrigue. Mozart was barely dead when rumors started that Salieri had poisoned him. Rimsky-Korsakoff about a century later composed an opera based upon those rumors. Salieri died at seventy-five, twenty-eight years after his opponent, and his last words are said to have been: "I did *not* poison Mozart."

The Mozartian adult years were marked by the continuing decline of the man and the continuing rise of the genius. Within two months in the summer of 1788, just three years before his death, he composed his three last symphonies which, when taken together, illustrate why there can be no reconciling of the man and the genius. The man was ill and harassed by debts and poverty and enemies. In the second of the three symphonies (No. 40) the genius seems in a titanic struggle of soul beneath a veneer of resignation. In the third of the three (No. 41, *Jupiter*) the genius achieves a kind of cosmic benediction. To believe these superhuman expressions came into being because the man was in the straits he was in is to believe ill-health and poverty generate great art. But even if you believed that you would have to account for the first of the three (No. 39) which is an outpouring of unadulterated happiness.

He died in Vienna on December 5, 1791, fifty-three days short of being thirty-six years old. Whatever tears Constanze shed were perfunctory. So was the funeral. The widow went home. A few associates set out to accompany the body to the grave in potter's field. The weather was inclement and the escort turned back at the city limit. It is true that Constanze was not well at the time. But she could have prevented her husband's body going to a pauper's grave. And she could have seen to it that the grave was marked while that was possible. So the grave has been lost and there is now no remnant of the man Mozart. The genius flourishes still, honored, even worshiped, by all to whom the art of music has meaning.

9

Beethoven

O NE of the very few simple facts about Ludwig van Beethoven is
that he was deaf through the years he was changing the course
of music. You'd think a composer would have to have functioning
ears. He didn't.

One of the many complicated facts is that he was obsessed with
fathering. You'd think such a man would have been driven into
parenthood by that—assuming he was able to avoid being led into it
by feminine stratagems.

He was able, and he wasn't driven. But from no absence of
feminine trying. On the portrait of herself which she gave him,
Countess Theresa von Brunswick wrote: "To the Unique Genius, to
the Great Artist, to the Good Man." (She died a spinster, at
eighty-six.)

Oh, but he was complicated, this Beethoven! Like his music, he
teemed with forcefulness. To give you an idea, he flung a would-be
patron down the stairs. Yet his tenderness was tender tender, especially
with a woman, a child, or any other object of his fathering.

His voice was raucous (due to his deafness); his untidyness, scarcely
believable; his temper, volcanic; his manners, abominable. Yet the
Archduke Rudolf of the Imperial Hapsburgs was proud to be his
piano pupil and his friend.

That in a day, mind, when musicians were ranked with servants.
Beethoven changed that. You dealt with him as an equal or you dealt
with him not at all. Not only the archduke, but assorted princes,
princesses, and personages in and out of the nobility accepted the
condition—gladly.

It was almost a full-time job to be his friend. Despite that, he had
many and rarely lost one. His endearing qualities and his exasperating ones worked together, like a hand and an arm. He wrote his
friend, Johann Hummel, "not to come to me again" because "you're
a treacherous dog." When he cooled he wrote Hummel again, saying:

"you are an honest fellow and I now see you were right. Come, then, to me, this afternoon." He promised to "bump, thump, and pump you to your heart's delight," sent him a kiss and signed himself "Beethoven also called mehlschöberl"—a mehlschöberl having been a kind of dumpling which floated in soup.

This fathering-obsessed nonfather was himself fathered by a court singer with a cook's daughter, and was born on December 16, 1770, in Bonn, a Rhine River town near which Robert Schumann died eighty-six years later. His father was a heavy drinker and so accounted a weakling, but there is no evidence he was an outstanding villain otherwise. The small boy was quite musical, enough so for Father to think he might be "another Mozart." Father saw to it he worked hard at the piano, beginning at five. And Father was forceful about it, disciplining the lad with a whip and a heavy slapping hand which were accepted approaches to child-rearing then. Nor was Father dealing with any sweetly agreeable child, but with a defiant one who seethed with resentments—of what, we do not know.

His childhood musical progress was impressive but he was no child prodigy in the way Mozart was, since he was driven rather than driving. But he was pleased to begin contributing to the family's support from musical earnings at fourteen because Father squandered most of his fixed income from the court on drink. When he was seventeen his adored mother died. The following year the eighteen-year-old had Father declared incompetent due to alcoholism and had himself appointed guardian of his two younger brothers.

Thereafter, and for the rest of his life, he played the part of father, never successfully but always to the utmost limit. He played it against his brothers and against the son of one of them, with domineering, possessive fury. As father he was all forcefulness which alternated between phases of strength that verged on savagery and phases of protective, strength-giving love. That is many a small boy's conception of his father. It also is an easily recognizable description of the typically Beethovenesque in music.

At twenty-two he went from Bonn to Vienna for the second time (the first time, he saw Mozart), this time to stay for good and to study counterpoint for a little while with Papa Haydn. That humane and wise master had more than just an inkling of how very complex his new pupil was. The young man asked and so Haydn told him: "You make upon me the impression of a man who has several heads, several hearts, and several souls."

He played the piano as the musical Viennese had never heard it played before, that is, with wild, ferocious abandon and limitless and often lawless imagination. Soon he was astonishing them further

—and upsetting some—with compositions which showed evidences of veering away from the polished formal perfections of Mozart and Haydn, into entirely new and so unknown directions.

Meanwhile, his father died back in Bonn although he had died long since in his son's heart. Brothers Karl and Johann, twenty-one and nineteen, went to Vienna from Bonn to be fathered by a brother who was only twenty-five. He tried to own them like chattels and direct them like puppets. They were not exceptional human beings, not in self-pride, especially. They objected and gave their brother endless trouble.

They gave the most trouble when he asserted a prerogative which neither granted even a little bit, which was to overrule their choices in the matter of wives. Like many another who has tried to exercise that kind of power, he was frustrated but he detested the wives as long as he lived. The quarrels were many and violent. He never gave up his brothers to their women.

In the midst of his first big musical triumphs he had the first premonitions of approaching deafness. You can understand how such an eventuality would prey on the mind of any musician. A deaf musician! To a nonmusician, the idea is ridiculous. To a musician, it suggests a hideous disfigurement, like not having a nose. And Beethoven felt himself growing steadily more and more deaf. For six years he saw doctor after doctor and hid as best he could from his musical friends, afraid this ultimate disgrace would be found out.

He reached bottom when he was thirty-two, in the Viennese suburb of Heiligenstadt where he was living and where he wrote his *Heiligenstadt Testament*. As a human document it matches any for depth of despair and intensity of suffering. The spiritual agonies of coming deafness are recounted, and he arrives at the contemplation of self-destruction. But he rejects that way of avoiding his fate.

"I would have put an end to my life," he wrote. "Only art stopped me. It seemed impossible for me to leave the world until I had produced all that I felt called upon to produce. And so I endured this wretched existence." Yet death still was in his mind, because he went on: "With joy I hasten toward death. If it comes before I shall have had opportunities to show all my artistic capabilities, it will still come too early for me despite my hard fate, and I shall probably wish that it had come later—but even then I will be satisfied. Will it not free me from a state of endless suffering?"

The tone is of self-justification. "O you men who think or say that I am malevolent, stubborn or misanthropic, how greatly do you wrong me." If these "men" would only understand the horror of being deaf they would appreciate that from childhood "my mind and my heart were kindly disposed and I longed to perform great deeds." He invoked God to bear him witness. "Almighty One. Thou knowest. Thou canst see into my innermost being. Thou knowest what love of man and desire to do good live therein."

The testament is disjointed and contradictory. It never quite makes sense but head-on, rushing emotions frequently don't. Obviously it reflects a major crisis in Beethoven the man, but we can't know the true nature of the crisis because he never interpreted his testament for anyone. It was not known to exist until it was found among his papers after his death. You have to be impressed that it was addressed to his brothers, who were never able to share any part of his ways of feeling. In fact, it seems clear they are the "men" who don't realize "how greatly do you wrong me." He wills to them all that he has and he enjoins them to "divide it justly, be friends, and help each other. What you may have done to hurt me, has long since been forgiven, as you know."

If he had killed himself then, at the age of thirty-two, his name hardly would be more than a name in a footnote in the history of music. His typical works and all his masterpieces were still ahead. These typical works began soon after he crawled out of his personal hell there in Heiligenstadt. Quite quickly his characteristic musical voice came into being. It is that of argument. The music hammers at you like vehemently eloquent words from an inspired disputant. The argument mounts in intensity and fury. Suddenly it dissolves and there is a quietly flowing river of milk and honey. All is sublime, all is serene. Evidently Beethoven has resolved his torments and reassured himself.

Two years after the *Testament*, his third symphony, **Eroica**, burst out of him, and music was never the same afterward. Music had been tightly bound to forms and to conventions, and it had been freed. **Eroica** and what followed closed the "classical" era of music and opened the "romantic." After **Eroica** there were only masterpieces—some lesser, some greater, to be sure—all hewed and shaped from the quite personal materials of a creator.

There were six more symphonies, for a total of nine, culminating with the overwhelming **D Minor**, the **Choral**, which can be heard a half hundred times without extracting its full content; eleven more piano sonatas for a total of thirty-two; ten more string quartets for a total of sixteen; his only opera, **Fidelio**, his fourth and fifth piano concertos, the latter called **Emperor**, and many smaller and lesser works. Among these is a song cycle, called **An die ferne geliebte (To the Distant Beloved)**.

Whether its yearnings for a beloved too distant to be attained have anything to do with his "Immortal Beloved" is unknowable. The "Immortal Beloved" has fascination because she was real, whoever she was. She lives now only in a letter which he wrote to her during the year he was forty-two, but never posted. It was found in a secret drawer of his desk. Again there is head-on emotion and contradiction. But it is most apparent that this is the passionate love of a man for a woman. The wording suggests that barriers exist between them, and a superficial view is that the woman was so high-placed she couldn't possibly have married a "mere" musician.

That is made silly by the fact that by the time he was forty-two to know Beethoven was a greater distinction for whoever knew him than any distinction which even the Archduke Rudolf could have conferred on Beethoven—and Beethoven and his friends, including the very high-placed ones, knew it. The Countess von Brunswick and her family maintained no barriers, and she certainly was a "beloved" of his and he, a "beloved" of hers. He conferred immortality on her with the dedication of the piano sonata in **F-sharp Minor**, Opus 78. But the "Immortal Beloved" could have been her sister, Josephine, or her cousin, Guilietta Guicciardi, to whom is dedicated the piano sonata in **C-sharp Minor**, Opus 27 No. 2, the so-called **Moonlight**. There were still other women who could have been, since he was devoted to them in a Beethovenesque way. He was no Don Juan. His moral sense was too strong and too inflexible. No one understands how he escaped matrimony. To be sure, he was extremely busy synthesizing himself in music and butting into the affairs of his brothers and their families.

He loved the idea of relentless "fate." So there is irony in what befell him when his brother Karl died. Karl in his will appointed him guardian of nine-year-old Karl Junior. Knowing his brother's low opinions of the boy's mother, Karl specified that the child was not to be taken from her and she was to be his guardian, too. That happened in 1815, when Beethoven was forty-five years old. Karl barely was in his grave when Beethoven was in court obtaining an order that dispossessed the mother. She appealed and won. He went back to court and after several years of litigation succeeded in excluding her for good.

Poor Karl Junior! Uncle took him over, body and soul, with ferocious hunger and fierce, terrifying love. Furthermore, the late Karl Senior was excluded, as the mother had been excluded. The youth was required to call his uncle "father" and Beethoven always wrote him, "dear son," and signed himself, "your father, Beethoven." Many of his letters to the adolescent and the young man exist and they add up a list of reproaches and complaints, mingled with prodigious generosity. From them you get the impression that young Karl was an ingrate, an idiot, and something of a scoundrel. That probably isn't altogether true. We have one record of Karl's point of view, from one of his deaf uncle's "conversation books." Karl wrote, for Uncle to read: "After you have upbraided me for hours undeservedly, you consider it insolence if this time at least I turn to jocularity from my bitter feeling of pain." The following year Karl shot himself in the head with suicidal intent, but recovered.

After his Heiligenstadt low, Beethoven made no more ado about his deafness, beyond pitying himself now and then. In his letters are many references to everyone's need for "resignation" to "fate," yet no one could possibly say he was ever truly resigned to anything. Even after he became stone deaf and lived in a silent world, he encouraged Johann Nepomuk Maelzel to try to invent a hearing trumpet that would help him, which he knew was impossible. Yet he had reason for a little hope because Maelzel was an inventive fellow who, among other things, invented the metronome. Maelzel was abused and even insulted in the process, but Beethoven gave him a magnificent recompense which he called "consolation for Maelzel." It is the second movement of the eighth symphony, which floats airily and delightfully along to the seeming beat of the metronome.

There were many consolations for the friends of this great genius and great eccentric. He lived alone in two or three rooms, usually amidst disorder and filth, with books and papers piled every which way, remnants of old meals here and there, ink pots spilled into pianos, the laundry scattered on the floor. He was constantly moving from one set of rooms to another, sometimes without reason, sometimes because the neighbors were up in arms over the shouting, singing, and pounding through the hours of the night. It was almost impossible for him to keep servants, because when they exasperated him he flung books at their heads, or even chairs, if chairs were nearer at hand.

His last years were marked by a series of illnesses of vague types, and also by compositions of extreme profundity—the last quartets and the **Grosse Fugue**, for instance. Karl's attempt at suicide upset him. When the young man recovered, he took him to the home of his brother, Johann, with an idea of somehow straightening him out but quickly fell to quarreling with Karl, with Johann, and with Johann's wife in the old familiar way. On his return to Vienna, he got pneumonia. Recovering from that, he took to his bed because of an illness whose nature we don't know although it may have been cirrhosis of the liver. It went on for months. In bed, he received a worshipful young man, Franz Peter Schubert, and said nice things about his compositions. (Beethoven often praised other musicians; it was part of his boundless generosity.) On March 26 1827, at the age of fifty-six, he reared up from his bed quite suddenly, lifted a clenched fist at the ceiling, and fell back. After that there was "not another breath, nor a heartbeat more," said a witness. The defiant child and the defiant man left life with defiance. But of whom? Of what?

10

Weber

Franz Anton Weber, musician, composer, inventor, actor, financier, impresario, braggart, strutter, and liar—but not very good at any of these things except the first and the last three—made himself both a baron and father of a musical genius.

This flamboyant charlatan with a handsome face and a charming tongue inserted a "von" into his name, preceded his name with "freiherr," appropriated the pedigree of an extinct noble family, and that easily he became a baron.

Nor was it difficult becoming a father. But he intended fathering a musical genius. All eight of his children by his first wife were blanks in this regard. Yet he persevered, and when the wife died, he lost no time in taking another. He was fifty-one and she was a fragile little waif of twenty-one who had missed many a meal and was cowed and furtive, like an abused kitten. Their first child was born with a laming hip defect. He was undersized, frail, and sickly from his first breath. No one would have given a dime for his chances even to survive. And this was the one of ten children in whom the father succeeded in sparking genius.

He was Carl Maria von Weber, composer of **Invitation to the Dance**, prototype of the lilting waltz, of **Der Freischütz**, an opera from which stemmed the whole school of German opera, and a large body of other works which are not now in fashion. His influence on music has been considerable.

Franz Anton came of a lower-class family. Both he and his brother, Fridolin, had marked musical ability. Fridolin was content to be a plain (and coarse) Weber all his life. By a drunken wife he sired a bevy of cantankerous daughters who could sing like angels. One was Constanze, who married and plagued Mozart.

To himself, Franz Anton was the leading actor in a melodrama of which he was also the playwright. He created the action as he went along and assigned roles to the people around him without asking or telling them, and then manipulated them into playing their roles unwittingly for as long as gullibility endured. His energy was inexhaustible. He would have done well if he had been clever.

Luck was with him, however, when he chanced to be a musician-servant to the prince-bishop of Cologne and Hildesheim at the time the court financial officer died. The prince bestowed the office on the deceased's daughter, Maria Anna Fumetti, provided she married a man who could do the work. Franz presented himself in haste and carried the day. He was secure then for a number of years, doing his work sloppily if at all, devoting himself to small-scale wanderings and adventures, and trying to develop musical genius in the babes who were arriving with clocklike regularity.

He wanted something to exhibit, something which would cause the world to gape with astonishment. At the time, the meteorlike flight of Mozart was running its course. Child prodigies were the rage. A really impressive one was a ticket to fame for its exhibitor.

Finally Weber was fired from his job, for sheer incompetence. Even more than before, Maria Anna had to content herself with seeing him only now and then. Her death seemed to trouble him not at all. He happened to be at anchor for the time, as town musician in Eutin in northern Germany not far from Hamburg, and a starvation job it was. Wandering off to Vienna, he returned with the emaciated and tubercular bride, Genofeva. He installed her in a dirty four-room flat where also lived two of his grown sons and two of his grown daughters, all as blatantly vociferous as their sire. In this place, on December 18, 1786, Carl Maria was born. (Mozart was then thirty years old, Beethoven was sixteen, and Schubert's birth was eleven years away.)

It would have been a wonder if the boy had survived even with the most skilled and hygienic care; that he survived without it is a miracle. He was four before he could walk. After that he always walked with a limp. In addition to the handicap of a substandard body, he had to contend with his strenuously eager father. He had hardly drawn his first breaths before Father was staring into his puckered face, looking for signs of genius.

Certainly, music was being thrust at him before he could talk and before he could walk. He was still a small child when he was having violin lessons and was getting his fingers rapped by a bow in a big brother's crude hands for every mistake he made. Father was drilling into him the elementary rudiments of composition. Also, there were unending and insistent lessons in piano playing.

All this was in the midst of the tearing uncertainties of a vagabond life. He was a year old when Father joined an operatic and dramatic

troupe. His mother could sing, so she went along. But her disease
was progressing and she was dead by the time her son was twelve.
Home became a succession of dingy theaters and rooming houses all
over Germany.

Fortune was up and down, but never very far up and usually down.
Father might be the orchestra leader, a viola player, an actor, or even
the impresario. On the side, he was making small and shady deals.
He dabbled in ancient Hebraic music and in chemical experiments.
He was a most remarkable man, but failure and half-failure attended
his efforts without ever dimming his self-confidence or his optimism.
But the small boy couldn't conceive of the big, exuberantly rough and
kind man being wrong about anything. He focused upon him as a growing plant focuses upon the sun. And what was important was not
that which was being done to the child, but how he was responding
to it. He was becoming wiry and tough—and supremely self-confident.

By the time the boy was eight, Father was exhibiting him and soon
made this his principal occupation, although, of course, he had side-
lines. After his wife died, Father and his son traveled around Germany
giving concerts for any who would listen—son playing the piano and
Father turning the music for him. Some of Carl Maria's compositions
were published, and at fourteen his first opera was produced.

The public was conspicuously disinterested. There was no doubt
of the child's being advanced beyond his years, but clearly his musical
development had been forced. The more often this opinion was
expressed the louder became Father's ballyhoo of another Mozart.
Whether Father knew he was making believe we cannot tell, but
neither criticism nor anything else could put doubt into the boy's
mind. He saw only lack of appreciation. Father had found him to be
a musical genius—and Father had to be right. All his life he was
going to feel insufficiently appreciated, although he would be floated
on an ocean of appreciation.

In time he justified Father, and in more than this one way. Having
swallowed Father's claim to the nobility, he lived up to the invented
heritage with his every fiber. It would have been impossible to tell
him from a genuine aristocrat, and during his lifetime no one doubted
his claim. It is all the more remarkable when it is remembered that he
was not properly educated, either for music or for the aristocracy.
Father was no gentleman. The son's education was principally the
education he gave himself, by experiencing, observing, and feeling.
His knowledge of the theater was intimate, detailed, and penetrat-
ing. In music he had a scattering of lessons, from a heavy-handed half
brother, from Father, from a few other pedagogic incompetents. Only
during his middle teens did he study under proper teachers—Michael

Haydn, brother of "Papa" Haydn, and the Abbé Vogler.

Vogler had connections, and the Webers, father and son, had brass. As a result the eighteen-year-old Carl Maria was appointed conductor of the Breslau Opera. Men twice his age and more had aspired to the post—men who were eminently qualified and famous. There were outcries of anguish, which the boy drowned very quickly by proving himself worthy—worthier than they, indeed, for he was inspired.

His methods were those of an autocrat. He was the presiding genius and from every person, whether singer or player or set designer or curtain raiser, he demanded absolute and unquestioning obedience. Discipline was his watchword, and his idea of discipline was not unlike that of an army sergeant. At first he was bitterly resented. His thin, small body and his pale complexion made him look even younger than he was. But his will was iron, and his stubbornness and endurance were unbreakable.

Away from the opera house he was more of a charmer than his father had ever been, because he had genuine consideration and feeling for human beings. The aristocratic outlook seemed as native to him as his skin, so it never obtruded and was never used to put an associate in his place or for self-aggrandizement. He loved to play the piano and sing for his friends. With an air that he owed it to his birth and breeding to do so, he indulged languidly in (as they were then considered) the aristocratic vices of wine, women, and gambling.

He lived with his father still, of course. Father now was seventy and was playing enthusiastically with acids, hoping to invent something sensational in engraving techniques. In his sloppy way, he left acids in wine bottles among bottles which contained wine. One evening Carl Maria chose the wrong bottle, and it almost killed him. His fine singing voice was ruined, and for the rest of his life he found it difficult to speak above a straining half whisper.

After two years, he left Breslau—evidently because his creditors were dunning him. No doubt they thought him a deadbeat, but they were very wrong. It took him years but he paid all his debts to the last penny. His honor was very important to him, and he guarded it zealously.

For a while he was private secretary to a younger brother of the bestial king of Württemberg, who earned his disgust and has since earned the disgust of history. Then for a few years he made his living as a touring pianist and conductor. Having been a vagabond throughout childhood, he found this life suited him well. Musical audiences, which refused to accept the child, accepted the adult as a first-rate musician. Notoriety solidified into fame.

In 1813, when he was twenty-seven, the celebrated Prague Opera hired him as its director, at a fat salary and with complete powers. It had been slipping; he restored it to its former place, by imposing his own musical and dramatic skills and tastes with steely arbitrariness. He was the czar in that opera house and there was no one, not even among the prima donnas, who cared to dispute it. But he was working much harder than even a robust young man should. From this period on it was always downhill for him physically. Yet his spirit hid it for the most part until the very end.

One of his young singers was Caroline Brandt. She had made her first stage appearance at the age of nine, and so they had much in common. His father had died, and he decided it was time for him to take a wife. She was his candidate. He wanted a wife who would give up any thought of a career and devote herself to bearing and rearing children and serving him. She declined what he considered to be a stupendous honor.

He didn't give up, he merely suspended the matter to give the foolish girl time to come to her senses. Meanwhile, he resigned from the Prague Opera, because he felt he had accomplished all he could after a little over three years, and so there was no reason for remaining. The German world was in foment and he was caught in it.

The German states had been repeatedly invaded and turned upside down by Napoleon. Now Napoleon was finished, and a fierce wave of Germanic nationalism was running. Weber already had composed several rousing choruses on patriotic themes which had profoundly impressed German emotions and made the composer a musical hero. While he was casting about for some way to do something outstandingly German, the king of Saxony asked him to go to Dresden, the Saxon capital, and establish a German school of opera.

The king wasn't too serious. He was making a sagacious nod to popular opinion and still preferred Italian opera and French culture. Weber had to insist upon equal status with the court's Italian *Kapellmeister*, and thereafter the king and the court did little to encourage him. But he created a German opera company out of nothing. Meanwhile, he began composing **Der Freischütz**.

He worked slowly because of the press of other duties. In 1817, Caroline did come to her senses, or at least changed her mind. She was rewarded with his tender and abiding love. But she was inevitably doomed to early widowhood.

After more than three years of intermittent work, he finished **Der Freischütz**, and since the Saxon court was so lukewarm toward German opera, it was given its first performance in Berlin on June 18,

1821. It swept Germany with the power of a tornado, overwhelming every German heart.

During his Dresden years he composed many other works that were to make a tremendous impression on composers who came afterward, although they are now seldom played. Der Freischütz was followed by Euryanthe, which was first produced in Vienna in October, 1823. Its libretto was unbelievably bad. The music was bright and arresting in places, but no music could have given such a libretto operatic vitality. Anyway, the composer was now conspicuously dying on his feet. He was wasting away, to the horror of Caroline and his friends, but not to his own. This was what the fates ordained and he accepted it.

Here was the aristocrat at his most courageous and at his best. He understood he might prolong his life a few years by allowing himself to be an invalid. What, then, would be the future of a penniless widow and his two children? So he drove his declining body into a frenzy of work.

From London came a generous offer, moneywise. For a new opera, for his personal supervision of its staging and first performances, and for some piano concerts, he could earn several times his annual salary as Dresden *Kapellmeister*. His doctors told him what he knew—the English climate was murderous for one in the advanced stage of tuberculosis. Yet he completed the opera in a year, while performing his court duties conscientiously and giving concerts, and in February, 1826, set out for London.

Rossini saw him during a short stopover in Paris and wrote in his diary: "He was in a pitiable state, livid of face, emaciated, with a terrible, dry cough, a heart-rending sight. . . . Aghast at the thought of him undertaking such a journey in such a state, I tried to dissuade him, telling him he was committing suicide, nothing less. But in vain. 'I know,' he answered. 'I shall die there. But I must go.'"

He went, he staged the opera, Oberon, he gave the concerts, he did everything required of him. It was amazing. He even bought tickets for his return to Dresden. But during the night of July 4-5, 1826, he died in his sleep. If he had lived a few months longer, he would have been forty years old.

11

Rossini

AFTER composing thirty-eight operas in nineteen years, Gioacchino Rossini stopped composing operas—bang—just like that, and for no reason apparent to him or to anyone else. Although only thirty-seven years old, he was the most famous and idolized musician in the world. There were going to be thirty-nine years more in his life. He was like a field which, after being wonderfully fertile through many seasons, suddenly sours and becomes desert sand.

From our distance in time, he and his works loom like magnificent ruins. Among these ruins are a few wholly intact structures, such as **The Barber of Seville**, one of the finest and most enduring operas. Mostly, however, there are exquisite and exciting bits and fragments from structures that didn't have the vitality to stand up against time. **The William Tell Overture** is one of these. For a reason unknown, but probably the same reason that suddenly made him musically sterile, this man fell far short of his potential.

Rossini was born on February 29, in the leap year 1792, in Pesaro, on the Italian Adriatic Sea coast. His father, Giuseppe, was the local inspector of slaughterhouses and also the town trumpeter. His mother, Anna, was a cook's daughter. They were cheerful of disposition and quite irresponsible. Shortly after their son's birth, they became theatrical troupers, he as a horn and trumpet player and she as a singer, although she couldn't read music and had to memorize whatever she sang.

A faltering grandmother and an aunt looked after the young child while his parents were on their theatrical circuit. He had energy, imagination, loved pranks and daring deeds. Anna and Giuseppe tried twice to correct his behavior by apprenticing him to blacksmiths, but even blacksmiths couldn't manage this lad, who was so very handsome people called him "the little Adonis" and so charming they were inclined to forgive his persistent badness.

He was getting just about no education, since he wasn't interested and his would-be teachers were incompetent. His first music teacher taught four-finger spinet playing, using the thumb and forefinger of each hand. All this was before he was ten. Already, however, he was devoted to beauty in women. According to him, one of Giuseppe's impulsive thrashings was more acceptable than the kiss of a woman he thought was not beautiful. He was convinced his mother was the most beautiful woman on earth or in heaven. He continued to believe this the rest of his life.

At about the age of ten, he received his first intelligent instruction in music, from a priest. Then, when he was twelve, the family moved to Bologna, where an outstanding music school, the Liceo Musicale, took him in. Only two years later he was elected a fellow of the Accademia Filarmonica which had similarly recognized the boy Mozart but did not deal out such honors lightly, certainly not to children. In addition to attending school, he worked evenings in the theaters, playing the horn or viola or the cembalo in the orchestra.

The pittances he earned helped support the family. Anna's voice had failed. The musical services of Giuseppe were not in demand. Their poverty was pathetic. The devoted youth would have liked to contribute more, but he knew what he wanted and he clung to the Liceo to get it. He wanted to master the composer's tools: counterpoint and harmony.

When he decided he had mastered them, although his pedantic teacher didn't agree, he left the Liceo. He now was eighteen. That year he composed his first opera, which was staged with fair success. The next year, he composed another; but the following year, he composed five! In his twenty-first year, the total was four!

Among them were several which excited people to their toes. Fame had come to him with the suddenness and in the volume of an avalanche. Crowds of admirers followed him through the streets; admiring throngs gathered under his windows at night and serenaded him with his own tunes; in Venice, where his ninth opera, **Tancredi**, was first performed, even in the law courts audiences, witnesses, and lawyers hummed its arias, and the judges were constantly compelled to call for silence.

Rossini remained extraordinarily handsome. His eyes seemed to light up a room, and his smile had the permeating warmth of the Italian sun. Women were wild about him, and there were many women in his life, then and later. They flitted in, then flitted out. There isn't an iota of evidence that he ever knew love of the kind we readily identify as a man's consuming love for a particular woman. But he loved his mother with a single-mindedness that was fanatical.

Always, he was gracious and kind to admirers. Still, he had little time for them. Operas were pouring from him as from a hydrant, while he divided his time among the opera houses of Rome, Venice, Milan, and Naples. **The Italian Girl in Algiers** took twenty-seven days to compose. But the masterpiece, **The Barber of Seville**, required only thirteen! It was first performed in Rome on February 20, 1816, when its composer was not quite twenty-four years old.

Among his prima donnas was Isabella Colbran, of the San Carlo Opera in Naples. She was thoroughly accustomed to having her every whim treated as law; she was a woman of whims—wild, extravagant whims. Rossini created operatic roles that fitted her temperament and her art and her German goddess figure as a glove fits the hand. Finally, in the year 1882, when he was thirty and she was thirty-seven, they were married.

Although she ruled any operatic world of which she was a part, Rossini ruled her—but softly, with a delicate, velvety touch; he was a sophisticate, with beautiful manners, brilliant wit, subtle tactfulness, exquisite tastes—especially in food and wines—and ever-increasing cynicism. Isabella loved him. He seemed to regard her as a very good friend. He showed her, and everyone, what he wished them to see. He kept people at a distance with his good-natured tolerance of any and every foible of the human race.

By 1822, he had written thirty-two operas, at the rate of more than two a year. It hadn't been an easy life. Composers, then, had to adjust themselves to the requirements of singers and impresarios. The system was a high-speed treadmill. To keep pace, Rossini resorted to all kinds of expediencies, like "borrowing" the overture from one of his old operas for a new one and fitting words of a new opera to music he had composed years before for another. Yet he seemed to thrive spiritually and physically.

The pressure of work is not enough to explain what was soon to happen. He gave us so few clues we must wonder if he himself knew of any explanation. Years later he confessed that along about this time he was finding out that with a mask of gaiety one can conceal fear and by laughing divert attention from matters of grave importance one wishes to hide. At this time, too, he was becoming more and more disparaging of himself. The rapier of his wit was cutting up the man who wielded it.

One incident—in 1819—foreshadowed the future. A stagehand came to him, at the end of the first performance of a new opera, and asked him to step out on the stage and take his bows, since the audience was shrieking for him. His instant response was to knock the man down, which was most un-Rossinian.

In 1822, he and Isabella went to Vienna, where he was received like a hero. He saw Beethoven, who admired **The Barber;** Schubert was too shy to present himself, although he thought that Rossinian music was wonderful. Through weeks of lionizing by the court down through the masses in the streets, he conducted himself impeccably.

Returning to Italy, he gave thirty-three days to composing **Semira-mide.** Its first performance, on February 3, 1823, was another great triumph. No one could have known that Italy's then most beloved and most successful composer would never again write an opera for Italians.

Later that year, he and Isabella went to London, where she had a singing engagements. Among the pleasures he seemed to have there was singing duets with King George IV.

After London came a long stay in Paris, where the court was eager to attach such a cultural asset. He was given an official position. For three years his surface life was one of seemingly unruffled and un-rufflable amiability. He staged and conducted Italian operas; he seemed to enjoy people and society. Privately, he was mastering the French language and assimilating French operatic forms. In 1826 he re-worked one of his old Italian operas so thoroughly it was both a new opera and a French opera, not only in its name, **La Siège de Corinthe,** but in every particular. Within six months he had another French opera ready—**Moïse,** based upon his old Italian opera **Mosè in Egitto** —and it appeared he was launched on a second successful career.

While working on **Moïse** word reached him that his mother was very ill back home in Bologna. Friends restrained him from rushing to her, saying she was excitable and his sudden appearance might make her worse. Just before **Moïse** had its triumphal first performance in the Paris Opera, he learned of her death. As he took his bows before a clamorous audience, tears streamed down his face. Oblivious of time and place, he murmured, "She is dead!"

After that he made little effort to appear lighthearted. More than a year passed before his next opera, **Le Comte Ory,** which was entirely new and very French. It was produced in 1828. That year he buried himself in the country and, in six months, composed his last opera, **William Tell,** produced the following year to the vast admira-tion of musicians and musical people. Soon after the first performance, he and Isabella set out for Bologna. There wasn't the slightest sign the great Rossini was through—or that the great Rossini had any intima-tion of being through.

Isabella was rich by her own earnings. He was rich by his. They had an estate outside Bologna and a palatial house in the town. He seemed to be enjoying leisure, of which he had had very little in his life so far. He returned to Paris the next year. Isabella stayed in Bologna.

Her relations with Rossini had been strained for some time, ever since she made the mistake of quarreling with his mother.

Charles X had been overthrown as king of France. The succeeding government nullified Rossini's long-term contract as a state composer, and he sued. Despite this vexation, he seemed his old self for the most part, though very nervous. Through a mutual friend, a Spanish prelate asked him to write music for a medieval poem, **Stabat Mater.** He refused, until he was promised it would never be performed in public and would remain in the prelate's possession, as a souvenir. With this guarantee of secrecy, he got to work. And here is another indication of his state of mind, for we hide the things about which we feel guilty. Rossini now was hiding the art that had made him.

Trying to maintain his front of *bon vivant*, he also composed little pieces, now and then, to be played at parties. But, as more time passed, people began to understand something was wrong. He sought to avoid their questions by talking about his "laziness" and his "love for idleness," which everyone knew were no qualities of his. When people dared to ask about his "next" opera, he changed the subject.

Meanwhile, he permitted Olympe Pélissier to enter his life. Her background was sordid; she was a Mary Magdalene seeking redemption through great love and great service. To her, Rossini was a god she wished to protect, to serve, and generally to mother. He was very much in need of what she wanted to give, and she quite quickly earned his gratitude—and dependence.

At about this time he had a nervous breakdown. The doctors ordered complete rest, and rest seemed to remedy his troubles, although he remained highly nervous. After trying to interest himself in travels, he drifted back to Bologna, arranged a legal separation from Isabella, and sent for Olympe. Isabella was both loving and understanding. She even invited Olympe to lunch.

Now Rossini interested himself in his old school, Liceo Musicale, and was, in time, its unofficial director. He seemed to want to make Bologna a world music center. This was his principal occupation, aside from social life, until 1848, when he was fifty-six. That year the fever of revolution swept Italy. Quite unreasonably, some hotheaded citizens decided Rossini wasn't patriotic, and there was a hostile demonstration in front of his house. The next day he and Olympe left for Florence. He had finished forever with Bologna.

In Florence his nervousness increased. In 1852 he had another breakdown, which carried him to the brink of madness. Indeed, some people said he was mad for a time. By his own later account, he stood in front of a mirror, cursing himself because he lacked the nerve to kill himself. "What am I doing in the world?" he asked himself.

"What will people think when they see me reduced, like a small child, to having to rely on a woman?" Olympe acted the part of a mother frenzied over a hurt child, with all her heart and energy. When all kinds of cures failed, she got him back to Paris, where the doctors had succeeded before and now succeeded again, unless Rossini's malady subsided on its own.

Within a year he was more or less his old self. His gleaming bald head he concealed with a fine collection of plain and fancy wigs. He began going out and entertaining in his home and even listening to music and accompanying singers on the piano. For a long time he had been as uninterested in hearing music as he had been in composing it. Now he could talk about what had happened to him as a creator. He still liked to say he was lazy. But to one of his oldest and closest friends, he said: "Believe me, it was a sentiment of delicacy, rather than vanity, which led me to renounce money and fame. Otherwise, I should not so soon have hung my lyre on the wall. Music needs freshness of ideas. I knew nothing but lassitude and crabbedness."

Through his years and his secret suffering he had grown enormously as a human being. A list of all the young and unknown composers he befriended and helped would run to considerable length and include many names which musical people now revere.

Isabella had died in 1845. Her last word was "Rossini." A year later, he had married Olympe. In April, 1857, when he was sixty-five, he gave her a musical manuscript with the inscription: "I offer these songs to my dear wife, Olympe, as a tribute of gratitude for the affectionate and intelligent care she lavished upon me in my long and terrible illness." It was just about the only music he had composed in almost thirty years.

Now he began composing again and at a great rate, mainly curious little pieces—for voice, piano, and other instruments—many with strange titles, such as **A Deep Sleep, Tortured Waltz, A Caress for my Wife, A Hygienic Prelude for Morning Use, The Radishes.** Rossini still was Rossini's severe critic. He called these pieces, which eventually reached a number approaching two hundred, "The sins of my old age." And on the margin of one of his very last works, the **Petite Messe Solenelle** (which wasn't *petite* at all), he addressed himself to God: I was born for *opera buffa*, as Thou knowest. Little skill but some heart and that about sums it up."

He died on November 13, 1868, in his seventy-seventh year.

12

Paganini

Nicolo Paganini was the greatest master of the violin the world has known so far, and also among the strangest of great men. He took pains to persuade people that his genius would have been impossible without supernatural sponsorship.

He endeavored to resemble the popular conception of the devil. He starved himself and looked like a clothed skeleton. His long bony face was wax colored and mask-like, and his eyes glittered balefully. He seemed a container of smoldering diabolical intensity, ready to burst at any instant into hell-fire.

This was the Paganini he chose to present to the world. Since the choice was his, you are compelled to believe it had undeniable appeal to him, especially when he took the trouble now and then to bolster his satanic appearance with a satanic deed—nothing imaginative or even unusual, however, always a commonplace satanic deed. His knowledge of the potentialities of evil was slight and childlike.

But his concentration upon the violin was much too furious for there to have been energy left for the study of either good or evil. It began in childhood, and by his early teens he was inventing playing difficulties that would have appeared impossible to any experienced violinist. But he solved them by working at them ten hours at a stretch for weeks and months.

There was nothing mysterious about how he acquired his mastery, really; but he made it mysterious—and strange and weird. Born in Genoa, Italy, on February 18, 1784, he was the child of ignorant and superstitious parents. That is not said unkindly. It is essential to know it. We all get our first ideas from our parents, and some of them stay with us all our lives. In the minds of his parents the world was almost as well populated with spirits, good and evil, as with people. They believed people could have personal, face-to-face dealings with Satan, and they believed in signs, omens, and the evil eye.

His mother, Teresa, was given to hysterics and to dreams in which angels and demons soothed and terrified her. In one of these dreams, angels invited her to choose the future of her youngest son, then seven. Since her husband, Antonio, loved music and dominated her every fiber, and since little Nicolò had already taught himself to play the violin, we can understand why she said she wanted the boy to become a great violinist.

Antonio believed angels could accomplish anything. But, being a two-fisted, hairy-chested dock-walloper, he was an actionist and eager to help. He helped the angels with a leather strap whenever his son showed signs of skimping his practice. In that way, and also by depriving him of food. It is interesting that starving himself was a lifelong practice of Nicolò Paganini, the man, and also that he rejected his mother's angels and chose instead to suggest that his genius had been contrived in hell.

From the beginning Nicolò had been a most unusual child. Musical sounds set him trembling and perspiring; he would seem on the verge of convulsion. He was subject to cataleptic seizures, and in one gave such a realistic appearance of being dead that Teresa began working on a shroud.

After Teresa's dream, Antonio must have felt he and the angels were working together most effectively. At nine, the boy gave his first concert and astonished a home-town audience. Antonio took him to Parma when he was eleven, to put him under Alessandro Rolla, a foremost virtuoso. Rolla heard him play, threw up his hands, and said he could teach him nothing.

In a few years Nicolò was composing his twenty-four **Caprices** which form one of the most amazing "opus ones" in music. Not only are they extremely difficult to play; they are rich in dramatic musical ideas and have influenced and inspired all violin players since, and many composers.

At this time—Nicolò was in his teens—something happened between brutish, muscular father and frail, sickly son. We don't know what it was, but it caused Antonio, who had been ferociously possessive, to abandon the possession. Thereafter the youth was his own man, and Antonio bowed to his will. Already cultivating a devilish appearance and rumored to have an evil eye, it is quite likely Nicolò had frightened his superstitious sire out of his wits. Once free of paternal tyranny, the boy-man embarked upon what a child might consider an evil life and an adult would consider a foolish one. Gambling was his devilment of choice, then; later, it was shoddy treatment of women.

At eighteen or so he was the darling of a provincial princess. His next patron was another princess, Maria Elisa, sister of Napoleon. He treated them badly, naturally, yet behind his craftily self-cultivated reputation as an archdestroyer of women was a pathetic fear of them. He attributed to women all kinds of evil of both action and intent. Never could he bring himself to have even a little faith in their love— and this man, behind the satanic mask he chose to wear, longed for faith in love, any love.

By the age of twenty-four he was deep in the rut of his permanent way of life, which was traveling from one town to the next and giving as many concerts as there were audiences. Now and then he would be prostrated by the peculiar trancelike illness of his childhood, or he would retire for a few months to work out even more incredible feats of violin playing. For nineteen years he traveled up and down Italy, building a mountainous reputation as a violin virtuoso, sorcerer, and devil. After that, he achieved no less fame in Austria, Germany, France, and the British Isles.

We can judge the hypnotic effect he had upon audiences by the fact that many contemporaries considered him exceptionally tall. Yet the French critic, F. H. J. Castil-Blaze, certified he was only five feet six. One contemporary description of him: "No one was ever so incredibly thin. He had a pale complexion, a sharp, prominent nose like an eagle's beak, and long, bony fingers. He seemed too frail to bear the weight of his clothes. When he bows to his audience, his movements are so strange that one dreads lest his feet should detach themselves from his body and the whole man disintegrate and crumble to a heap of bones. . . . His face never loses its deathlike impassiveness except when the storms of applause break out, then it lights with a peculiar smile. He pushes out his lips, his eyes dart hither and thither, but there is no trace of benevolence in them."

In his youth he played well-known and well-loved works for the violin but showed no respect for the intentions of the composers, and recomposed them, in effect, as he played. Then he began playing only his own compositions, which were loaded with amazing effects, some beautiful, some painfully ugly, replete with what his audiences felt were visions of hell, including the shrieks of the damned. Going to a Paganini concert was like going to a musical circus. For instance, the master's violin strings were forever breaking. He used very thin ones to produce some of his strange effects and also, no doubt, so they would break. When they did, he continued to play, on three strings, then on two, then on only one.

Whether he played on four strings or one, the fireworks were always brilliant. The steely fingers of his left hand ran up and down the fingerboard, plucking with a speed and sureness that matched his flying bow, and giving the effect of two violins played together. No one ever heard him tune his instrument; that he always was careful to prevent. It was years before other violinists discovered that some of his most amazing effects were brought about by tricks in tuning, one of which was to tune a semitone higher than the accompanying orchestra, and so his playing would leap out from the orchestral backdrop as vividly as a comet.

Inevitably, a man who looked so sickly, who displayed so much genius and sorrow, and who had such a reputation as a destroyer of women would attract many women. As he said himself, "I am not handsome, but when women hear me play they come crawling to my feet," which also is an accurate statement of the role he assigned the female sex. It also was inevitable that he should come across a woman who would be a match for him—for a time, at least. She was Antonia Bianchi, a singer, whom he met in Venice. He always concertized with an assisting artist, who filled in while he took breathers off the stage. Antonia had the job.

This relation bloomed into a personal one. In July of 1825, when he was forty-one, she gave birth to his son, who was named Achileo. We get an idea of Antonia from Paganini's letters to the only long-term intimate friend he ever had, Luigi Guglielmo Germi, Genoese lawyer and amateur musician. In one of them Paganini said he and Antonia were at a party, and for no reason at all she asked him to take her home. He merely asked her why. "Whereupon she slapped my ears violently and gave off such infernal screams that she alarmed the whole assembly. She shrieked until she nearly burst, and we thought we would never bring her to her senses."

This was the one woman who held him for a period longer than weeks. She held him for years. But the time came when she couldn't any longer. He wrote Germi: "I have washed my hands of her. She is a beast, an iniquitous beast." Although he made a handsome settlement on her, he took their child and during all his remaining years directed an unending torrent of affection at the boy. His profession of love for his mother had been at best formal. He never made a profession of love for his father. He had great regard for Germi as an only friend. But on the child he lavished his deep capacity to love. As an example, here is a letter he wrote the seven-year-old:

My Dear Son, My Darling Achillino:
These few days which I have spent away from you seemed to me like ten years. Heaven knows what it cost me to leave you. . . . Not a day goes by without my thinking of you. I pretend that I am talking to you and hugging you. Tomorrow evening I shall have the joy of clasping you in my arms and of saying things which are too heartfelt to put into a letter. I hope you are being good and getting on well at school. I long to press

you to my heart again. Believe me, with deep devotion, Your Papa,
Paganini.

We may contrast this pure affection with his attitude toward a
Miss Charlotte Watson, which was quite typical. She was seventeen
when she eloped, to her subsequent sorrow, with the then fifty-year-old
Paganini. It made a frightful scandal, monopolizing newspapers for
days. He coolly wrote a newspaper that Miss Watson said "she followed me because I had promised to marry her in Paris and give her
jewels and a rich dowry. Her acts, therefore, were voluntary and by
no means disinterested. Let the public draw its own conclusions. As
for me, I have said my last word about this tiresome business."

Miss Watson, so far as we know, was his last escapade of this sort.
Over the years various doctors had had their chances to improve his
health. To their amazement, they'd found nothing wrong with him
aside from malnutrition. One had even written in a newspaper article
that, miraculously, this consumptive-looking artist was not in the least
tubercular. But his health began to fail now. A wealthy man, he
bought a rich estate near Parma and tried to play the role of a lord
with his money and fame, his many decorations, which included
one from a petty German state that carried with it the title "baron."

That was not his taste, however. He became involved in a scheme to
operate a gambling palace in Paris and eventually lost a great deal of
money. No one had any sympathy for him, since he had a reputation
for extreme stinginess. Yet during this period, he heard Hector Berlioz
conduct the first performance of **Symphonie Fantastique** and presented the astonished conductor-composer with twenty thousand
francs. That piece—made up of visions of hellish scenes and hellish
torments—would have appealed immensely to him.

By now he had lost his voice. The doctors had something to treat
at last—a severe infection of the larynx and throat—but they couldn't
treat it effectively, and Paganini went into slow decline during which
he was tenderly cared for by his son, now in his teens.

In 1840 he was in Nice, and dying. He commended his soul to God
and in his will left money for Masses for his soul's repose. He died, on
May 27, 1840, at the age of fifty-six.

He had built his devilish reputation solidly. The archbishop refused
permission for his body to be buried in consecrated ground. For thirty-
five years the leaden casket was stored, until at last the faithful son
got the edict reversed by the Pope, and Paganini was interred in a
churchyard in Parma. We can regard Paganini as sufferer rather than
sinner. His lasting importance as a composer proved to be rather slight.
It is no wonder. By the time he reached his end the romantic masters
were flourishing—Berlioz, Mendelssohn, Schumann, Chopin, and

Liszt. As a composer he was never in their league. What remains healthily alive of his are the **Caprices** and a number of violin concertos which can be fun for hearers—and for a violinist able to play them. Yet the art of music is greatly in his debt. He was the goad which sped both the development of composing for and the techniques of playing the stringed instruments.

13

Schubert

FRANZ PETER SCHUBERT was the unalloyed poet among the five supergiants of the musical art (Bach, Haydn, Mozart, Beethoven, and Schubert)—the poet in the sense of Plato when he said that "poets utter great and wise things which they do not themselves understand."

Schubert seemed to understand very little. For the business of living, he had not a semblance of competence. He was hardly five feet tall. He was near-blind and wore his thick-lensed spectacles even in bed. If he had taken them off he might not have been able to find them. His shyness and meekness were extreme enough to suggest the morbid state. As a man, nature shortchanged him outrageously.

But nature compensated by letting him feel sunnily happy through just about every hour of his short life. He had every reason to suffer piteously from poverty, frustration, and worry. So far as we can tell, he never had enough plain sense to know it. Perhaps he would have had enough of that kind of sense, at least now and then, if he hadn't been so incessantly ridden.

The rider was his genius. It was energized by as much instinct and intuition as was ever compressed within one human being. A friend described his creative process as "hurling"—for eighteen years he spent most of his time hurling musical notes onto paper, and then he died after only thirty-one years of living.

Six years after Mozart died in Vienna, Schubert was born there, on January 31, 1797, which was the year two eminent Viennese-by-adoption, Haydn and Beethoven, became sixty-five and twenty-seven years old, respectively.

The new arrival was the thirteenth of the fourteen children Franz Theodor Schubert, a schoolteacher of mediocre ancestry and deficient education, fathered with Elisabeth née Vietz who had been a servant girl. Of this bountiful crop (Franz Theodor was going to father five more by his second wife!) only five survived to adulthood. Vienna was a filthy city in a filthy age. Infectious disease was everywhere, especially among the herd-living lower classes. Babies arriving and babies dying; that must have set the tempo of the small Schubert home. Individuality among children couldn't have counted for very much.

Father Schubert lived long enough to know he had sired genius and so he liked to indicate he had had a hand in its nurture. Beyond teaching the child the rudiments of music, there is no evidence he had a hand or was capable of having one. He himself played the stringed instruments but was a musician only of sorts. No doubt he was kindly disposed when he had time for it but he had his rigidities and his moments of violent temper. As for the mother, very little is known about her. She died when her genius son was fourteen. Yet it seems quite certain she was a nonentity in the home. Whatever was the cause or causes of it, we can't forget the man part of the genuis was milk toast.

At least Father recognized in the boy's superb singing voice the wherewithal for a better education than he and other Schuberts had had. At the age of eleven the lad's voice got him admitted as a free boarding pupil in the school which provided boy singers for the Imperial Chapel. Father wasn't particularly interested in its facilities for the boy to learn music. His interest was in his learning enough Latin, theology, mathematics, and grammar to become a schoolteacher.

Now we have our first clear view of Schubert, while he still was a child, as other pupils and teachers saw him. His sweet cheerfulness was never known to diminish or fail. His musicality was quite tremendous. There was a wistful helplessness about him. Clearly he needed to be looked after. That's irresistible. There were plenty of volunteers.

Mozart's old opponent, Antonio Salieri, had been one of the judges who admitted Schubert to the school. That excellent technical musician endeavored earnestly over the following six years to make a first-class musical technician out of him. He didn't succeed, nor was Schubert ever one. But as his first music teacher in the school remarked, "the boy knows everything already." He did, in the special sense of genius. In any conventional sense, he was largely uneducable. When his voice broke, his marks in nonmusical subjects weren't high enough to get him a scholarship which would have kept him in the school, and out he went.

Already he was hard-ridden. He had been in his thirteenth year when his genius really straddled him. There had been preliminary seizures of creative frenzy but now the unceasing pace was a full run.

When, at sixteen, he was finished with school, he seemed hardly aware of it, or of other events. He became an assistant in his father's school, where he quickly demonstrated his complete inability even to maintain order among children, much less teach them anything. During the second of the two years in which he was making an ass of himself as a teacher, which was the year he was eighteen, he composed 148 songs, 2 symphonies, a string quartet, 2 Masses, 4 dramatic works, 4 piano sonatas, and a miscellany of other pieces. That year he composed **The Erl King.** The year before, **Gretchen at the Spinning Wheel** had been in his output.

Something happened in the Schubert home about this time. We don't know what. At nineteen, Franz left the home, never to return as a resident although it was much superior, plain though it was, to some of the "homes" he had thereafter. Father was living with his second wife but Franz was on amiable terms with her—he was on amiable terms with everyone who met him even one one-hundredth of the way. We know Father didn't approve of professional musicians. They fell far short of the respectability which schoolteachers enjoyed. And we know Franz left to live with a friend who realized he was a musician—and absolutely nothing else.

Let's have a look at his genius at work. It need not detain us for long because it has a monotonous sameness. When he got out of bed, he went right to his worktable and for five hours or six hours or even seven hours, he "hurled." Whatever came up out of his mind was what he hurled. The process was so extremely rapid, we have every right to doubt that his conscious mind was often aware of what was going on. Never did he look at what he had done, to see if the hurled notes had made a proper impression upon the paper.

Perhaps a friend had said to him in the tavern the night before, you ought to compose a symphony—Beethoven's symphonies are sensations. So the morning after, he composed a symphony. Or a friend might have said, look at Rossini! His operas make him rich and famous. You ought to be rich and famous! So Schubert composed opera. Just anything could give direction to his compositorial torrents which were going to spill out with or without direction.

His friends were singers who loved nothing more than to sing his songs and poets who were honored to provide his lyrics. That was the directing stimulation which made him the greatest song writer who ever lived. Perhaps a friend had given him a manuscript or a book of poetry in the tavern, or he had copied the poetry a wine-warmed friend was reciting. It could be the poetry of Goethe or doggerel. Consciously he exercised no literary taste whatever (which is the basis of the aphorism, "Schubert could set even billboards to music—and did!"), although his greatest songs are set to the best poetry which came into his hands.

Schubert himself explained himself quite simply—and most cryptically. "When I finish one piece," he said, "I begin another." His awareness of the worth of Schubert's utterances was just about zero. The following little story is telling: he picked up a copy of a song, read it with interest, remarked it was a good song, and asked: "Who wrote it?" You can imagine the tone of voice with which his friend exclaimed: "Why, you did!" Rather than try very hard—or even try at all—to get his output performed or staged or published, he dumped it in closets where, in time, considerable heaps accumulated.

That was his genius at work. At other times, when freed from his genius for the time being, the man was living passively—watching, not participating; listening, hardly ever asserting; dreaming, rarely doing. After his withdrawn hours of "hurling," he'd become suddenly gregarious and rush into the warming, comforting closeness of herds—herds of poets and painters and such "Bohemians" or of musicians. The former he herded with in taverns and made himself their beloved by his rapturous listening to their feverish discussions of the meanings of life and of art and to their recitations of their poetry and dramas. The latter he herded with in musicians' homes, where the company sang and played the music of Schubert and tried not to embarrass the composer too painfully by giving undue notice of his presence.

He loved all these friends with the sweet amiability of a child. They loved him protectively, as a child is loved, called him "Little Mushroom," and tried among themselves to see to it that he was cared for. Occasionally, one of them tried to get him a job as a music teacher or performer; now and then, one of them took him on a holiday in the country. Thanks mainly to their efforts, his music was published and performed professionally. But their watchfulness over him failed frequently. He lived in a succession of rooms, shabby and shabbier. We know he went without food frequently. Occasionally, a harlot made sport of him in a tavern-made rendezvous. But there were decent and sensitive women who longed to shield him from every chance of harm. The man whose genius created so many poignant songs but nothing of genius in love songs was as incompetent with feminine overtures as he was with less obvious phenomena. All adult relations baffled him.

In these ways Schubert lived his two lives, the inner one of incredible richness, pulsating with countless and overwhelming beauties; the outer one, that of a timid child. To say he was unappreciated in his lifetime is to speak nonsense. He was appreciated to the fullest extent he allowed. The recognition he had was the recognition his admiring friends pushed him into taking. The instant the push was taken away, he stopped moving. Even so, he would have been swamped with fame if he had lived a few years longer. Genius such as Schubert's can't possibly be hidden for very long.

During his last year of life it occurred to him he might profit by knowing more about counterpoint, and he arranged for some lessons. He composed the "Great" **C Major symphony** and the **C Major Double Cello Quintet** which have to be counted among the finest masterpieces of music. While he "hurled," typhus microorganisms were in even greater circulation than was usual in that age. They had killed his mother, and they killed him on November 19, 1828. Beethoven had died the year before. Schubert carried a taper in the funeral procession. Now Schubert's grave was made, three graves from Beethoven's. A poet friend composed the epitaph: "Music has here entombed a rich treasure, but still fairer hopes."

Which was quite true, but the poet and the rest of Schubert's friends had no idea how very rich was the treasure. In his lifetime only 187 of his 603 songs were published, only three of his 21 piano sonatas, only one of his 7 Masses, only one of his 19 string quartets, not one of his 10 symphonies, and only about half of a miscellancy comprising some three hundred items. Ten years after his death, Robert Schumann heard a rumor there were piles of Schubert manuscripts lying around Vienna and he went to have a look. Fanatical musician and music-lover that he was, he danced for joy over the treasures he found in the dusty piles, particularly over the "Great" **C Major Symphony** which, thanks to him, was launched into immortality by a first performance conducted by Felix Mendelssohn on March 21, 1839.

Anything so incredible caused skeptical people to check back. The old friends strained their memories and it came back to them. A Vienna orchestra had asked Schubert for a symphony. He composed it with his usual dispatch. At rehearsals, they found it extremely difficult—too difficult, in fact. Schubert said, in effect, Don't bother. Why not play one of my earlier symphonies? And so they had and Schubert had carried the new one to his room and dumped it on the pile of castoffs.

But that was by no means an end of the incredible. In 1865, thirty-eight years after Schubert's death, Johann Herbeck, a conductor picked up a rumor that a friend of Schubert's, Amselm Hüttenbrenner, had among his private papers a symphony of Schubert's. He journeyed to Hüttenbrenner and inquired. Hüttenbrenner said, Yes, he did, and produced the score of what many a musician has considered the masterpiece of all musical masterpieces—the **B Minor Symphony, The Unfinished.** Hüttenbrenner was a composer himself, a somewhat pedantic one. He considered the "unfinished" condition of the symphony a fatal flaw. It turned out that Schubert had composed two symphonic movements with which to thank a provincial music society for electing him a member. He gave them to Hüttenbrenner to deliver for him—and Hüttenbrenner hadn't.

Two years later Sir George Grove, the English musicologist, and Sir Arthur Sullivan, of the Gilbert and Sullivan operas, went to Vienna to look for the complete score of the incidental music Schubert composed for a short-lived drama, **Rosamunde.** Only a fragment existed and it obviously had been torn from a masterpiece. They rooted about in closets and came at last upon the part books, just where the composer had tossed them after **Rosamunde** closed—that treasure and many another.

To this day pedantic musicians will point to "faults" in Schubert's music. Listeners who neither play nor sing do it, without realizing it, by calling the **B Minor Symphony, the Unfinished.** To be unfinished is a tremendous fault—Hüttenbrenner was quite right about that. But the "unfinished" state is our opinion, not Schubert's. His musical instincts and intuition humble all learning and his technical imperfections are quite often exquisite perfections, which isn't a paradox. Alexander Brent Smith, a musicologist, said if he were asked to pick out genius on the basis of a bar or two of music, he'd pick Schubert instantly from a bar in **Death and the Maiden** quartet. "No wrenching, aching harmonies! Only a *faultily* written chord."

14

Berlioz

We're not going to understand Hector Berlioz, but we can try, and a good place to begin is with a pair of pink shoes. They were on the feet of the eighteen-year-old girl he met and adored when he was twelve, or so he thought. A year later, she disappeared from his life. Forty-nine years later, he traveled hundreds of miles to find this girl, who now was a widow and the mother of four men. He assailed her with ardent protestations of love. She was "a shrine," he said; he was "a worshiper." To her, he was a wild stranger from out of the blue, and she was positive she had never owned a pair of pink shoes in all her life.

She did not return his feelings, and he suffered. But could it have been otherwise? That question is as good a key as there is to this man. His affairs were always arranged—by him—so they'd return a high yield of suffering. He must have fancied suffering very much, to have given himself so much.

He was inclined to shrieks of anguish, to sobs and tears, to wild laughter, to grotesque antics and sudden whims. If we judged Berlioz only by these things, we'd have to think him a madman. We must also keep in mind that he had an unflagging capacity for enormous and painstaking labor, a mind that was capable of philosophical thought and courtierlike intrigue, too. He also had musical genius to burn.

The most extraordinary feature of this extraordinary man was his hair—his red hair. The poet Heinrich Heine, who knew him well, said it was "a forest overhanging a precipice." Beneath the hair were piercing blue eyes and a large Roman nose. His body was skinny and angular; taken altogether, he presented a most memorable appearance.

Even more memorable were the moments when his emotions overflowed, which were frequent. For instance: One evening in the opera house, the orchestra was beginning an aria and the singer was about to come in when a shaking figure arose from the audience and, in "a voice of thunder," filled the house with his shouts: "You don't want two flutes there, you brutes! You want two piccolos! Two piccolos, you hear!"

Listen to Berlioz telling how he responded to "good" music: "My arteries quiver violently. My tears show only that the condition may become intensified. If that further stage is reached, my muscles contract spasmodically. My limbs tremble, and my feet and hands are numb. I cannot see perfectly. I am giddy and half faint."

When not in emotional eruption, he was cold and withdrawn. Either way, he was difficult for all concerned, and especially for himself.

Hector Berlioz was not quite eighteen years old when he arrived in Paris from La Côte-Saint-André, the village where he was born on December 11, 1803. His mission was to study medicine, and he had learned the rudiments from his father, Louis Berlioz, a physician. He also had had a little musical instruction. He could perform on the flute, the guitar, and the drum.

In his *Memoirs*—his lengthy and detailed account of what he considered a life of constant suffering and all but continuous martyrdom—Berlioz tells us his mother disowned him because he insisted upon becoming an artist and his father tried to force him into following in his medical footsteps. He is consistently antagonistic toward his mother and as consistently friendly toward his father. His *Memoirs* strain our credulity; we have to suspect they often present the facts not as they actually were but as he thought they were.

There is no doubt, however, the medical student was irresistibly drawn to music. He spent his days in the Conservatoire library, poring over the scores of the masters, instead of in the dissecting room. But two years passed before he put himself in the hands of his first really good music teacher.

Three years later, at the age of twenty-three, he was admitted to the Conservatoire, the cradle of French musicians. He needed a dispensation, since he was far beyond cradle age. But one year after his admission he passed the rigorous examination and was permitted to compete for the Prix de Rome, the highest possible award for the finished music student. He didn't win it that year, but he did win three years later, on his fourth try.

All this time Berlioz was composing feverishly and learning hungrily. Operas, Masses, oratorios poured from him. When musical authorities and musicians did not leap to perform them, he credited their reluctance to malice, envy, and a determination to frustrate his genius. Yet very little of this early work survives in its original form. Some he reworked into his later compositions; the remainder he destroyed.

At the time, however, he was shrieking for performance, scheming and even borrowing money to get it. When his father objected to some of these maneuvers and cut off his allowance temporarily, Berlioz sang in a theater chorus in order to eat and live in flamboyant and vocalized misery.

In the midst of all this he heard an English company perform Shakespeare—he understood not "one syllable" of English—and instantly fell in love with the leading lady, Henrietta Smithson.

Being Berlioz, he didn't seek a way of getting himself introduced to her. Instead, he blundered backstage and found her and the leading man rehearsing a love scene, reciting their lines in each other's arms. Berlioz gave off a bloodcurdling shriek and ran out the door. He roamed the streets and fields day and night for weeks, his mind burning with torturing thoughts.

Years passed. Now and then he managed to get Miss Smithson's attention directed toward him from afar—they still hadn't met—and each incident seemed calculated to frighten her as much as the shriek had. Berlioz' state of mind he expressed in a letter to a friend: "Can you explain this power of emotion, this capacity for suffering which is killing me? Oh, sublime beings of the infinite, exterminate me! Summon me within your golden clouds that I may be set free! Reason speaks, 'Be tranquil, fool! In a few years there will be no more question of your sufferings.' Trust me, Henrietta Smithson and Hector Berlioz will be reunited in the oblivion of the tomb."

At last he was ready to translate these morbid thoughts into music, into his first enduring masterpiece, **Symphonie Fantastique (Episode from the Life of an Artist).** He wrote out the program, which should be read in full for its illumination of his emotions toward Miss Smithson. In outline, it is the story of a young musician tortured by unrequited love, who takes too much opium and dreams of his beloved from the near side of death. These dreams are increasingly feverish and culminate in a march to the scaffold and a witches' sabbath. Whatever may be thought of the program, the music is informed by high-order genius and the beginnings of a technical mastery over large forms that has never been surpassed—indeed, has very rarely been equaled.

Having put Miss Smithson into music, he set his thoughts of her to one side for the time. He had met Marie Moke, a young and pretty pianist and the girl friend of Ferdinand Hiller, a pianist who was to attain sufficient stature to be remembered today.

Hiller was one of a few Berlioz intimates who were able to listen to his endless tales of suffering and remain sympathetic. He told Miss Moke about all this pain, but when she met the sufferer her reaction was to smile at his troubles. This endeared her to Berlioz, and he proposed and was accepted, much to the distress of her mother.

While all this was going on, he was competing for the Prix de Rome for the fourth time. This time the vote of the judges was unanimous—he was the winner. He instantly revised his prize-winning cantata for the required public performance. The judges had seen a relatively tame piece, calculated to do no violence to conservative tastes. Now he inserted an orchestral "conflagration" that might have caused them to regret their decision. But one of the musicians missed his entry. That upset the whole orchestra; the "conflagration" was hardly a wisp of smoke. The composer screamed in anguish and threw his score at the musicians. There was a scramble in the orchestra. Music racks were upset. The house was in an uproar.

Miss Moke's mother persuaded the prospective bride to put off the wedding until he got back from the stay in Rome to which his prize entitled him. Mother kept right on working on daughter, evidently, because not long after Berlioz arrived in Italy he received word that his beloved had decided to marry another. His instant decision was that mother and daughter must die for their perfidy and he would die with them.

He bought a lady's-maid costume—that was going to be his disguise in order to get near them—and put pistols and poison into his valise. Then he set out on the long journey to Paris by stagecoach. Before he got out of Italy, hunger overtook him. He paused to eat and lost his resolution. According to his own account, he then tried to drown himself in the sea.

This episode of suffering subsided, but he was instantly deep in another. Student life in Rome was hateful to him. He ignored his fellow students and took to roaming the Roman hills with a fowling piece and a guitar; when he wasn't shooting birds, he was singing and playing to Italian peasants and brigands. Whatever embellishments he may have added to these adventures when he came to write his *Memoirs*, the impressions were eventually to go into another of his major works, **Harold in Italy.**

In 1832—when he was twenty-nine—he returned to Paris. Now he set out to court Henrietta Smithson in a more or less conventional way. First he contrived to meet her and then showered her with attentions, sympathy, and expressions of regard. The upshot was that they were married on October 3, 1833, and their only child, Louis Berlioz, was born the following August. But within a few years they were becoming estranged. By 1842 they were living apart.

Berlioz said in his *Memoirs* that her jealousy was unbearable. He stopped living with her, but he supported her to her dying day, in

March, 1854. At that time, he wrote to their son: "You will never know what we suffered, your mother and I. It was as impossible for me to live with her as it was to live without her."

He had long since taken up with another woman who, according to the testimony of friends, made him suffer with her malicious tongue and shrewish disposition. A few months after Henrietta's death, he married her.

The years after his return from Rome were made miserable by "abject slavery" and grossly insufficient appreciation, he tells us in his *Memoirs*. Whatever the accuracy of his description, he was productive. He took up musical journalism and practiced it for more than thirty years. At one time he was writing for five journals and was also the music editor of a Paris newspaper. He hated just about every moment of his writing; yet he wrote well, with violence and color, and was both informed and scrupulously fair to performers and to the music they performed.

He was also composing great music, though complex and difficult to play. Many of his contemporaries expected him to be "the successor of Beethoven." But the simple essence of Beethoven is as close as a piano and a pianist; the complicated essence of Berlioz is hardly to be had short of a big orchestra augmented by a big chorus —or choruses.

His **Requiem**, or **Messe des Morts**, written for five orchestras and bands and hundreds of singers, was first played in 1837, when he was thirty-four, and the composer remarked that "its grandeur was terrible!" His inspiration, in creating it, had flowed like a torrent— he'd had to invent a musical shorthand in order to write it down as fast as it poured forth.

His opera **Benvenuto Cellini** was a failure when produced in 1838—and remains a failure to this day. But his symphony **Romeo and Juliet**, for full orchestra and two choruses, was a big success when first played in Paris the following year—and today is considered a masterpiece. These comments are needed only because Berlioz himself maintained that all his works were masterpieces but some didn't obtain their just appreciation because envious musicians conspired against them.

The sufferings of Berlioz should not be minimized. They were extremely real to him, and extremely painful. And he did have failures where he had every right to expect success. **The Damnation of Faust** —a concert opera for soloists, chorus, and orchestra—failed miserably in 1846, all but ruining him.

His reputation as a conductor was growing; and by the time he was fifty his services were in demand just about wherever there was an

orchestra. He toured Germany repeatedly—his most devoted followers
were there—and he was greatly admired in Russia and England.
Even in France his music was played more, and he himself was more
appreciated than he would have you believe in his *Memoirs*. But,
without doubt, he had his enemies in Paris. He made them with
freely rendered insults.

France honored him as much as, if not more than, any of her other
musical geniuses. He was made a chevalier and afterward an officer
of the Legion of Honor. He received a seat in the French Academy.
Midway in his career he was given a sinecure, the post of librarian for
the Conservatoire. In 1855 his mighty **Te Deum**—for three choirs,
soloists, organ, and orchestra—was given an official performance, and
the government rewarded the composer richly. The year before,
L'Enfance du Christ—an oratorio for soloists, chorus, and orchestra—
had had "*un succès extraordinaire*" (his words) when first performed
in Paris.

As he grew older, his symptoms changed. Instead of clamoring for
the performance of his works, he held the new ones back, sometimes
for years. He began suffering more and more from what modern
medicine classifies as psychosomatic disease—that is, disease whose
physically painful manifestations are produced by the mind rather
than by any organic disorder. The suffering is genuine, of course, and
Berlioz relied increasingly on opium to silence his abdominal pains,
while constantly inviting flare-ups by ignoring his diet.

His second wife died in 1862, when he was fifty-nine, and he
became involved in a pathetically foolish love affair with a girl in her
early twenties. This ended badly. Then he was off in pursuit of the
girl of his boyhood and her pink shoes. Meanwhile, he was composing
his last works: an enormously long and complex opera, **The Trojans,**
and an uneven comic opera based upon Shakespeare, **Beatrice and
Benedict.**

After the pink shoes turned out to be another mirage, Berlioz
declared, "God how I suffer!" His philosophy degenerated into this:
"Life is nothing. Death is no better. Worlds die as we die. All is
emptiness." On the state of the world: "Everything is dead except
the authority of fools." About himself: "I am in a hurry to untie or
cut all the bonds which chain me to art, so that I may be ready at
any time to say to death, 'Whenever you please.'" And so he wasted
slowly away, and on the morning of March 8, 1869, he died, in his
sixty-sixth year.

Poor Berlioz! He was both a tremendous man and a tremendous
genius. You could weep for him, as he wept so often for himself.
But not for the same reasons!

15

Liszt

WHEN Franz Liszt was very young, no one expected him to live. When he was very old, it seemed he couldn't die.

The young child was cataleptic, like Paganini. No bodily phenomenon is more strange or more alarming. The victim collapses suddenly, every muscle rigid. This rigidity binds him motionless for an indefinite time. To the unknowing eye he may appear to be dead. Conflicting forces in the unconscious mind produce catalepsy—a dramatic demonstration of the power of the mind over the body. The cure comes if and when one force finds the strength to overcome the other.

Franz's seizures disappeared when he was six years old. At that age he turned to piano playing, and he'd play until he was exhausted.

This occurred in 1817 in the village of Raiding on the vast Hungarian plain, where Franz was born, October 22, 1811. His father, Adam, was rents agent on one of the estates of the princes of Eszterházy, who had been Haydn's employers and patrons.

Adam and Anna Liszt were as delighted by their son's piano playing as by the disappearance of catalepsy. Adam played the piano well enough to feel he should have been a professional musician. Under his tutelage, but powered by a relentless inner drive, the child developed brilliantly. At nine, he was the talk of the countryside. The local nobility put up the money for his musical education.

The Liszts moved to Vienna and engaged the most famous of piano teachers, Karl Czerny, and a famous master of harmony and composition, Antonio Salieri, who had been Mozart's opponent and one of Beethoven's teachers. The boy became a sensation. After some three years his parents took him to Paris, where he was an even greater sensation. He played in the salons of the musically minded nobility and was asked to compose an opera to a sophisticated libretto called **Don Sancho, or The Castle of Love.**

The result showed that a thirteen-year-old boy couldn't know anything about that kind of love. But Liszt, the man, who was to be frantically and fanatically adored by hundreds of women, would never know a great deal about it either. The boy's intimates feared for him in this respect. His father, on his deathbed, said to him, "You have a good heart and no lack of intelligence. Nevertheless, I dread women on your account. They will trouble and dominate your life." He died when Franz was not quite sixteen years old.

The lad gave piano lessons there in Paris to support himself and his mother. His pupils were the daughters of fashionable families. One was Caroline, daughter of Count de Saint-Cricq, a minister to Charles X. She was as romantic as he; it wasn't long before they fancied themselves in love. When the count found out, he sent Liszt on his way with a courteous reminder that counts' daughters were not for musicians.

Liszt wanted to renounce the world and become a priest. His confessor told him emphatically that a religious life was not for him. "You must serve God as an artist," he said. Cataleptic seizures reappeared. He went into a semiprostration, a prolonged languor, that lasted for eighteen months. Suddenly he returned to the piano with voracious intensity; worked at it like a galley slave. He wrote a pupil, "If only I don't go mad, you'll find me an artist."

This went on for two years. When he emerged from his retreat he was quickly accepted as the greatest pianist. He was twenty-two and strikingly beautiful—not effeminate, yet not handsome in any conventional he-man way. He was tall, his shoulders were narrow, he was slender and straight, and his face exuded a passive spirituality. To the type of woman whom poets liken to a spider, a lynx, or other beast of prey, merely to look at him was to be a devastating experience.

It is an error to think of Liszt as a Great Lover. He was no devourer, no consumer; rather, he was the devoured and consumed. Woman, he said, speaking of an idealistic embodiment of the sex, was "the redemptress." Through woman, as well as through religion and music, he sought his redemption. From what, we cannot know.

Marie, Comtesse d'Agoult, was not the first of his redemptresses; but she left the longest and best record, since under the pen name, Daniel Stern, she was a prolific novelist and essayist. Daughter of a count, she was also the wife of a count, twenty years her senior, and the mother of his three children. According to a friend, she was "six feet of ice on top of twenty feet of lava."

In August, 1835, she and Liszt, who was six years younger than she, slipped out of Paris. The next Parisian society heard of them, they were sharing a flat in Geneva. It was an immense scandal. Their first child, Blandine, was born in December. Their second, Cosima, was born on Christmas Day, 1837. Their third, Daniel, came two years later.

To both of them, it all was very beautiful and satisfying. She enjoyed renunciation—retiring from the world. As he was, by common consent, the greatest living pianist, his renunciation was of no small order either. It lasted four years, until 1839, when they parted without rancor and without finality, as though they were mutually weary.

From then until 1847, he gave concerts—earning the appellation "the indefatigable vagabond" from Berlioz. He crisscrossed Europe many times, was forever on the road. Wherever he went, he was assailed by hysterical admiration. Adulators paved the streets with flowers. His carriage, drawn by three pairs of white horses, would be followed by miles of carriages filled with adoring fans. Great and small kings loaded him with decorations and, creaking with hardware, he'd wear them all when making his appearances on the concert platform.

He played, mostly, compositions and arrangements of his own that were deliberately designed to exploit his dazzling virtuosity. Musically, they were largely noise, yet he carried them off with overwhelming effect.

Another pianist, Josef Fischhof, described it in a letter to Robert Schumann: "When he seats himself at the instrument, he strokes his hair behind his ear. His glance is staring, his eyes hollow, the upper part of the body quiet, only the head moves, and the expression of the face changes and mirrors every passing mood that seizes him or that he wishes to call forth, wherein he always succeeds. This fantastic exterior is only the covering of an interior volcano from which tones are hurled like flames and gigantic ruins, not caressing, but with the force of thunderbolts. One thinks neither of his hands, nor of the mechanism, the technique, nor the instrument. He seizes our soul, carried away by an unknown impression, and raises it violently to his own height, making all Philistines giddy."

There were predatory females wherever he went. Some concealed bottles in their gloves, hoping to capture his tears. Suddenly he renounced all this to retire once more from the world—this time with another high-placed lady he met during his tour in 1847. She was the Princess Carolyne Sayn-Wittgenstein, who was twenty-eight and had a husband, a child, and a vast feudal estate near Kiev, Russia, where, in moments of relaxation, she'd lie on a bear skin, smoke long black cigars, and contemplate the sadness and futility of life.

She renounced her husband, her secure position in the Russian nobility, and her fortune to accompany the 36-year-old Liszt into retirement. They settled in Weimar, Germany, where he intended to advance the art of music by directing the grand duke's orchestra and opera house, and by setting forth in musical compositions all the emotions he was feeling. The greatest living pianist—indeed, the greatest piano virtuoso who has so far appeared—was never to cut a public figure as such again. Now and then over the succeeding years he'd give a concert for charity, play for friends and for pupils.

And he did advance the art of music. Anything new and worthy got a friendly hearing in Weimar, even though it met with hostility elsewhere. Schumann's music came into prominence years earlier than it might have without Liszt's patronage, although Schumann treated him shamefully. Berlioz' music, too—and Berlioz was often contemptuous. And Wagner's music, most of all. Wagner admired and loved him with a wild extravagance and "borrowed" large sums of money. There was a host of lesser new composers he helped, too, but without neglecting the old. He was the first mighty popularizer of Beethoven, and he knew the music of Mozart, Bach, and the other older masters intimately.

During these years, his three illegitimate children by the Comtesse d'Agoult came back into his life. In 1857 he saw Blandine married to Emile Ollivier, a French politician who was a minister to Napoleon III; Cosima ("admirably my daughter," he said of her, which was to have an ironic twist, as we shall see) married to his pupil and friend, Hans von Bülow. Daniel became a brilliant law student, but died at twenty.

In 1859, after eleven years of it, he gave up his musical directorships (alleging that the grand duke hadn't supported him properly) and went into deeper retirement—in the mansion he and the princess shared, to the scandal of the conservative ducal court.

She, meanwhile, had become deeply interested in theology and church government, as she wanted to marry him. To do this she needed a church annulment of her marriage to Prince Wittgenstein. She pursued her goal all the way to Rome and the Pope. For a while it looked as though she finally might succeed. She summoned Liszt to Rome from Weimar and paid to have a church decorated for their wedding, which she scheduled for his fiftieth birthday, October 22, 1861.

But the church authorities were not to be hoodwinked. Liszt was passive as always, and she sank deeper and deeper into eccentricity. Entombed in a flat sealed against fresh air, she scribbled away for years on her magnum opus, *The Interior Causes of the Exterior Weaknesses of the Church*, which eventually reached twenty-four volumes. Visitors had to sit for ten minutes in a kind of decontamination chamber, to rid themselves of the outside air, before they were admitted to her sanctum, where she sprawled, smoking her long black cigars, amidst piles of books, papers, busts and portraits of her most prized possession—Liszt. She seemed contented now to possess him in the abstract, and his status became that of occasional caller and reporting correpondent. This arrangement was to continue all the rest of his days, and most of hers—she survived him only a year.

Her renunciation was complete and final. He would have liked to go as far, and made another approach toward the priesthood. But if he had been unsuited for it in his youth, he was doubly so now. He could only reach the outer circles—the third order of St. Francis. His head was shaved to a tonsure, he wore a Roman collar and a cassock, and he assumed the title "*abbé*."

He was supposed to be entirely dedicated to the spirit—and he was, by and large, although an occasional redemptress took him over. There was at least one after he was seventy. He became reconciled with the Grand Duke of Weimar, who gave him a cottage on the palace grounds. The Hungarian nation, bursting with pride, appointed him director of a national conservatory. For the last nineteen years of his life, he divided each year among Rome, Weimar, and Budapest and devoted himself to teaching and composing.

In 1867 he received word that "admirably my daughter" Cosima had left her husband and was living with her father's close friend and beneficiary, Wagner. Shocked by such behavior, he had nothing to do with them for five years, until von Bülow had got his divorce and Cosima and Wagner had married.

The years passed, and Liszt seemed to get stronger rather than weaker. In 1886, his seventy-fifth year, he added a long, tiring visit to England to his full routine. He left England on April 22, and by the time he reached Cosima's home in the Wagnerian capital, Bayreuth, Germany, he was exhausted. A widow now, she was the reigning empress of all the Wagnerites. Busy with the preparations for the annual festival, she had little time for her father. He was dying before she noticed. Her belated nursing couldn't save him. He died on July 31.

Liszt has four aspects: personality, piano virtuoso, teacher, composer. The personality can be baffling or it can be childishly simple. He was neither charlatan nor poseur, even though people say he was both. Once you grant a Liszt his natural right to be Liszt, inconsistencies and contradictions vanish. He was a rich brew. To many of his contemporaries and their descendants, it was and still is indigestible. This is the fault of the stomach—not of the brew.

Liszt knew from childhood that he was a genius, and accepted the status. But he also accepted the responsibilities of genius. "Genius obligates," he always said—and this was his code, to which he was true. He felt obligated to serve both music and musicians, and the sum of his selflessness, his generosities, his kindnesses, and his forbearances approaches saintliness.

One of his pupils, the American pianist Amy Fay (1844-1928), gave us a sharp picture of him: "tall and slight, with deep-set eyes, shaggy eyebrows, and long iron-gray hair which he wears parted in the middle. His mouth turns up at the corners, which gives him a most crafty and Mephistophelean expression when he smiles. . . . Anything like the polish of his manners I never saw. . . . But the most extraordinary thing about Liszt is his wonderful variety of expression and play of features. One moment his face will look dreamy, shadowy, tragic. The next he will be insinuating, amiable, ironic, sardonic; but always the same captivating grace of manner. . . . He is all spirit but half the time at least, a mocking spirit."

Miss Fay also is an excellent witness to his piano playing. She wrote: "All playing sounds barren by the side of Liszt, for his is the living, breathing embodiment of poetry, passion, grace, wit, coquetry, daring, tenderness and every other fascinating quality that you can think of. I'm ready to hang myself half the time when I've been to him." All this some twenty-five years after his retirement as a piano virtuoso.

Of course, no one living today heard Liszt in his prime. But the record left by his contemporaries is overwhelming, and practically every pianist then living—including Clara Wieck Schumann, who grew to dislike the man intensely despite all the kindness he paid her —acknowledged his supremacy. He taught hundreds of pianists, many of whom became famous. Through them and their pupils, we are thoroughly familiar with the Lisztian piano; we know he was the greatest of all, and realize the debt the art owes him.

From youth onward, he took the trouble to teach any talented person who came to him and, once he was famous, refused to accept a cent from any. As he grew older, his pupils didn't even have to be talented to stay with him; in his kindness, he couldn't bear to tell aspiring human beings they were not likely to reach their goals. Some of his pupils were imposters. Some were thieves who stole his property. Some were moochers who lived off him. Yet he never complained, and was happy with the talented ones—among whom were more than half the renowned pianists of the last quarter of the nineteenth century and the first quarter of the twentieth.

Liszt the composer is quite a different matter. In public esteem, a few of his pieces rank at the very top. To pianists, quite a number of his piano compositions are among the most ingratiating. Nevertheless, no major composer is under such constant and embittered attack on aesthetic grounds. He was prolific; his total reaches well over 1,300 items. But most are fantasias and fanciful piano arrangements of other composers' opera and symphonic scores and songs.

His big orchestral works are marked by daring and originality. Many of his technical devices found their way into the music of others, especially Wagner, who borrowed lavishly, and Richard Strauss.

His piano works are notable for their breath-taking exploitation of the instrument's endless capabilities, many of which were not obvious until he found them and are not now obvious unless properly played.

True, most of his compositions are dead—although it is rash to predict the tastes of the future. In my opinion, the following are among the comparatively small remainder that keeps Liszt's name, as composer, alive and respected.

The **B Minor piano sonata; Années de Pèlerinage** including **Au lac de Wallenstadt, Eglogue, Au Bord d'une Source, Gondoliera, Il Penseroso,** and **Canzonetta di Salvator Rosa; Two Legends—St. Francis Preaching to the Birds** and **St. Francis Walking on the Water; Sixth Hungarian Rhapsody; Les Preludes; The Dante Symphony** and **A Faust Symphony.**

16

Wagner

ACCORDING to the rules most of us live by, Richard Wagner was a scoundrel. He embezzled his friends' money and stole their wives. He was completely lacking in loyalty, scruples, and common honesty.

According to Wagner, there were no rules other than the one he made for himself—his wishes, even his whims, were law. In his own eyes he was so many cuts above others, it was as though he alone occupied the world. He considered himself the greatest poet, greatest composer, greatest dramatist, greatest actor, greatest thinker, greatest writer, greatest lover, greatest anything else that interested him. Thus, from his point of view, it was only proper for others to strain and suffer so he could have whatever he wanted.

From our point of view, he resembled an intensely self-centered small child forever at the brink of a tantrum and frequently falling over. And, although the world kicked him around no little, he remained convinced of his supremacy. So did many others. If Wagnerism is madness, as has been said, it is a highly contagious disease.

In social gatherings at which he was present, no one talked but Wagner. He talked for hours and hours, always about himself. A friend once said, "The least contradiction provoked him to incredible anger. He would leap like a stag and roar like a tiger. His voice became hoarse and the words came out like screams."

He was irresistible to himself, but repulsive by our standards. Nor was he prepossessing physically. He was smallish, his head too big for his torso, and he had a chronic, unsightly skin infection. Nevertheless, he generated awesome force. To many, he was hypnotically fascinating.

An artist who painted his portrait said, "You lose your identity when in his presence. . . . You are under an influence which sets every nerve at its highest pitch." This helps to explain why so many eagerly volunteered to serve as his carpet. They thought him much more than human, and agreed he couldn't be held to our rules.

Of course, he had countless enemies. But if he was a madman, he was a madman only incidentally. Primarily, he was a great creative artist—a genius of the first rank as composer and dramatist. So let's try looking at him from his viewpoint, if we can.

He was born in Leipzig on May 22, 1813, the birth year of another major force in opera, Giuseppe Verdi, and the year in which Liszt was two years old, Schumann and Chopin three, Mendelssohn four, Schubert sixteen, and Beethoven forty-three.

Of his mother's children, he was the ninth. His ostensible father was a police clerk, who died when Wagner was six months old. Less than a year after becoming a widow, his mother married a family friend, Ludwig Geyer, actor, singer, and painter. Wagner never hesitated to tell people he suspected Geyer was his father and his mother was the illegitimate daughter of a prince. It did not seem likely to him that a police clerk and a woman of ordinary parentage could have produced such a god as himself.

He grew up in the theater, theatrical boardinghouses, and an assortment of schools. Now he was more incorrigible, now less. His formal education was poor, but his eagerly grasping mind was as retentive as a bank vault.

Drama and poetry were his first loves. At twelve, he composed a prize poem. At fifteen, he wrote a play in which forty-two characters died—he had to bring some back as ghosts to keep the thing going. Music was a belated passion; he was in his mid-teens before he took it seriously.

At eighteen, he learned in six months all a competent master could teach him of harmony and counterpoint. At twenty, he became chorus master in an opera theater. A year later, he was conductor. Opera was his life from then on. But he was already a financial dead beat and making enemies left and right by his insistence on treating everyone as subhuman. He wanted to live like a prince—with other people's money.

So, periodically, he fled to another town, with creditors at his heels, for in those days you could be imprisoned for debt. He fell in love with an actress, Minna Planer. She didn't seem pleased when he asked her to marry him, but few people found it possible to oppose his wishes. At length she succumbed, and he made her miserable for the rest of her life.

They settled in Riga, where he had a conductor's post. Pursuing creditors forced them to flee to Paris. There they half starved for a few years. When his opera **Rienzi** was produced in Dresden, October 20, 1842, it brought in money and got him a job as second conductor at the court opera. This enabled him to stave off existing creditors while acquiring more.

When a revolution broke out against his employer, King Frederick Augustus II of Saxony, he joined it, and when it failed, he had to flee again. He went to Weimar, where Franz Liszt had settled. He was an ardent admirer of Wagner the artist and kindly made excuses for Wagner the man.

Minna sent word from Dresden that a warrant had been issued for his arrest, which meant he was not safe in Weimar. This time he fled to Switzerland, where she joined him. And so began eleven years of exile, mainly in Switzerland, but with sojourns in Paris.

Poverty dogged him, but the eleven years weren't all bad. By now, many people saw he was a genius, and some felt an obligation to support him, even in the profligate style on which this genius insisted. One of these, Otto Wesendonck, deserves special mention, because he gave his all. He provided Wagner a sumptuous villa, innumerable and uncounted sums of money, and finally was compelled to yield his pretty young wife, Mathilde. He would have lost her for good if it hadn't been that, in the end, she was unwilling to give up children and wealthy husband for an egomaniac.

Meanwhile, Minna suffered and made trips to Germany to try to get Wagner's exile lifted. That would get him away from Mathilde. They returned to home grounds when he was forty-six, to the usual poverty and troubles with creditors, interspersed with luxury when Wagner found more genius-struck rich people to "lend" him money.

Foremost of these was Ludwig II of Bavaria, known to history as "the mad king," which disparages him unfairly. He was intelligent, sensitive, and decent, as well as "mad." In 1864, when he was nineteen and Wagner was fifty-one, he heard Wagner's music dramas, was swept off his feet, and entered the ranks of Wagnerites. In a magnificent royal gesture, he invited Wagner to live in Munich as adviser and intimate friend.

Wagner was delighted. Now he had his hands in a royal treasury. He became music dictator of the kingdom and at once added Hans von Bülow, pianist and conductor, to the payroll. Bülow was among his most active and influential artistic supporters. He also had a pretty young wife, Cosima—daughter of Wagner's good friend and admirer, Liszt.

The Bülows were hardly settled in Munich when Wagner began paying open court to Cosima. Daughter of a genius who had paid very little attention to her, she had a fierce, inner drive to serve genius at whatever price. Wagner, twenty-four years older than she, became her idol, and she became his sanctified priestess. However, this arrangement was not understood by the world. It set off a scandal that shook Ludwig's throne. The upshot was that Minna died, Bülow got a divorce, and Cosima, after bearing Wagner two daughters and a son, at last became his wife in 1870.

But let's backtrack now and see what the artist was doing all this time. Wagner was nineteen when he created his first opera, twenty-one the second, twenty-three the third. They were imitations of existing operatic forms and were stillborn. **Rienzi**, his fourth, completed when he was twenty-seven, is the earliest Wagnerian opera that still gets performed. Not often, to be sure, because it, too, is an imitation—of Italian and French romantic opera. But it has touches that proclaim the budding of original genius.

This originality burst forth in his next opera, **The Flying Dutchman (Der fliegende Holländer)**, which he finished only one year later. Here we find, for the first time, the essential quality of Wagnerian opera. Dramatic purpose is served; music is made to serve.

Keep in mind that, to himself, Wagner was the greatest dramatist, greatest poet, and greatest composer. He fashioned his own opera stories; he wrote the verse that told the stories—the librettos. With **The Flying Dutchman** the Wagnerian ideal of music drama was forming, in which there are three equal components—music, drama, and poetry—all subordinated and disciplined and so merged into each other that the blend is indissoluable and becomes, truly, a new art form.

Tannhäuser came three years after the **Dutchman**, and **Lohengrin** four years after **Tannhäuser**. The ideal is advanced, but is still not perfected. There are "set pieces." Singers, in solo and in chorus, have moments of dominance over the orchestra, at the expense of the union of the three arts.

Wagner now was thirty-five years old. His ideas were revolutionary; they crossed the vested interests of established singers, musicians, and opera companies. Of course, he was criticized. But criticizing Wagner was like twisting a tiger's tail. In defense of his ideas, in his single-minded determination to make them triumph, and in vindictive passion to destroy his critics, he poured forth words in geysers.

Words—words—hundreds of thousands of words. The total is incredible. Indeed, no one can be quite sure of the total, except that it approaches the astronomical. They were written for music journals, for any newspaper or periodical that would print them, for pamphlets and books published at the expense of creditors and friends—even at Wagner's own expense. That was how strongly he felt. And the people he vilified retorted in kind. Music has never known any other controversy of such violence, unreason, and length.

In the dire poverty of his exile, after the fiasco revolution against King Frederick Augustus, these writings provided some income, more than his operas, in fact. Yet, despite poverty and his literary labors, Wagner was at work on one of the most grandiose creations in music, drama, or any other art—the opera **The Ring of the Nibelung**, which has four parts, each longer and more complex than other operas, except Wagnerian operas. In its entirety, it takes sixteen hours to perform, and tells a story of gods and demigods that requires thousands of words even to outline.

This gigantic opera took twenty-one years to complete, and during that time it generated for its creator no glory, no compensation of any kind from the outside world. This is a point to note: if Wagner the man had not been an egomaniac, there would have been no Wagner the artist to interest us. His art was Wagner's justification for his scoundrelly ways. What he felt he needed in order to create, he didn't hesitate to take—with ruthless brutality.

Wesendonck's wife, Mathilde, for example. Her love provided the inspiration for **Tristan and Isolde**, which is music's matchless love drama. Therefore, if she and her husband were hurt in the process, they had no right even to complain. She also gave him the impetus to work on **The Mastersingers of Nuremberg**, the other towering masterpiece he created during the years he was working on **The Ring**.

He needed Bülow's wife, Cosima, to complete **The Mastersingers** and **The Ring** and the grandiose plans he had for the latter. Therefore, why should Bülow object when "the greatest genius" had found the right inspiration and emotional support?

While the Bülow scandal unfolded, Wagner was stirring up a hornets' nest for young King Ludwig. Ministers and other influential people were not immune to the royal favorite's savage insults, nor did Wagner have the sense not to dabble in politics. Finally, Ludwig had to ask him to live in Switzerland again, until the situation cooled —with Ludwig still paying his bills.

Wagner was fifty-seven when Cosima at last became his wife. **The Ring** was nearing completion, and he felt it was a work of art of such sublime and tremendous proportions that only its own theater would be worthy of it. To this theater only the elite would be admitted, and every year there would be a festival in honor of Wagnerian art. In his transport, his was the only German musico-dramatic art, and therefore it deserved to be enshrined and worshiped.

By unflagging drive, unscrupulous manipulation of people and their money, and with the princely help of Ludwig, this theater was built at Bayreuth, an out-of-the-way town in Ludwig's kingdom, Bavaria. It took years; but there, during the summer of 1876, before an audience of emperors, kings, princes, and Wagnerites, **The Ring** was unwound for the first time in all its fantastic length.

Wagner's idea was that **The Ring** would be performed only in its own theater. But he was compelled to abandon this plan by the enormous debts he piled up in getting the theater built. He now set to work on his last opera, **Parsifal**, which was to be as sacred to Bayreuth as its theme was sacred to Christianity. Less than seven months after its first performance at Bayreuth, Wagner died in Venice of a heart attack—on February 13, 1883, almost three months short of his seventieth birthday.

Cosima survived him for forty-seven years, dying in 1930 at the age of ninety-three. She remained the high priestess of Wagnerian religion to her last breath, and attended the Bayreuth altar. You get an idea of her fervor from this: Johannes Brahms, who was no Wagnerite, but was not the foe of Wagner that some people claim, sent a wreath when he learned of Wagner's death. Cosima eyed it icily and said, "We won't acknowledge it, because he did not love the master's music."

17

Verdi

Giuseppe Verdi composed 26 operas. Gioacchino Rossini composed 38 and Gaetano Donizetti got up to 67 before he became as mad as his heroine, Lucia di Lammermoor. Of the vast Rossini-Donizetti total only two remain fully alive, but eight of Verdi's are world-wide favorites to this day and most of the rest are in the living repertoire.

This is to give suitable emphasis to the staying powers of an Italian peasant who was born in the same year as Wagner. He is the most popular composer, with Irving Berlin or any other "popular" composer included in the reckoning. No matter how popular "popular" composers get to be, their popularity rarely lasts longer than they do. Verdi's enormous popularity dates from 1851.

Admirers of "serious" music usually are not admirers of Berlins. Admirers of Berlins rarely are devoted to Bach. Yet this man Verdi appeals to the most accurate, the most sensitive, and the most cultivated ears as well as to the musically unknowing, the musically uncaring, and to persons who are all but tone-deaf. If art is universal, here is the universal artist.

In life he matched no standard of the artist. Rather, he was a craftsman as a tailor is a craftsman who cuts the cloth and makes the seams so the finished product will hang right and fit. He was a bootstrap man who lifted himself bodily by means of a steely will and inexhaustible energy. Among musical geniuses he is a sport. He composed by calculating, and he revealed little of his spark until he was very well along—until he had learned to draw up artistic calculations. Mozart had created the Mozartian world and was dead before he was thirty-six. Verdi was thirty-seven before he produced his first masterpiece, which was **Rigoletto,** and he was seventy-three and seventy-nine when he created his last two, which were **Otello** and **Falstaff.**

He was born in Le Roncole, the name of a cluster of peasant

houses in northern Italy, on October 10, 1813, in the poor inn operated by his father and mother, Carlo and Luigia. It was little more than a hovel and the livelihood his father earned barely supported hovel living. The small child was overwhelmed when he heard music for the first time. Since the place was Le Roncole, the music came from a barrel organ. When he heard the gaspy church organ he all but collapsed in his ecstasy. Everyone was impressed. Father scraped pennies and bought him a wreck of a spinet. The hope was that he might grow up and earn his living as a performing musician, since that clearly was a better way of doing it than keeping a poor inn or laboring with the poor soil.

The nearest sizable town was Busseto. There he was sent at ten to learn to read and write and cipher while living in the home of a cobbler who was a family friend. He attracted the attention of Antonio Barezzi, a grocer and fanatical lover of music in the Italian pattern. But Barezzi was attracted to a serious-minded boy who happened to be musical, rather than to a boy whom he suspected of harboring musical genius. He gave the lad an after-school job in his grocery and took him into his home, where it pleasured him to listen to the fourteen-year-old playing piano duets with his thirteen-year-old daughter, Margherita.

When the boy began composing and stuck to it, Barezzi persuaded the local music lovers to subscribe to a scholarship, added generously to it, and sent him to Milan to be educated in the splendid Conservatory there. Barezzi's maximum expectation seems to have been that his protégé would become a "maestro," of which Italy always has thousands, and, with luck, the leading musician of Busetto—and also the husband of his daughter.

The Conservatory's faculty examiners had not even that expectation. The young man was taciturn and clumsy. They found nothing in him which suggested unusual talent. He was nineteen. That was over-age for ordinary pupils, and they refused to admit him. But young Verdi was going to become a maestro or burst. Hardheadedness always was a notable trait of his. For two years he studied with a private teacher, composed doggedly for his own instruction, studied operas and operatic techniques from the galleries of the opera houses, and at last found a group of amateur musicians who had faith in him. They gave him a libretto and asked him to make an opera of it.

He was called back to Busseto to take a musical post which Barezzi had gotten for him, and soon thereafter married Margherita. He composed marches for the town band, among other chores, and worked on the opera, even after word came that his sponsors no longer had funds with which to produce it. He had agreed to stay in the Busseto job for three years, and Verdi never in his life permitted himself the slightest deviation from his given word. At the end of three years he returned to Milan, where fortuitous circumstances put his opera into a first-rank opera house, La Scala. It was fairly successful and he was made—as an ordinary composer of ordinary operas, of which Italy never has a lack.

He was twenty-six. The year before, his infant daughter had died and this year of his first success also saw the death of his two-year-old son. His new commission was for a comic opera and while he worked out its humor and high spirits, Margherita died—all this in less than two years. He kept right at his comic composing and delivered the score when he had promised, to Bartolomeo Merelli, Scala's impresario. He told Merelli to forget him because he was never going to compose another note.

We may make of that anything we wish. He never explained what or how he felt. A striking thing about Verdi always was his reticence —Verdi never explained Verdi and rarely talked about Verdi. Merelli evidently knew his man. He gave him a good libretto and insisted that he take it home and at least read it. Within a few months Verdi had it set to music. It was **Nabucodonosor** now usually called **Nabucco.** It was a terrific success. Scala gave him a contract for his next opera in which the space for composer's fee was blank, for him to fill out.

But it must be kept in mind that opera making is a business as well as an art. Italy at the time was a mass of tiny principalities dominated by foreign powers. Lombardy, of which Milan is capital, was under the Austrian boot. Italian sensibilities were raw and aching; Italian patriotism bubbled furiously under tight official repression. There was one sure-fire way to fill opera houses and that was to make operas which catered to these sensibilities through enough of a disguise to get by the censorship. Impresarios had hacks who concocted the formulas, and in Verdi they had the composer to give the formulas sincere, from-the-heart expression. He believed in what he was doing, without the slightest questioning. He always did.

Between **Nabucco** and **Rigoletto** were nine years and eleven operas, notably **I Lombardi, Ernani, Macbeth,** and **Luisa Miller.** In that time Verdi was making himself both a masterful musical technician and a master opera maker. That was his development as a craftsman. His development as an artist—as creative genius—is not nearly so clear. But it amounted to a matchless ability to use music to make common emotions seem uncommon and precious and to deal in such imponderables as love, hate, patriotism, jealousy, pride, and ambition with a directness that is blunt but produces an effect that is vivid and unmistakable. To get full value from **Nabucco** you should be a resentful Italian living in Lombardy in the 1840's. To get good value from **Rigoletto** you can be an Eskimo.

Rigoletto marks his maturity both as a genius and as a man. As a genius he now was tailoring art to fit human beings. As a man he had given himself certain godlike aspects, particularly those of being all-knowing and all-powerful. The rigidity of his character was self-advertising—people surrendered rather than risk getting lacerated in a collision with it. Mariana Barbieri-Nini, one of the best of the Italian prima donnas of the mid-1800's, described it well in her memoirs. She was the first Lady Macbeth of his **Macbeth** and recalled that the maestro required well over one hundred rehearsals of the entire score. "It sounds almost incredible, but the fact is that the sleep-walking scene alone required three months of study . . . it was enough to drive you crazy." That scene and her duet with the baritone, Varese, bothered Verdi. At the dress rehearsal, which in Italy is before a paying audience, he held the first curtain because he wanted the singers to "work over that accursed duet once more." She continued:

"Varese, indignant at the strange and unreasonable demand, could not refrain from saying in a loud voice. 'For God's Sake, we've re-hearsed it one hundred and fifty times!' The maestro replied, 'In half an hour you won't be saying that any more—because it will be one hundred and fifty-one times!' There was nothing to do but to yield to the tyrant's will. I still remember the furious look Varese threw at his back while walking after Verdi into the rehearsal hall, his hand on his sword hilt as though he intended to strike down the maestro. Nevertheless he resigned himself at last and the hundred and fifty-first rehearsal took place while the public fumed impatiently, milling about the parterre."

Verdi was even more painstaking and much less considerate of himself. While educating himself in opera and music, he also was educating himself in other matters, but strictly practical matters having to do with his two abiding interests, opera and Italy. Poetry and drama are of the operatic essence, and the peasant from Le Roncole absorbed the poetry and drama of all languages and times. He was particularly attracted to Shakespeare and kept returning to that master throughout his life. As for Italy, it was obvious to him that if she ever was to be united and free, her patriots would have to understand history and the intricacies of politics and diplomacy. Therefore, he absorbed those understandings.

While he was going outward toward the wide world, he also was turning inward, back to the Italian soil. With his first successes, he bought a farm near Busseto and that was the base from which he operated thereafter. **Nabucco** had given him fame throughout Italy and **Ernani,** produced when he was thirty-one, spread his name through Europe. At thirty-three he went to Paris for the first time and the following year visited London. Thereafter, he was a citizen of the world in one of his aspects, sophisticated and cynical in his comprehension of the affairs of nations and of men, yet a peasant still in another aspect—a hardfisted, suspicious, and narrow-minded peasant who trusted nothing he couldn't test in his own two hands.

The original farm, Sant'Agata, grew with the years as he bought adjacent farms, until it was a considerable estate worked by large numbers of tenants and farm hands. Blanche Roosevelt, an American singer and contemporary, who admired Verdi fervently, could never quite reconcile his aspects. "On looking at Verdi, I defy any human being to think him a man either of genius or any uncommon talent," she wrote. "His face is pleasant but rather stolid, his smile develops a certain cunning. . . . Verdi lives in such quiet at Sant'Agata that he is rarely disturbed. In fact, the only persons whom he ever allows to interrupt him are his farmers or tenants, and any day he would stop in the midst of the divinest phrase to see if one of his men had sharpened the second scythe, if another had mowed a meadow patch, or another had planted early seed for an early harvest."

After **Rigoletto,** opera making was easy for him. He had learned the trade. During the year following **Rigoletto**'s stupendous success he composed simultaneously, and within a few months, **Il Trovatore** and **La Traviata,** which hardly can be considered lesser masterpieces. This was the time when he installed Giuseppina Strepponi at Sant'Agata although she was not his wife. She was a prima donna and had been his mistress for several years. Verdi had gone to Paris and there he received a letter from his father-in-law, Barezzi, informing him that the countryside was scandalized. His reply revealed a highhanded indifference to public opinion and also his profound respect and gratitude for the man who had helped him so much. At this time, his aged parents also were installed at Sant'Agata. Verdi took care of his own.

No one understands why he waited so long to marry Giuseppina formally. "Peppina," he called her. She was his mistress and then his wife for well over fifty years, his closest and dearest friend, his artistic and personal confidante, the one person who ever attained to genuine intimacy with him. It has been suggested that after the tragedy of Margherita and her babes, he could have had an idea that tragedy would have to befall any wife of his. Since he was contemptuous of dogma of any sort and quite irreligious (despite composing in his old age exceptionally moving religious music, especially his **Requiem**), it is said that perhaps he couldn't accept a ceremony in which he had no belief. However it was, he was forty-six and she was forty-four when, at last, their marriage was legalized.

Il Trovatore and La Traviata were followed by **Sicilian Vespers, Simon Boccanegra, The Masked Ball, The Force of Destiny,** and **Don Carlos.** These five operas took twelve years (he also revised two earlier operas during this time), whereas two and even three operas a year had given him no strain. But now he was deep in conspiratory intrigue with the odd array of intellectuals, politicians, and adventurers who brought about, after many a setback, a free and united Italy.

All this time he had been a hard man in business and money matters. Impresarios had been squealing for years under his insistence on the financial rights of the creator of operas which jammed the opera houses. As a very wealthy man, he was less inclined to hurry along with artistic production. Four years passed between the production of **Don Carlos** and his next opera, which was that creation of amazing depths and beauties, **Aïda.** It was first performed in Cairo, in a new opera house built to commemorate the opening of the Suez Canal, in 1871. Its composer was fifty-eight years old.

Since no new opera was forthcoming after **Aïda,** it became accepted that Verdi was through. The master of Sant'Agata lived serenely, kept his own counsel, permitted himself to be lionized up to a point but not beyond it, and, as his years piled up, began distributing his wealth in philanthropic enterprises. He had admitted to his intimacy a remarkable man of many talents, Arrigo Boïto, composer, poet, soldier, scholar, and philosopher. When he first met Boïto, years before, he hadn't liked him. He reversed himself. That Verdi could always do, although he didn't do it often.

Boïto was a devout admirer of Shakespeare. In that he and Verdi had affinity. These two conspired in great secrecy. Boïto provided a libretto based upon *Othello* and Verdi set it, while telling people he would never again compose anything for the stage. He was quite aware he was an old man and he wanted no dotage works to survive him. But **Otello** was no great task—he finished it in less than a year, even though he was seventy-three! With care he decided it was up to his standard, and permitted it to be produced. Nor was that all. Boïto put together a libretto from *The Merry Wives of Windsor* and called

Falstaff, which Verdi composed slowly but with deep satisfaction. It took two years. He was seventy-nine when it was finished and eighty when it was produced.

Giuseppina died four years later, at the age of eighty-two. The rugged old man stood up to the blow, since it was his way to stand up. Four years later, in January of 1901, he had a stroke and died six days later, on January 27, without returning to consciousness. He was eighty-eight years old.

18

Mendelssohn

FELIX MENDELSSOHN's life was in fast time. He was mature at ten, produced his finest masterpiece at seventeen, and died at thirty-eight of a weariness resembling that of old age.

Superficially, he seems to have been the happiest and most fortunate of men. Certainly he had everything to make him so. He was born to wealth and position. His parents were loving and kind. In addition to genius, he had charm, good looks, and a cheerful disposition. His wife was distinguished for her beauty, good sense, and selfless love for him. His five children were all delights.

Yet you can hear the reproving voice of his mother, Leah, exclaiming at the small child: "Felix! Are you doing nothing?" To her this was an offense, and rarely were any of her children guilty of it. Even when he became a man, Felix was never guilty of doing nothing. He worked under unceasing pressure to fulfill the high expectations of others.

The Mendelssohns' expectations for their children were high as a matter of course. Leah Salomon Mendelssohn was an artist and musician, well versed in four modern languages and their literatures, and a Greek scholar. Her husband, Abraham, had taken his high standards from his father, the renowned Moses Mendelssohn, scholar and philosopher called "the wise," whose force of love, character, and intellect lightened the burden of persecution borne by Jews in eighteenth-century Germany. Abraham and his brother, Joseph, founded the banking firm, Mendelssohn and Company.

Abraham and Leah's first child was Fanny Cäcilie, born in Hamburg on November 14, 1805. Felix—Jakob Ludwig Felix, to give him his full name—came along on February 3, 1809. Rebecka was born in Hamburg, too; but the youngest, Paul, was born after the family had moved to Berlin.

Old Moses had believed in the brotherhood of Jews and Christians. Leah's brother embraced Christianity and exchanged his name,

Salomon, for Bartholdy. His mother cursed him for this; but years later she became reconciled with her Christian relatives, through the strong-minded Fanny. Each of Leah and Abraham's children was baptized soon after birth under the name Mendelssohn Bartholdy, and in due course both parents became Christians, too.

The children were brought up amidst princely luxury. But it wasn't free. They got up at five each morning (except Sundays) because so much was expected of them. There were tutors to instruct them in art, music, literature, philosophy, languages, and mathematics. By example and admonition, their parents showed them how to be perfect little ladies and gentlemen, against a never-ending stream of guests, who were among the leading lights of the arts, politics, and commerce. Even the children's games were elevated, built around poetry and drama, and intended to instruct. Yet they liked it. Never was there a whisper of rebellion, so no harsh words were spoken to them, just pure reasoning.

Years later, Abraham analyzed a particular action of the adult Felix, found the action erroneous, but added: "If I view this matter incorrectly, then teach me a better mode of judging." With his mixture of autocratic reasoning and humility, he was a master of the overwhelming and unanswerable argument.

From birth onward Felix was thoroughly regulated. Yet it would seem he dearly wanted to be. To him, regulation was a condition of life. When it was withdrawn or withheld, he was at his wit's end. His regulators were his father, his mother, and his sister, Fanny, who had her father's force and strength of mind and the advantage of almost three and a half years in age.

At seven he was taking piano lessons from the celebrated teacher, Marie Bigot, in Paris. His teacher of harmony and composition was Carl Friedrich Zelter, composer, conductor, and among the top pedagogues of the age. Zelter, who was a friend of Goethe, decided his twelve-year-old pupil would be a fit companion-of-mind for the 72-year-old wise man, then reigning over culture from Weimar.

Accordingly, he took Felix to Goethe, but not before Abraham admonished his son: "Every time I write to you, dear boy, I shall remind you to keep a strict watch over yourself, to sit properly and behave well, especially at dinner, to speak clearly and suitably, and try as much as you can to express yourself to the point."

Zelter was quite right; Goethe was fascinated. He remarked on how very expressive the child was. His mind was quick and sharp; his charm was irresistible. He played the piano exquisitely; knew and understood music, especially the works of Bach and Beethoven; drew and painted with craftsmanship, and was familiar with the aesthetics of

art; was versed in literature, particularly poetry; and wrote so vividly
that a marked literary talent was obvious. The old man kept him
around for two weeks, after which they were firm friends.

When Felix returned to Berlin, he had more than fulfilled the expectations of Fanny. She had expressed them thus: "When you are
with Goethe I advise you to keep your eyes and ears wide open and
when you come home if you can't repeat every word that fell from
his mouth, I will have nothing more to do with you."

For a lad of such tender years he was remarkably industrious. He
had books filled with his drawings. He had written piles of descriptive
letters during travels with the family, in Switzerland and elsewhere.
He had composed a great mass of music, including quartets, trios,
sonatas, symphonies for strings, three parlor operas, and songs—and
among them are no small number that even now sound good enough
to do credit to an adult composer.

His fourth small-scale opera, **Der Onkel aus Boston,** was staged
privately in the Mendelssohn mansion when he was fifteen. It caused
the severe Zelter to say: "My dear boy, from this day you are no
longer an apprentice, but an independent member of the brotherhood
of musicians. I proclaim you independent in the name of Mozart,
Haydn, and old father Bach."

On Sunday mornings at the Mendelssohns' the leading musicians
performed in the "garden house," which was a small theater, and the
hosts provided a small, high-quality orchestra. In the mansion proper
was a salon the size of many a recital hall, and music was performed
there several times a week or oftener. Some of this music was Felix's.
He and the other children often played the piano, or cello and
violin, or sang. Felix always conducted the orchestra.

At one of these family musicales, his first and—as it is usually
acknowledged—finest masterpiece, an overture for Shakespeare's **A
Midsummer Night's Dream,** was performed. Whenever great music
is discussed, this piece will come into the talk sooner or later. And the
composer was only seventeen! What is even more astonishing is that
comparatively few of his adult compositions equaled it and none
truly surpassed it. **A Midsummer Night's Dream** overture compares
favorably with the teen-age masterpieces of Schubert and Mozart, the
other shining examples of youthful musical genius. Both went on to
much greater masterpieces. Isn't it odd Mendelssohn didn't?

On the surface this youth was like quicksilver, shimmering, always
in movement. He eyed people with warmth and interest; his smile was
like an embrace. His talk was likely to be gay. Laughter came from
him easily. In a regulated, gentlemanly way, he seemed to enjoy
whatever he did.

Such was the consistent surface, which is why he is called the happiest of men. Maybe he was like that under the surface, too. But there is cause to wonder. Mozart and Beethoven were anything but serene, yet both composed much music of heavenly serenity. Mendelssohn, who almost always seemed serene, displayed very little, if any, serenity in his music. A common playing direction was *agitato*.

You wonder about the time Ignaz Moscheles, a leading piano virtuoso, was a guest at one of the Mendelssohn recitals, and Felix was asked to play for the master. All eyes were on the lad as the guests expectantly waited for him to astonish the established artist. Felix burst into tears and fled the room. Such an incident was most untoward in the Mendelssohn parlors; it was a rare departure from regulation.

And you wonder about the time it looked as though the key singer might be late for a private performance of one of Felix's little operas. His composure vanished. He began muttering senseless phrases—in English, although the company around him was German speaking—and had to have a night's sleep to recover. Again, order and regulation appeared endangered—which Mendelssohn could never abide.

After he completed his formidable education at Berlin University and acquired even more polish with broadening travels, he began his career of professional musician. He played the piano and conducted in the capitals; he became music director at Düsseldorf, later at Leipzig; he conducted the German music festivals; was court composer to the King of Prussia; founded the Leipzig Conservatory. And he made frequent visits to England. The English loved him and his music—and he loved them. In all, he visited England ten times.

He had a regular schedule for composing, and year after year his compositions piled higher. He was also punctilious about taking holidays. As he was not the relaxing kind, he used these times to paint water colors of the landscapes, to compose, to do things. He passed up very little socially, and was a darling of the drawing rooms. He danced expertly, could take most of the gentlemen at billiards and lawn bowling, and was an excellent horseman. All these things he seemed to enjoy. Yet there was no bubbling enthusiasm; one might suspect they were accepted obligations.

All this time he was never without regulatory (and loving) advice from father, mother, and sister. It is interesting to read the letters of the brilliant Fanny—who was all but on the genius level herself—reproving him for being intolerant, which he was. He was intolerant, for example, of people who didn't share his worship of Bach and, to a slightly less extent, of Beethoven. He was offended by the "frivolous" music of Italy and France, by the antics of the wild Bohemian, Berlioz, by the flamboyant immorality of Liszt, by the "spasmodic and impassioned" style of Chopin, which, he thought, lost sight "too often of time and sobriety and true music."

When he was twenty-six, his chief regulator, Abraham, died suddenly, and he was all but prostrated for months. Fanny had thought for some time he ought to be married, and now marriage seemed a way of lifting him from depression. He went from Berlin to Frankfurt and began calling at the home of Madame Jeanrenaud, youthful and lively widow of a minister of the French Reformed (Protestant) Church. But the object of his interest turned out to be her beautiful seventeen-year-old daughter, Cécile. To make sure of his feelings, he stayed away from Frankfurt for a while. But since she persisted in his thoughts, he returned, proposed, and they were married on March 28, 1837.

It all sounds most deliberate to us today. Yet Cécile turned out to be the perfect wife for him, and he the perfect husband. Their children finally numbered five—Carl, Marie, Paul, Felix, and Lilli. Among them were Heidelberg and Oxford professors, who, in turn, were parents of a line of professors and learned doctors.

When Felix was thirty-three, his mother died. This was another devastating blow. Here was a man in his physical prime, who had always taken excellent care of himself. Yet he was suffering more and more from a weariness for which rest is not a lasting cure. True, he worked hard, but work doesn't kill. Never had he been able to take criticism of his work; never had he been able to maintain his equanimity when crossed or thwarted. Now this quality became exaggerated.

On his last visit to England, people said he looked tired and old. They wanted him to stay longer. He replied: "One more week of this unremitting fatigue and I should be killed outright." He arrived in Frankfurt in May, 1847. A few days later word reached him that Fanny, the last of his regulators, had died suddenly of a stroke while conducting her amateur choir.

He dropped to the floor, like a man shot through the heart, and was unconscious for some time. Cécile took him to Switzerland, but he remained tired and depressed. By September he was having chills and had to take to his bed. He died on November 4. The prime cause was cerebral hemorrhage. Cécile died of consumption less than six years later.

During the Nazi horror in Germany, his monuments were destroyed, his music was burned, and performances of his works were forbidden. Yet this Jew was a Christian from birth, and a sincerely practicing one, whose upright life was a credit to Christian morality.

To himself he was Felix Mendelssohn Bartholdy, and thus he presented two names to the world, one Jewish and one Christian. Posterity has chosen to remember him by his Jewish name—Mendelssohn, meaning Mendel's son.

To **A Midsummer Night's Dream** overture he added incidental music for the same play sixteen years later. This includes the **Nocturne** and the **Wedding March** which has kept his name alive even for unmusical people.

The twelve string symphonies of his childhood are never played; his **1st Symphony** for full orchestra, the **C Minor**—composed when he was only fifteen—is seldom heard, and for good reason, since it isn't interesting. His high reputation as a symphonist is based on the **3rd in A Minor** (the **Scotch**); the **4th in A Major** (the **Italian**); and the **5th in D Major** (the **Reformation**).

The 3rd and 4th are called **Scotch** and **Italian**, respectively, because they contain the composer's musical impressions of these countries. The 5th is difficult music. It is heavy with counterpoint, which Mendelssohn always employed with great skill, yet often with vaporous emptiness, and very scant on melody.

The **Violin Concerto in E Minor** is uniformly pleasurable from beginning to end. Of Mendelssohn's vast amount of piano music, very little holds its own today. The **Variations Sérieuses** and the **Rondo Capriccioso** are the most consistently admired.

His gigantic oratorio, **Elijah,** which takes well over two hours to perform, remains almost as popular in England as Handel's **Messiah,** but unless you're especially fond of choral singing and the effects of masses of shifting harmonics, you may find the whole too much.

Walpurgisnacht, a full setting of a Goethe text for alto, tenor, and baritone, plus choir and orchestra, is an exciting example of the *agitato* Mendelssohn at his best.

19

Schumann

As a composer, Robert Schumann is among the immortals, but we might never have heard of him if it hadn't been for his wife. The way to Schumann—man and artist—is through his Clara. She is also the way to another composer of genius, Johannes Brahms. But that is another story.

Clara Wieck was nine years old and already a remarkable pianist in 1828 when Schumann, a handsome young man of eighteen, applied to her father, Friedrich, for piano lessons. The place was Leipzig, where Bach lived, fathered modern music, and died in 1750.

Let's have a close look at this young man. His ideals were high-flown, and he was intolerant of challenges to or contradictions of those ideals. His thoughts were elevated, and his tears flowed easily; he was proud to weep. Indeed, he enjoyed feeling sad. All this was going to be reflected in his compositions and become the much-loved elements of Schumannesque romanticism.

His widowed, well-to-do mother back in his home town—Zwickau, 41 miles away—thought he was in Leipzig to study law at the university. The law was stable, and she thought he needed a stabilizing anchor. But behind her back he was seeking the unstable life of a musician.

Wieck was an excellent teacher. His daughter was a testimonial to his skills. He also was a self-trained psychologist with an understanding of minds that was far in advance of his times. From the very start he had no doubt of Schumann's musical talents, and pledged to turn him "within three years into one of the greatest pianists now living."

He took him into his home to teach him better. There Schumann met Clara, who was sharp far beyond her years. All her life she was to regard herself as a dedicated servant to the art of music. Thus Schumann's talents entailed obligation.

They became like brother and sister in their devotion to the highest ideals of their art. But, as he had done before and as he was to do again and again, Schumann found the means of self-defeat. This time he invented a gadget that held his fourth finger rigid while he exercised the others. In a very short time, the fourth finger of his right hand became permanently crippled.

A disaster! He was only twenty-two, but he could never be a great pianist. His calm, maintained by dignified melancholy, was amazing. He decided to devote himself to composing and music journalism. He believed music was comparable to a fair maid of matchless virtue being held captive by coarse ruffians, and these included some of the most successful performers and composers of the day. This point of view he elaborated in barrages of high-flown prose in a music journal, *Neue Zeitschrift für Musik*, which he founded with other young "radicals" and quickly made influential.

He had been composing in fits and starts since he was nine. Now the idea of plumed knights versus despoilers of the fair—Philistines, he called the latter—also began appearing in his music.

His nature was not one and indivisible. One part of himself he personified into an individual named Florestan. Another part he called Eusebius. They agreed there should be everlasting war on the Philistines, but essentially they were in conflict. To reconcile these two, there was a third personification—Master Raro.

Encouraging, sympathizing, and agreeing wholeheartedly with these fantasies, was his little "sister," Clara. He needed what this child priestess of music gave, and, of course, its value in stabilizing Schumann in sustained composing is incalculable. Like her father, she was a keen judge of minds. When she was fourteen years old she began calling him "my old moonstruck maker of charades."

You can see how things were going with them at this time, when he was twenty-three, in this passage from a letter he wrote his mother:

Clara is as fond of me as ever, and is just as she used to be of old, wild and enthusiastic, skipping and running about like a child, and saying the most intensely thoughtful things. It is a pleasure to see her gifts of mind and heart keep developing faster and faster. . . .

The other day, as we were walking back from Connewitz (we go for a two or three hour hike almost every day) I heard her saying to herself, "Oh, how happy I am! How happy!" Who would not love to hear that? On that road there are a great many useless stones lying about in the middle of the foothpath. Now, when I am talking, I often look more up than down, so she always walks behind me and gently pulls my coat at every stone to prevent my falling, meantime she stumbles over them herself.

She had just returned to Leipzig from a concert tour—already she was a famous pianist.

Eventually came the day when Friedrich Wieck realized these two were no longer regarding each other as sister and brother. By then she was seventeen and he was twenty-six. You'd think Wieck would have been delighted. He wasn't. He ordered Robert to leave and commanded Clara never to communicate with him. For some four years he maintained an embittered opposition, resorting to tactics so despicable they indicate the measure of his desperation.

These were years of cruel trials for the tenderly sensitive Robert; for Clara, too, although she was made of more stable stuff. Occasionally she wavered; but even in her indecision she realized his creative genius and his need for her. When she was twenty-one and no longer needed her father's consent, she married her "moonstruck maker of charades."

All sorts of motives have been assigned to Wieck's opposition, none very plausible except the one that should now be obvious. In all fairness it should be said that events justified him—assuming he was acting as a loving and protecting father. Schumann's remaining road was downhill.

He now was thirty years old. During his twenties, epecially while suffering from Wieck's attitude, he had created some of the most emotion-charged compositions, suffused with conflicts and strange, original beauty, in piano literature. With the winning of Clara, he turned to songs. Soon it was chamber music, then symphonies.

This was typical of him. It was always all of one thing and little, if anything, of other things. As a music journalist, he had made and was making notable contributions to the appreciation of musical values. He supported Mendelssohn, who came to Leipzig when Schumann was twenty-five to conduct the Gewandhaus Orchestra. He campaigned for the music of Schubert and Berlioz, also for the works of many composers now forgotten. He wrote, "*Hats off, gentlemen—a genius!*" in referring to a young and then unknown Pole, Frédéric Chopin.

Clara kept the creative genius prolific for three years. Compositions poured from Schumann, all challenging, but not all easily comprehensible. Then, very suddenly, something happened to his internal harmony. He fell ill. The illness was called mental exhaustion. Sad, suffering creator! He had been ill all along, and only a few—including Clara and, probably, her father—and Schumann himself knew it.

The following year, when he was thirty-four, he had to give up his editorship. They moved from Leipzig to Dresden and later to Düsseldorf. Babies came—in all there were eight, although one died in infancy.

Clara mothered her growing brood. She struggled to help Master

Raro restore and maintain internal harmony, and the two of them succeeded for brief periods, during which compositions would pour forth again. Between and among these duties, she was giving concerts —the family needed the money.

More and more Schumann was turning inward on himself. He would sit for hours in company without contributing one word to the conversation and without seeming to be listening to it. There would be a sweet, half-smiling expression on his face. He went with her on some of her tours, and she had to heal his hurts. She was much more famous than he; actually, she was famous and he was not, although, since childhood, she had been playing his music at every opportunity, despite the cold reception it was given.

In 1853, when he was forty-three and she was thirty-four, there arrived one day at their home in Düsseldorf a young man of twenty. He had a letter of introduction from Joseph Joachim, who was then only twenty-two, but was going to make musical history as one of the great violin virtuosos.

The young man wanted to play some of his own piano compositions. Glumly taciturn, Schumann agreed to listen. In a minute or two, his face lit up with excitement. He called Clara to listen with him. They asked the young man to play on and on; they kept him as a house guest.

Roused from his lethargy, Schumann sent his first contribution in ten years to his old journal in Leipzig. He wrote that there had to appear "a musician called to give expression to his times in ideal fashion; a musician who would reveal his mastery not in a gradual evolution, but like Athene would spring fully armed from Zeus' head. And such a one has appeared; a young man over whose cradle Graces and Heroes have stood watch. His name is Johannes Brahms."

He never wrote again. Clara could no longer communicate with Master Raro. Schumann thought musical notes sounded in his ears continuously. In February of the year he was forty-four he left his bed and rushed to his writing table, saying Schubert and Mendelssohn had sent him a theme from heaven and he must write it down. On February 26 he flung himself into the Rhine. Rescued, he begged to be placed in an asylum, where he could not harm himself. He was placed in one near Bonn, the birthplace of Beethoven, and there he lived, more like a vegetable than a man, for over two years, until July 29, 1856, when he died in his sleep.

Clara had been summoned from a concert tour. She was now the sole support of seven children. She held him in her arms, and later wrote in her diary:

"His head was beautiful, the forehead so transparent and slightly arched.

"I stood by the body of my passionately loved husband, and was calm. All my feelings were absorbed in thankfulness to God that he was at last set free, and as I kneeled by his bed I was filled with awe, it was as if his holy spirit was hovering over me—Ah! if only he had taken me with him."

This same year, when she was thirty-seven, she wrote in her diary for her children:

"You hardly knew your father, you were too young to experience deep grief; and so, during those terrible years, you were unable to bring me consolation, but only hope, which could not sustain me in the midst of such suffering.

"And then came Johannes Brahms. Your father loved and admired him as he did nobody else save Joachim. He came to help me, and like a faithful friend, to bear all my distress; he gave strength to my heart when it bade fair to break, he raised my courage, and cheered me so far as he was able. In short, he was my friend in every sense of the word."

When Schumann died, she had forty more years to live; she died at seventy-seven, in 1896. She was one of the greatest pianists of the nineteenth century and probably the greatest woman pianist of all time. Just as Schumann might never have composed many of his masterpieces if it hadn't been for her, these masterpieces might be unknown and forgotten today if it hadn't been for her. Public recognition of Schumann came slowly. She was his always-persevering popularizer and succeeded so well that she lived long enough to see him ranked with Beethoven.

The great Schumann tide of the last of the nineteenth century has receded now, and we accept Schumann's music for a value which is considerably below that of the greatest masters, including Brahms, yet has values all its own. His music has intensely individualistic qualities. At first, people considered it radical and its composer a revolutionary. They are nothing of the sort. Schumann was a romantic, but he was strictly a Schumannesque romantic.

Almost all his best music was for the piano and the voice. Many of the songs are distinguished by exquisite piano accompaniments and by a deep insight that enables the music to convey the same sentiment as the words.

The finest of his piano music is to be found in such compositions as the **Fantasiestücke, Die Davidsbundlertanze (Dances of the David League), Fantasia in C Major, Kinderscenen (Scenes from Childhood),**

Carnaval, Kreisleriana, Papillons, and the Symphonic Etudes. They're made up of short, little pieces strung together like beads.

Some of the beads affect us more than others, and some are singularly unattractive. But the latter are few, and the episodes of emotional power—sometimes overwhelming or brightly gay, or like pleasant dreams, or remindful of one's most valued memories—are many.

Dichterliebe (Poet's Love), a setting for a series of poems by Heine, displays Schumann's genius for song consecutively over a considerable stretch. Another important Schumann song cycle is Frauenliebe und Leben (Woman's Love and Life). The A Minor Piano Concerto is tremendous and moving, and its popularity has never waned. It was played for the first time by Clara with the Leipzig Gewandhaus Orchestra on January 1, 1846. Another Schumann masterpiece is the Piano Quintet in E-flat, one of the most compelling chamber works composed after Beethoven and before Brahms.

20

Brahms

ON May 31, 1856, while Robert Schumann was dying, Johannes Brahms wrote Schumann's wife, Clara, "I wish I could write to you as tenderly as I love you." Don't misconstrue. He loved Schumann, too. His love was spiritual. As a matter of fact, all his loves were spiritual.

When Schumann died, Brahms was twenty-three. Clara wrote in her diary that his love for her and hers for him were "the most beautiful spiritual harmony." She reiterated this sentiment forty years later, in 1896, the year of her death, and through all the years between. Spiritually, they couldn't have been closer. But that's all it ever was. And therein is the real tragedy of Johannes Brahms.

He had the brightest blue eyes anyone ever saw. Everyone remarked on them. He was brought up in a Hamburg slum, spent many childhood hours in sailors' dives, had every chance to be a delinquent. His father, Johann Jakob, played bull fiddle in a theater orchestra, an untalented orchestral drudge. He thought little Hannes might become the same "success." His horizons were narrow.

The first outsider to have a hand was Otto Cossel, a piano teacher. In 1840 he gave ear to seven-year-old Hannes and recognized genius. The next teacher was Eduard Marxsen, the best in Hamburg. He didn't want to take on a free pupil—until he heard the boy. In 1853, Schumann heard him and proclaimed the twenty-year-old youth to the musical world as "a young eagle."

Thus, recognition came early and easily. He hardly had to ask for it. He went from success to success. He was lionized, idolized. Concert halls were packed for him. His music was played everywhere. His fees and royalties made him rich.

But the man who died at sixty-four, in 1897, wifeless and childless, died with regretful tears in his eyes. If he had had it all to do again, he would have wanted it to be different. And not without good reason.

A slum child can have a rough time. He had one. The family was made up of an older sister and a younger brother (neither had a shred of musical talent), and a mother and father who didn't get along. It was always touch and go with the wolf at the door. Well-meaning, hard-working, miserably paid Jakob couldn't cope with life or wife. Thirteen-year-old Hannes wanted to help, which was characteristic of him. He had one skill. He knew how to play the piano.

So into waterfront bawdyhouses he went, on his own. His wages were pittances, plus all he wanted to drink. Night after night, well into his sixteenth year, he kept at it—hammering tawdry tunes out of shaky pianos for the benefit of prostitutes and their clients. This was the furnace in which he was forged. The acute sensitivity all creative artists must have became sheeted over with the steel of contempt.

He tried to conceal his contempt behind irony and mock geniality, but now and then it broke out. He railed at men as fools. What he said of women is unprintable. Yet no man could be more humane. Behind his protective sheeting were idealism, nobility, tenderness, honesty, forgiveness. Most of the people who knew him knew this. They overlooked his coarseness. A few even got through to the inner artist.

Of these, a few were women. Although Clara was not the only one, she was the first and the last. He often wrote her such sentiments as this: "Let this deep love of mine be a comfort to you, for I love you more than myself, more than anybody or anything whatsoever in the world."

The creator of **Brahms' Cradle Song** never had any personal connection with a cradle after he outgrew his own. Yet he loved children and all that pertains to childhood, especially tin soldiers. He preserved his own childhood battalions well into his adult years. The old man with the long beard was always happy to get down on his hands and knees when tin soldiers and children were on the floor.

One spiritual love of his youth was for a pretty young singer, Bertha Porubszky. For a time it looked as though his love might become more, but eventually she married another man. On the arrival of her child, she received a present from Hannes—a song for her to sing to her babe. It was **Brahms' Cradle Song.**

Another recipient of a song was Julie Schumann, daughter of Clara and Robert, who was twelve years younger than he. When she came into young womanhood, he fell in love with her, since she was the image of her mother. When she married another man, he sent her a wedding song—the **Alto Rhapsody**—filled with longing and sorrow.

Meantime, even in his last years, he was entering into passing liaisons with women of the street; and bitterly flaunting them at the respectable world. For decent women he was impotent.

Nobility he had in full measure. For example: He loved his mother. During his twenties, she reached the point where she no longer could tolerate his father. He loved his father, too. Unlike his sister and brother, he couldn't bring himself to take sides. So he tried to be a peacemaker. Failing, he supported his parents in separate establishments. When mother died he grieved. Yet when his father decided to marry again, less than a year later, he was delighted. He took his stepmother into his heart, along with her son by her first marriage. His father lived only six years to enjoy his new happiness. His widow and her son retained Hannes' love for the remainder of his life.

All this helps in understanding Brahms, who was not easy to understand. When he was around thirty, he began to move with the high and mighty of the world. To his credit, he never concealed his origin, although it might be said he overdid letting people know about it.

He enjoyed having his uncouth father as his guest in Vienna and displaying him to the highly cultured, the noble, even the royal. A story is told that the father would shout at his celebrated son, "Hannes! Mind your tongue!" Hannes would subside into silence.

He should have minded his tongue more than he did. One evening, in a fashionable drawing room, he lashed out at a circle of friends. Stalking from the room, he paused long enough in the doorway to say to them, "If there is anyone here whom I have not insulted, I beg his pardon." So he knew what he was doing. He was under a strange compulsion to prevent people from intruding on his secret self. He destroyed musical sketches, letters, personal papers, and much of his music. His existing music he published only after long deliberation, so the works we know may be a relatively small percentage of those he created.

In 1886, he persuaded Clara to return a thirty-year accumulation of his letters, which he threw into the Rhine. In reciprocation, he returned hers and she burned them. But many of his letters were too precious to her to part with. He let her keep them when she insisted. These and some others, which somehow escaped destruction, fill a huge volume.

Outwardly, his adult life was one of routine. Winters he toured, conducting orchestras, playing the piano. Summers he spent in country resorts, composing. Usually Clara summered nearby. Winters she toured, too, playing the piano music of Schumann and Brahms up and down and across Europe.

He was forty-five when he grew the beard with which we identify him. He said he liked neither shaving nor wearing collars. As he grew older, he became more and more untidy. The Viennese referred to some of the ancient coats he wore as "landmarks." And as he grew older, he grew stouter. Good food and drink had greater and greater appeal. He was self-educated in literature, history, and political science. Among great composers, his was one of the impressive intellects.

In May, 1896, he received a telegram from Frankfurt am Main. It was from Marie Schumann, eldest child of Clara and Robert. It said, "Our mother fell gently asleep today." Older than his years—he had aged rapidly—the old man with the pot belly and the beard set forth on a long journey.

In Bonn, he watched Clara's coffin lowered into a grave beside her husband's. He picked up a handful of soil and let it run through his fingers into her grave. We can only imagine what futile regret ran through his mind. The following April he died—of cancer.

Brahms's idolators of his own time used the phrase, "The three B's —Bach, Beethoven, and Brahms." Adulation enraged him, and this phrase drew forth a favored expletive: "Fools!" He was a humble man about his own art and habitually underrated himself. Yet he knew his place in the hierarchy of composers; he knew it was below Bach and Beethoven, whom he adored.

This question of place remains controversial. There is still a small, hard core of "three B's" enthusiasts. There is also a larger group that maintains Brahms was an exquisite miniaturist, that his songs and small piano pieces are the purest of pure gems, but you can throw out most of the rest.

Neither position is reasonable. Isn't it quite enough to accept the fact that after Beethoven—considering Schubert contemporary with Beethoven, rather than after him—Brahms is the next great master chronologically in the classic-romantic tradition?

Brahms composed over two hundred songs, which range over all his creative life. Hardly one is unworthy of him.

The short piano forms, which he called intermezzo or ballade or capriccio or romance or rhapsody, are most beautiful. The best are unforgettable. Since the piano was Brahms's instrument, it is curious his writing for it didn't even come close, in volume, to Beethoven's. Beethoven's piano music may be the reason. It always awed Brahms. Among the piano music he did compose, **Variations and Fugue on a Theme by Handel** is the most powerful of the larger works. There are two piano concertos in which the piano is treated more as an orchestral instrument than as a solo one, both marred by disgressions and both distinguished by passages of passion or sublimity.

The **Alto Rhapsody** is a large work, for alto, male chorus, and full orchestra. The **German Requiem** has what some Brahms detractors call Brahmsian length, which is very long. Yet some of its passages are so moving they're not really long enough. These include a soprano solo, which the composer intended as a memorial to his mother. The **Song of Destiny (Schicksalslied)** is another choral work of heroic proportions, about which there can be little controversy.

The **4th Symphony** is, beyond questioning, one of the towering masterpieces in symphonic literature. It covers a range of emotions with unremitting concentration. The **1st Symphony** is shadowy, and only fanatical Brahmsians will battle for its every last note. The **2nd**, the jolliest, and the **3rd** still cause arguments. They meander. This invites boredom, say some; every sound is movingly expressive, say others.

Brahms composed twenty-four chamber works—from duets for violin or cello and piano, through string quartets, to two sextets for strings. It's hard to say whether anyone, aside from a confirmed Brahmsian, would be sure to like them all a great deal. But the one that has the most instant appeal is the **F Minor Piano Quintet**, for its many moments of force and beauty. It's a good place to start with the chamber music.

21

Chopin

LET US contemplate the secret life of Frédéric Chopin—and very secret it was. His best friends had only hints of its existence; most people knew merely the surface man. And the surface wasn't attractive. It was cold, pallid, and sickly. He was rigid and narrow in outlook, superficial, and a snob.

Only because of his music do we know he possessed bottomless depths. In it are evidences of his secret life. A poignant longing here, a bittersweet renunciation there. Here a spark of gaiety, but with the turned-down mouth of sorrow. There the flash of high resolve suspended by a chain of sighs. The emotional range was from stagnant melancholy to leaping, bounding passion and exaltation. But the strangest quality is one of contradiction; each emotion carries a specific denial.

The supreme contradictions are in the coldly impersonal and unemotional titles he gave to his music—titles like Waltz, Prelude, Etude, Polonaise, Mazurka, and Nocturne. Thus he avoided any definition of emotional meaning. Indeed, any suggestion that there was emotional meaning made him peevish. It impinged on his secret life, and he resented it.

We'll never know what made him tick. But, whatever it was, it must have been pretty much what makes us all tick. The musically veiled emotions of Chopin evoke similar emotions in all listeners who are not tone-deaf and insensible to rhythm.

Music and emotion were combined in him from birth, seemingly. In 1810 (he was born on February 22), in the pleasant, comfortable home of Nicholas and Justine Chopin in Zelazowa-Wola, Poland, the infant in his cradle burst into tears each time he heard music and cried as long as the music continued.

Both parents were musical. Their son's behavior distressed them. How could a child of theirs be pained by music when they loved it so? But they were soon reassured. He was hardly out of his cradle when he was picking out little melodies on the piano.

It was a miracle of affinity. When he was eight, a family friend wrote in her diary: "Not only does he play with complete facility and wonderful taste the most difficult compositions, but is already the composer of dances and variations which amaze the connoisseurs."

At nineteen, he completed a thorough education in music (and a sketchy one in other matters), and his music master wrote into the record: "Chopin, Frédéric (third-year student); outstanding abilities, musical genius." He told his master, he intended "creating a new world." And so he did.

His mother came of a poor but upper-class Polish family. His father, the son of a wheelwright, was French by birth. He went to Poland as a young man, became a French tutor and teacher of the children of the upper class, and learned to be as Polish as the Poles.

Their physically slight and frail child was brought up in the drawing rooms of high society. It wasn't so much they willed it for him as he chose it for himself. From the socially noble he acquired a glossy artificiality and superficiality that adhered to the surface. He learned the degrees of deference paid to a prince and to a mere baron. He learned how to condescend subtly to those he considered slightly inferior and how to be callously rude to those who were definitely inferior. He learned what clothes a gentleman wore for what occasions, and how a gentleman could make a little drama of putting on or taking off gloves. He could kiss a lady's hand or bow to a lord with exquisite grace. His small talk was spontaneous—and empty.

All this made up the exterior of the musician of twenty-one who, in 1831, arrived in Paris—which was to be his home thereafter and where he was to die eighteen years later, only thirty-nine years old. Death was already on him, and physical weakness and malaise exaggerated defects in his character. In his day, people weren't cured of tuberculosis. They often died by inches, and so did Chopin.

Franz Liszt, less than two years younger, was already in Paris, attracting considerable attention as an overwhelming piano virtuoso. Chopin played as well as any man who ever lived, but he played uniquely. His style was delicate, notable for the subtle nuance, the finely turned phrase. It was ideal for salons and small audiences, not for vast halls and huge audiences.

Thanks largely to his manners, Chopin quickly became the favorite music master of the daughters of the French aristocracy, while Liszt conquered the musical world at large. Chopin would have as many as eight pupils a day. No aristocrat would have insulted him by even mentioning money. After a lesson, he'd find a generous honorarium had been left discreetly on the mantel.

Very soon he acquired his own carriage, patronized the best tailors, owned innumerable pairs of gloves, lived in a sumptuously furnished apartment in a fashionable street, and had a staff of servants. Hostesses doted on him. Evenings he would honor one or another of them by appearing in her salon.

During this time he was excerpting from his secret life various emotionally charged commentaries that he called Waltz or Polonaise. The more sensitive among his intimates were aware of this secret life, notably Liszt, who, years later, wrote:

"No one ever asked him to give an account of his dreams, his wishes, or his hopes. No one seemed to wish to know what he sighed for, what he might have conquered, if his white and tapering fingers could have linked the brazen chords of life to the golden ones of his enchanted lyre.

"No one had leisure to think of this in his presence. His conversation was rarely upon subjects of deep interest. He glided lightly over all, and as he gave but little of his time, it was easily filled with the details of the day. He was careful never to allow himself to wander into digressions of which he himself might become a subject."

It is the custom of music commentators to find nothing wrong with musical genius. They love music so much, creators seem to have no flaw. But a fact is never ugly—it is only a fact. And the fact is, Chopin loved only Chopin and was concerned only for Chopin— quite understandable in a person who is able to measure the increasing shortness of his breath and knows death is that much nearer.

He treated Liszt's devotion with ingratitude. He did the same to Schumann, who was among the very first to hail his genius. But most glaring of all was his treatment of the woman who was the only fulfilled love of his life. When she needed his sympathetic understanding most, he simply didn't have it to give.

She was Amandine Lucile Aurore Dupin, who at eighteen had married a country squire, Casimir Dudevant. She bore him a son and a daughter, and then left him to assert her right to full liberty—which women just didn't do then—to become an extraordinary woman of letters and to acquire a succession of lovers, among whom was Chopin. Her collected works fill ninety-six volumes. We know her best by her pen name, George Sand.

The evidence is that she wooed Chopin. He was overwhelmed by her intellectual and emotional hardihood, as any man might have been. Yet he loved her, in his way and to his capacity. It is a gross libel to consider him effeminate. He was exquisite, true; superrefined. Liszt once said of him: "He never made use of an inelegant word, even in moments of the most entire familiarity. An improper innuendo, a coarse jest would have been shocking to him." But he had loved other women, although idealistically and timidly, before the cigar-smoking George Sand came into his life.

In 1838, when she was thirty-four and Chopin was twenty-eight, she wrote him a note—concise but eloquent: "I adore you. George." Soon after, they fled Paris, accompanied by her two children, for a hideaway love idyl on the island of Majorca in the Mediterranean. The islanders were unfriendly, the weather was abominable, and Chopin was ill much of the time, so the idyl was a fiasco.

But for nine years she took excellent care of him. She nursed him tenderly when he was ill, which was often. She relieved him of every care and arranged every prosaic detail of his life. She patiently coped with the difficulties arising from his temperament. During these years he composed some of his finest music and much of his total output.

Chopin the musician she worshiped. Chopin the man she mothered with fanatical thoroughness. She understood him as well as any contemporary, better than most. He was, she said, "the *poor* great artist." Nor was she unaware of his secret life, as this statement reveals:

"His creation was spontaneous and miraculous. He found it without seeking it, without foreseeing it. It came on his piano suddenly, complete, sublime, or it sang in his head during a walk, and he was immediately impatient to play it to himself.

"But then began the most heart-rending labor I ever saw. It was a series of efforts, of irresolutions, and of frettings to seize again certain details of the theme he had heard; what he had conceived as a whole he analyzed too much when wishing to write it, and his regret at not finding it again, in his opinion, clearly defined, threw him into a kind of despair.

"He shut himself up in his room for whole days, weeping, walking, breaking his pens, repeating and altering a bar a hundred times, writing and effacing it as many times, and recommencing the next day with a meticulous and desperate perseverance. He spent six weeks over a single page to write it at last as he had noted it down at the very first."

During these nine years, Chopin could have been a father to her children. But the boy, Maurice, grew up to dislike him intensely; the girl, Solange, to manipulate him and break the bond between him and her mother.

There was a long, violent quarrel between mother and daughter. Chopin displayed no rushing, impulsive loyalty and comfort for the mother, who wanted and felt entitled to his unquestioning support. Rather, Solange so maneuvered him he seemed to side with her—

and the mother was outraged. He made no effort to explain himself, no effort to assure a loved one of love.

It was the end of their life together. If it hadn't happened, he might have lived a few years longer than he did. Her care and protection were withdrawn. He had to deal with harsh realities himself, and now he gasped for breath. He continued to teach, but could no longer compose. The following year, 1848, he was persuaded by his adoring friend and pupil, Miss Jane Stirling of the Scottish Stirlings, to visit England and Scotland.

He left Paris in April. The English and Scots wanted to hear him. He gave a series of concerts that exhausted his little remaining strength. The autumn found him in London, where the seasonal damp and fog were murderous to a man in the last stages of tuberculosis. He left "this hellish London" in November, and the admirers who met him on his return to Paris found him "more dead than alive."

But he lived almost a year, dying on October 17, 1849. His sister, Louise, had come from Poland to nurse him. George Sand sent her a pathetic note, saying she had heard contradictory reports concerning his health. She went on: "I venture to ask you to send me word, for one can be misunderstood and abandoned by one's children without ceasing to love them." Louise did not reply. Whether she did this at her brother's direction or on her own is not known. But the note George Sand had sent him eleven years before—"I adore you. George" —was found in his purse.

As a creative artist, Chopin deliberately restricted himself to the piano. To a friend who urged him to expand, he replied, "Leave me to my piano. It is my business." On another occasion, he said, "Mozart encompasses the entire domain of musical creation, but I've got only the keyboard in my poor head. I know my limitations and I know that I'd make a fool of myself if I tried to climb too high without having the ability to do so. . . . I'm only a pianist, and if I'm worth anything, this is good, too."

He knew full well he was worth a great deal. Delicately phrased modesty was one of his social accomplishments. In a more realistic vein he once said that he would have "my little kingdom" in music. He has. Nothing that Chopin wrote could possibly be mistaken for the work of anyone else. Every piece of his bears his characteristic stamp.

There are some who would make him a salon composer of perfumed trifles. Others would have him a nationalistic composer because he used Polish dance forms so freely—the Polonaise and the Mazurka—and because he carried in his imagination an idealized Poland that never existed or could exist. True, his music reflects recognizable Slavic emotion and often displays his knowledge of Polish folk music. But those who would fit him to a mold deny his universality. His music transcends nationality.

Chopin's works are easily listed: 27 Etudes; 52 Mazurkas; 19 Nocturnes; 14 Waltzes; 8 Polonaises; 25 Preludes; 4 Ballades; 4 Scherzos; 3 Sonatas for piano and 1 for cello and piano; 2 Concertos "for the pianoforte *accompanied* by orchestra"; a **Fantasie in F Minor**; a **Fantasie-Impromptu,** from which was taken the tune of the erstwhile popular song, **I'm Always Chasing Rainbows**; a **Barcarolle**; and a miscellany of lesser works, including a couple of dozen songs that are rarely sung and more or less unknown today.

22

Offenbach

JACQUES OFFENBACH was breathless in his admiration of the musical
gift of Jacques Offenbach. There hardly was an adjective he didn't
employ at one time or another in his efforts to describe it ade-
quately. He was like a child with a marvelous toy of endless delights.

His happiness with his gift knew no bounds, and so he used it to
compose some of the gayest music ever written. As he himself said:
"I do not know what I've done to cause God to bestow so much happiness and so much melody upon me." Yet his gift gave him no rest,
permitted him no peace. Throughout his years, it obsessively drove
him—Compose, slave! Compose! A friend described a typical scene in
his life: "His children would be noisily playing, laughing, and singing all around him, and friends would call. He would talk and joke
. . . but his right hand would go on writing all the time."

At length, when he could feel death creeping close, he drew up a
horrible accusation against himself: He had never made proper use
of his wonderful gift. Although he was then the composer of more
than one hundred operas and operatic pieces which had made him
famous throughout the world, not one, he thought, would keep him
alive after he died.

In desperation, while ailing and failing, he composed yet another
opera as a bid for immortality. Amazing man! He succeeded by producing his masterpiece, one of the most enthralling and enduring of
all operas, **The Tales of Hoffmann,** which, as every school child knows,
contains an unforgettable barcarolle.

He was in the sunburst of genius-musicians which broke over music
during the first two decades of the nineteenth century. Berlioz was
born in 1803. Six years later came Mendelssohn. Both Schumann and
Chopin were born in 1810, and the following year Liszt was born.
Another pair-year was 1813—Wagner and Verdi. And in 1819 (on
June 20) arrived Offenbach, who because he composed music for
the cancan shouldn't be excluded from this company. He, too, left a

permanent imprint upon the art, if only by showing it could be infused with unalloyed gaiety and happiness.

Like Chopin, he spent his productive years among the French. Unlike Chopin, who was untouched by surroundings or anything else which was apart from Chopin, Offenbach became at least as French as the French and died a Parisian to his core. But he was born in the ghetto of Cologne, Germany, the seventh child of Isaac Juda Eberst, bookbinder, synagogue singer, and fiddler, and his wife, Marianne, daughter of a money-changer. They named their new child Jakob.

Isaac had been born in Offenbach on the river Main. When he was a young man making a precarious living as an itinerant musician, people called him the Offenbacher. As the years passed, Offenbach became his professional name, but as a professional musician he always fared poorly, and now and then he had to return to his trade. He loved music with a consuming love. That being so, the new child soon was brightening his life. The others were musical, but Jakob was phenomenally so, playing the violin at six and composing at eight.

When he was twelve he played the cello well enough to join his older sister and brother, Isabella and Julius, in a string trio which played in restaurants and bars and helped the family make ends meet. By fourteen, he knew more about music and its performance than did the Cologne teachers who were accessible to poor Jews. Only the French were willing to cultivate genius, or even talent, at the taxpayer's expense without regard to whether it reposed in a Jew. So Isaac took his brilliant child to Paris, where he was admitted to the Conservatoire.

Julius, who was now eighteen, went along to watch over his younger brother, while making his livelihood as a violin player. Isaac returned to Cologne and Julius' authority was not enough. In a year Jakob (whose name was being Frenchified into Jacques) left the Conservatoire.

We can't be sure why. He himself indicated the instruction was not absorbing. On the other hand, one of the most prominent aspects of his character was a panicky dread of depths, in emotion or thought. The Jacques Offenbach of the surface always seemed in head-on flight from the Jacques Offenbach of the depths.

From the Conservatoire, he went into the orchestra of the Opéra-Comique as a cellist, a routine and poorly paid job, but his surface energy and love of jokes provided his outlets. A typical joke, when the lights were down and no one was noticing, was to hook up the playing arms of the violinists and empty chairs with string. As the fiddlers played, the chairs jiggled.

He lived in a Montmartre room with his brother and two other young men. Low income dictated stringent economies, but he always surrounded himself with friends. He never could bear to be alone, even while practicing on the cello. This endless practicing was not to master deeply charged emotional music, but to achieve sparkle and polish.

The Paris of the time had sparkle and polish. The Napoleonic Wars had left France morally bankrupt. Wild and often fraudulent speculation created a feverish prosperity for the moneyed classes. There was a tomorrow-we-die spirit about, and the driving urge was to enjoy the day. Social extravagances were a matter of competition, and every lady who could possibly finance one, maintained a salon where she entertained as many persons as often as her energy and money allowed.

These perpetual hostesses labored to soak their guests in culture—it was the fashion—and musicians who performed brilliantly, although not necessarily with depth and perception, were much in demand. There was no pay; the musicians were honored guests. But they could play their own compositions, and when they gave public concerts, each hostess in whose salon they had performed was obliged to buy a block of seats, and at premium prices. It was a way of making a living which many used, including Chopin, upon his arrival from Poland.

After three years of being "riveted," as he put it, into the Opéra-Comique orchestra, Offenbach, lugging his cello, took to the salons. He was nineteen, and with his youth, strange looks, and native wit was an immediate success. He was tall and his thinness made him seem taller. His eyes were so luminous they could be hypnotic; his hair was wavy and he wore it long, and his nose reminded some people of a bird of prey. On the other hand, one contemporary remarked that he looked like "a cross between a rooster and a grasshopper."

His compulsion to compose intensified. Now he was running up sentimental ballads and dance music which got performed but with little profit for the composer, and pouring torrents of energy into music for the theater which he couldn't get performed. His trouble here was that he was a genius in this particular field and was ahead of his day.

What he was composing was "really gay, cheerful, witty music . . . music with life in it." He described it that way, railing at the Opéra-Comique, which would have nothing to do with his works but kept on producing "little grand operas," unconnected with anything comic. His brand of comedy was loaded with satire—it cut. The times were troubled; theatrical managements were afraid of satire.

For some seventeen years he fought this battle fruitlessly without ever losing heart and with steadily increasing energy. During this time he found the girl of his heart, Herminie. To marry her, he accepted baptism and became a Roman Catholic. Never a dogmatic follower of the Jewish religion, he couldn't very well become a dogmatic Christian. A simple, childlike man, he continued to speak of God as he always had—reverently, with unshakable faith in God's personal love for him.

The revolution of 1848 occurred four years after the marriage and he, Herminie, and their little daughter fled to Cologne where, for a year, they shared the dismal poverty of his parents. When they returned to Paris, matters became better because he was appointed conductor at the Théâtre Français, which meant an insured income, although a small one, since it was a dramatic theater and music wasn't too important. But this shrank when his musicians discovered he was a soft touch.

At last, in 1853, when he was thirty-four years old, he succeeded in persuading a theater to produce a one-act opera of his, and it had a short run. But his day didn't really arrive until two years later. Louis Bonaparte, through a *coup d'état*, had restored the Napoleonic empire and made himself emperor, as Napoleon III. To solidify his shaky throne, he organized a mammoth world exposition which opened in Paris in May, 1855. By that time Offenbach had concluded that if the world was going to be made to admire his gift the way he did, he would have to bring it about himself. Near the exposition grounds was an old and tiny theater, which had been unused for years. He rented it, refurbished it, and renamed it, Bouffes-Parisiens.

He was general manager, stage manager, composer, conductor, and just about everything else. His success in all those endeavors was instantaneous. Vast crowds clamored to get into the crackerbox; the house was sold out for weeks in advance. The multitudes of foreign visitors to the exposition carried word of his brand of gaiety to all the world. Recognition and fame had been a long time in coming, but now they came. Bouffes-Parisiens moved to a larger theater. Offenbach was turning out new pieces as though he were a factory rather than a man, meanwhile carrying all the production and business details and entertaining at home every Friday evening for scores, sometimes hundreds, of guests.

This was his life, with minor variations, from then on, but with more work and detail, never less. The Paris season was not enough. He began composing and producing operas at a German spa during its season. One city was not enough. He began duplicating his Paris

work in Vienna. Money was pouring in, of course, but money was
pouring out, and often the outgo was greater than the income. He
was no businessman. He thought so highly of his operas that only
the finest mountings would do for them. The story is told that two
seat covers in the theater were torn, so he ordered every seat in the
house covered. He helped out every friend in trouble, and every
troubled stranger about whose troubles he heard.

Inevitably, his successes were intermingled with failures. Since
he never put the profits of a success into reserve against the chance
of a future failure, the failures hit him hard. One such cost him the
control of Bouffes-Parisiens. Other failures put him deeply into debt,
but subsequent successes pulled him out. Neither success nor failure
disturbed him; he was always happy—he had his gift. As he grew
older, he was afflicted with rheumatism and gout, but they didn't
faze him either. His home life was ideal. He and Herminie became the
parents of four daughters and a son. To observe their twenty-fifth
wedding anniversary, they gave a dinner party for several hundred
guests and dressed up as peasant bride and bridegroom. A wedding
march was composed by the host for the occasion and was played on
forty reed pipes.

In 1873, when he was fifty-four, he again took full responsibility
for a theater, and four years later it was bankrupt. He assembled the
singers, players, musicians, and other employees. "My children," he
said. "You will all be paid to the last sou. I have been careless, but I
shall at least be honorable."

He gave up his property and mortgaged his royalties for three
years. To get even more money for his creditors, he accepted an
invitation to conduct in New York and Philadelphia. That was in
1876, and when he returned to Paris a change had come over him.
It had occurred to him that, like all mortals, he was going to die—
probably rather soon since he was fifty-seven years old. He looked
back over his successes, and there had been successes such as very few
composers ever have—**Orpheus in the Underworld, La Belle Hélène,
La Vie Parisienne, The Grand Duchess of Gérolstein,** and **La Péri-
chole** (to name those which have survived in whole or in part). All
seemed dead. *He* wasn't dead yet—but already the world had passed
him by, or so he felt.

Oddly, his mind went back twenty-five years to a play called *The
Fantastic Tales of Hoffmann,* based on stories of a German writer,
E. T. W. Hoffmann. For some reason, he decided that play and
none other was going to become the libretto of an opera which would
make him immortal. We can only guess why. The play's underlying
plot is that Hoffmann had four great loves, all of whom, actually,

were one woman—not a real woman but a creature of Hoffmann's mind. Hoffmann lost all four of his great loves because of the evil plottings of four devils who were actually one devil, also a product of Hoffmann's mind. It may be Jacques Offenbach of the surface was at last in touch with Jacques Offenbach of the depths.

He worked on this opera for three years, with unheard-of care and concentration for him, all the while composing operettas of his usual kind and supervising their staging, since creditors were still on his heels. The Opéra-Comique was going to produce **The Tales of Hoffmann** in the fall of 1880. During the summer, Offenbach sent word to the manager: "Make haste! Produce my opera! I haven't long to wait." Friends could hear him at work, polishing the piano score of Hoffmann, and the music would be mingled with frightening attacks of coughing. One said to another: "The musician at work! What an artist! When he is dead the world will appreciate him."

He died on October 5, 1880, at the age of sixty-one, without knowing he had no cause to doubt his immortality. Because of a delay in making costumes and scenery, **The Tales of Hoffmann** was not performed until February 10, 1881.

Offenbach was too pessimistic about his other work. While most of it is dead, a considerable part is alive and healthy.

23

Franck

Because simple goodness is hard to accept in a simple way, a great many people were bewildered by César Franck. He was simply good. They said he lived with the angels while he was, quite obviously, living with other human beings. They were always speaking of his otherworldliness although he was, most definitely, entirely of this world.

He loved God but he also loved people and all others of God's creatures. Earnestly and cheerfully he gave freely of himself, even to the unappreciative. He achieved a considerable measure of selflessness, resignation, and humility. When you combine this simple goodness with his having been a truly radical composer, you can understand why so many found him difficult to understand.

Some people idolized him as a saint, which was ridiculous. Others scorned him as incompetent, musically and personally. That was extremely ridiculous. But most people found it easy to ignore him. He was living his very last years before any sizable number began suspecting him of being an original genius who was putting a lasting mark on the musical art. By now this last view has been entirely confirmed.

He was all gentleness; there was no aggressiveness in him. Yet his names were César Auguste—Caesar Augustus, for the Roman emperors and ruthless men of power. What a laugh! Such names tell us nothing about him but they give us a pathetic insight into his father, Nicholas Joseph Franck, who chose them for him when he was born in Liège in Belgium on December 10, 1822. (This was five years before the death of Beethoven.)

Nicholas Joseph tried very hard to be a Caesar Augustus himself. Outside his home no one felt obliged to pay much attention to him. Inside the home he was a dictator. Wife and children were made to walk a straight line and to account to him for their every act and just about their every thought.

The highest station he attained on his own was that of petty bank clerk, and how that galled him. When he became a father, he got it into his scheming head that a way to riches and power was music—if it was produced impressively by attractive children. All he needed was the children. César was assigned to the piano. When Joseph was born, three years later, he was assigned to the violin.

Father pushed them both very hard. They had no playmates, except themselves, when he wasn't around, and no play when he was. They were in the Liège Conservatory as soon as they were old enough. It was lucky for them that they were able to go along with their father's dictates. If they hadn't been, he would have broken them. César was not yet thirteen when he was performing in public as a wonder-child, and Joseph was ten when he first played to an audience. But the then newly formed kingdom of Belgium was a small field. Encouraged by small successes, Father moved his prodigies and their sweet non-entity of a mother to Paris.

There the inevitable complexities of human nature began crossing him up. All he wanted was a pair of performing musical seals. What he had developed were children with the capacity, stamina, and desire to know everything there was to know about music. Their promise was even greater than their ability. That impressed the musical authorities and Father had to commit them to the full course at the Paris Conservatory with its array of dedicated teachers.

But he was not letting them retire to any secluded academic peace. Since César was the older, he was concentrating upon him. He had the colossal nerve to hire one of the biggest halls and went around town trumpeting the glories of the boy genius with all the energetic blatancy of the present-day press agent. The lad by now was fifteen and he played to an empty hall.

Father wasn't subdued. His ambition was propelled by ferocity. There were more concerts. And he press-agented the boy also as a master of piano technique, which he was or soon was going to be, and set him up in business as a private teacher. In addition to these labors, César had to practice for hours daily because his father insisted that he become a virtuoso at least equaling Liszt, who was dazzling Paris; also he was taking the required Conservatory courses and excelling in them.

To make it possible for him to do so much, Father scheduled every minute of his long day and enforced the schedule rigidly. Far from rebelling or even complaining, César opposed sweetness to harshness, kindliness to brutishness, selflessness to selfishness. The effectiveness of such weapons is a matter of opinion, but they preserved the lad. Indeed, they prevented him from realizing he had troubles.

Music absorbed him, particularly what he was learning at the Conservatory. We know that he became so profound in counterpoint and harmony that he greatly impressed his elders and confused some of them. He spent almost five years there. Before he could be graduated and just when he became eligible to compete for the grandest of prizes, the Prix de Rome, Father ordered him to resign.

That was astonishing. It has been suggested that if he had competed for the prize he would have won it (there was no one in the Conservatory at the time who even compared with him in later achievements), and if he had won it he would have had to go to Rome and would have wanted to give up playing in favor of composing. Father used his composing ability (he had been composing since he was ten) only for prestige building—what he wanted was a money-making pianist.

So Father took him off on a tour of Belgium. This came to nothing, and within a few months they were back in Paris. César was now twenty years old and a visiting teacher at several girls' schools. Young ladies charmed him. One charmed him even more than others. She was Eugénie Félicité Saillot, who was two years younger than he. Both her mother and father were actors at the Comédie-Française and her mother's family had an even longer and richer tradition in the French theater than the Barrymores have in ours.

When Félicité finished her schooling, she continued her piano lessons at home. She doted on her teacher, and she was quite musical. Her parents (who used their stage name, Desmousseaux, even in private life) learned very quickly to love her teacher. Already he was exercising, without being conscious of it, his second genius, which was to love and attract love.

So the complexities of human nature were setting up a second trap for Father. To him Desmousseaux was just another name on the long list of pupils, to whom a certain amount of time was allotted and not one minute more. César had to adhere to Father's schedule but the time he spent in the Desmousseaux home was hardly professional time. In due course Father began to understand that Félicité Desmousseaux was much more than just another pupil.

One day he found on César's worktable a newly composed song, **The Angel and the Child.** It bore this dedication: "To Mlle. F. Desmousseaux, in pleasant memories." Father tore it into shreds. For once, César showed temper. He raced off to the Desmousseaux and wrote down the song again. It wasn't published until years later and then it was dedicated "To Mme. César Franck, in pleasant memories." The dedicatees were the same person, it is hardly necessary to say.

Soon thereafter he left home for good—sneaked away while his parents were having their Sunday afternoon walk. This sneaking was done on the advice of his meek mother, who dreaded Father's temper. Father pursued only to the extent of requiring him to sign an agreement to pay over a small fortune to him through future years. The young man was locally famous as a pianist. Liszt, Mendelssohn, and other celebrated musicians of the day had praised him publicly as a composer. Father took all the credit and now was making sure he got his fees. He still had Joseph, who was not giving—and never gave—any trouble. Joseph won more honors at the Conservatoire than César had. He became a widely respected organist and composer but has long since been forgotten.

Félicité and César had to wait for more than a year before they could be married. French custom at the time prevented a man from marrying without his father's consent before he was twenty-five. As an independent being, he made certain changes. Father always promoted him as César Auguste Franck. The music critics had often been rough in commenting on such names. Now he began signing himself "C. Franck," and later, "César Franck." Father had required him to play the piano in public at every opportunity. Now he stopped being a professional pianist. Father had kept him in the limelight. Now he lost no time in disappearing, with his bride, into obscurity.

Obscurity was his chosen way of living from then on. He maintained it for as long as he could. When fame came to him again, it came slowly and entirely on its own and, toward the end, at the behest of fanatically devoted pupils and disciples who proclaimed him as one of the greatest of musical geniuses and also a saint. He became a familiar and rather eccentric-appearing figure in the Paris streets— a smallish, stocky man who always seemed in a hurry, who rarely walked but was usually trotting, whose pants were a little too short and whose coats were a little too long. His top hat was conspicuously outmoded. He never had the slightest idea of what the fashions were at any time.

Every morning he was out of bed at five-thirty. For two hours he composed, then breakfasted and was off on his busy day of one piano pupil after another. Late in the afternoon he might have a little time for composing. Evenings he usually was surrounded by pupils. Sundays he played the organ in a church—for a fee, of course. There was no end to his giving, no end to his love for all.

The years passed. His four children were born. Two died and two lived to grow up. Félicité had tried to teach him to dance. To console her for her failure, he composed a little polka for her. She took him to the theater, to interest him in the art in which her family had earned so much repute. He fell asleep while the actors declaimed. She was keenly interested in music, in the teaching of it, in the performing and the composing. She ran him, just as Father had, but was much more gentle and tender about it.

Ten years after their marriage he became organist in the church of Sainte-Clotilde, where he commanded a wonderful organ. Slowly the word spread among musicians and musical people that a master musician presided over this organ. Who was this C. Franck? Many had forgotten there had been once a brilliant Conservatoire student and pianist whose name was César Auguste Franck. The time came when every musician passing through Paris found Sainte-Clotilde a major attraction.

Fifteen years after he took over this organ, the professor of organ at the Conservatoire retired. Franck didn't apply for the post—such a thing wouldn't have occurred to him. No clique of academic musicians formed in his favor although they formed to back other men. But a musician went to the director and said quite simply, "There is only one person worthy of this professorship—M. Franck." The director reflected for a moment, then replied, "That is true." And so he was appointed.

By now he was fifty years old and his obscurity had lasted twenty-five years. The obscurity was over, because in Paris a full Conservatoire professor is a prominent person. At about this time he was ceasing to be a conventional composer and was becoming one of the most unconventional—although his innovations have since become more or less conventions. One might guess that more contemporary composers can find in Franck an artistic father than could relate themselves to Beethoven or Mozart.

He was beginning to challenge the "laws" of harmony. These laws were stern about such things as consecutive octaves and fifths. They were explicit about the relations of keys. Instead of following the laws, Franck did as it pleased him to do and the results were shocking to conventional musicians and incomprehensible to musical audiences. His new works were being performed. Audiences applauded only politely and hisses could be heard amid the subdued handclapping. Critics raged. The fanatical disciples came into being, led by Vincent d'Indy, a composer chiefly remembered today for his **Symphony on a French Mountain Air.** As a conductor, he conducted Franck, and one critic remarked that if he had been able to do so, he would have conducted Franck while on his knees.

Franck's serenity was not disturbed—no one could disturb it. Not even Félicité. As long as he had respected the laws, she had been with him. She couldn't go along with his lawbreaking. She started sitting in the next room while he was composing at the piano. Quite frequently, she flung open the double doors, exclaiming, "César! I do not approve of what you're playing!" She was a forceful woman, Félicité, as strong of mind as she was of constitution. (She outlived him by twenty-eight years and was ninety-four when she died in 1918.) While he was playing his piano masterpiece, **Prelude, Chorale and Fugue** for a friend, she burst into the room shouting, "Is all this hubbub going to stop soon?"

He stopped playing and said to the friend, "You see! What I write now is regarded as unpleasant noise." This piece was composed after he was sixty and in the last decade of his life. All the compositions upon which his high reputation is based belong to this period: the piano quintet, **Symphonic Variations** for piano and orchestra, the symphonic poem, **Psyche,** for chorus and orchestra, his one string quartet, and his one symphony. Félicité was outraged, in varying degrees, by all of them.

But she was by no means alone among musicians who couldn't change. When his symphony was given its first performance—the same symphony which orchestral audiences of today consistently rate as among the greatest in the literature—there were howls of indignation. Charles Gounod, composer of the opera **Faust,** said it was "the affirmation of incompetence pushed to the length of a dogma." Aging Ambrose Thomas, who was director of the Conservatoire and is remembered today as composer of the opera **Mignon,** felt very sad that a Conservatoire professor was guilty of such a thing. He noted that it passed back and forth through a dozen or so keys. He wanted to know why Franck called it a symphony in D Minor.

In April, 1890, his string quartet was performed for the first time. When it was over, the audience applauded—not only applauded but applauded noisily and kept right on until the composer came out on the platform, looking both astonished and pleased. He retired. The audience called him back for a second set of bows. He said exultantly to his waiting disciples, "They're beginning to understand me at last!" A few weeks later he was injured in a carriage accident and never quite recovered. In October he came down with a cold, which developed into pleurisy that soon affected his heart. He died on November 8, 1890 (seven years before Brahms died), less than a month before he would have reached his sixty-eighth birthday. His fame hasn't ceased growing from that day to this.

24

Bizet

IF YOU had known Georges Bizet when he was eighteen, you would have expected the musical world of him. If you had known him eighteen years later, you would have said he was just one more child prodigy who hadn't lived up to his promise.

Not until he was thirty-six did he crash through his self-built walls of doubt and fear with one of music's finest masterpieces. That work is **Carmen**. How did Georges Bizet understand so much about people and their emotions that he could make a gypsy spitfire of a woman, a soldier, a sweetly innocent country girl, and a bullfighter stand for the strengths and weakness of the whole human race? We will never know, but that is part of his fascination. Nor will we ever know why he produced only one masterpiece. He seemed to have the genius for a dozen.

Before he was eighteen he composed a symphony that will bear comparison with anything Mozart, Schubert, or Mendelssohn composed at this age. It seemed a harbinger of many masterpieces. But between it and **Carmen** passed eighteen years of frenzied labor that produced many stunted works, only a few of which bore even blossoms.

His father was Adolphe Bizet, a singing teacher. His mother was Aimée, daughter of a musical family, the Delsartes, and a pianist. Georges was their only child. He was born in Paris on October 25, 1838 (which was a year after César Franck arrived in Paris from Belgium), and took to music so easily he was admitted to the Paris Conservatoire before he was eleven. Within six months, he won first prize in scale exercises and went on to win many others.

When he was only fifteen, his composition teacher, Jacques François Halévy (later his father-in-law) pronounced him ready to compete for the biggest prize of all, the Prix de Rome. But he had to wait, because the judges were not likely to grant it to one so young. Meanwhile, he composed that wonder symphony which was to remain in the Conservatoire archives, unplayed and unknown, for over eighty years. There was no French audience for symphonic music at the time.

He competed for the Prix de Rome when he was eighteen. After long deliberation, the judges announced there wouldn't be any grand award that year. They gave Bizet second prize. The assumption has to be that the judges considered him too young. The following year he was awarded the prize that entitled him to government support for five years, three of them in Rome.

Now he was expected to prove himself. Almost at once a state of mind developed that nearly prevented him from doing anything. It was the result, Bizet thought, of a struggle inside himself between good and evil. The good was his genius. He knew it was there; he even considered himself an egoist. The evil was the force that mistrusted the genius, was afraid of it, and wanted to suppress it.

One can see these two forces battling within him—in the things he said, in the way he planned operas but never started them, or started operas but never finished them. Less than a year after he arrived in Rome, a youth of nineteen, he wrote about his newest composition: "I don't know what to think about it. Sometimes I find it good, other times I detest it." Ten years later he wrote of another work: "I have reviewed my first act on two different occasions. The first time I found it altogether admirable. The second time it seemed to me nauseating."

"Poor Bizet!" his friends often said, and well they might. His genius flowed spontaneously when, now and then, he didn't get in its way. His best works, including his masterpiece, were created quickly and easily. His worst came into being after prolonged and agonized struggles, in which practically every note was under constant challenge. Thus, the creator of **Carmen** was himself the theater for a struggle of mind and spirit hardly less dramatic and certainly no less tragic than his opera.

His capacity for happiness was enormous. He liked people, he liked conviviality. His spirit was exuberant. Beneath his mop of curly fair hair, his eyes were bright and alert, and his interest in anyone he chanced to meet was quick, warm, and genuine. He made friends with the greatest of ease. As soon as he arrived in Rome, he was deluged with invitations to parties. But he permitted himself very little fun and frivolity. "I am not here to amuse myself," he said.

He could have been one of the top piano virtuosos. Even the supreme master, Liszt, gave testimony to that. But he wouldn't even consider such a career. He was going to be a composer, and not for the piano, for which he had affinity. His obsessive drive was to write for the theater where, in his day, the competition was keen and the artistic standards so low that outstanding, high-caliber successes—the only kind he wanted—were extremely difficult to achieve.

One fair success, a little bit of fame, and his troubles would be over because then he would be sure of himself, he thought. Success and fame did come finally, but by then the struggle had been ended in a different way—he was dead.

While in Rome, Bizet projected operas based on Shakespearean plays, on *Don Quixote*, on the poem that was going to inspire Wagner's **The Mastersingers**, on Homer's Ulysses, and on Italian melodrama and comedy. But most were never begun and only one was ever finished—a one-act comic opera, **Don Procopio**, which the Conservatoire judges back in Paris thought was "brilliant . . . with precious qualities." Later, Bizet called it "extremely feeble."

His Rome years ended in 1860, when he was twenty-two. Three years later he managed to complete a full opera, **The Pearl Fishers**, which was first produced in Paris in September, 1863. The audience liked it well enough to call for the composer. But the critics were hostile; the opera had eighteen performances and disappeared from the stage until after Bizet's death. He wasn't surprised by its failure, since he considered it bad. He talked of giving up opera and writing symphonies, for which there was no market at all, but was soon at work on a five-act drama, **Ivan the Terrible**. Meanwhile, he was supporting himself as a musical hack. A sixteen-hour workday was usual for him.

Ivan the Terrible was scheduled for production in 1865; at the last moment the composer withdrew it—it seemed so bad to him. He next started an opera he couldn't finish. Then came **The Fair Maid of Perth**, produced in 1867 and also retired from the stage after only eighteen performances. But its creator liked it.

"I am sure of myself," he wrote exultantly. "The good has triumphed over the evil. The victory is won." In this same letter he vowed: "I am sticking to my path. Now, forward! I must climb, climb, always climb. No more evening parties. No more fits and starts. . . . All that is finished. . . . I have met an adorable girl whom I love. In two years she will be my wife!"

He did stick to his path, but not in the way he meant. During the next six years he planned ten operas, began five, and finished only one.

He did, however, marry the "adorable girl." She was Geneviève Halévy, daughter of his old teacher, pretty, tenderhearted, warm, and loving. They were to have six happy years together, and one child. There was not a single hour—indeed, not a single moment—of her life with him that she wouldn't gladly live over again, she said years after his death. She undoubtedly knew of his frightful inner struggles, and we can believe she helped the good.

Meanwhile, Bizet was laboring over **Djamileh**, produced at the Opéra-Comique in May, 1872, with the composer watching from the prompter's box and saying, as the final curtain fell, "There! A complete failure!" He was also composing incidental music for a play, **L'Arlésienne**. This work came easily and spontaneously; it is among his best. **Djamileh** was labored and is among his worst.

Yet now he was only a few months away from his masterpiece. His wife's first cousin, Ludovic Halévy, and Henri Meilhac, wrote the libretto for him, adapting it from a story by Prosper Mérimée. Bizet began working on **Carmen** in January, 1873, and by summer had much of it composed. Then he received intimations that the Paris Opera would consider producing a grand opera if he would compose one. So he put **Carmen** to one side and in a few months composed a piano score for a five-act tragedy, **Don Rodrigue**. He had no sooner finished than the opera house burned, and in a temporary theater the management was unwilling to risk a work by a little-known composer who had produced only failures.

Bizet was thrown into a deep depression. Never, he swore, would he compose another note for the theater. But soon he was back at work on **Carmen** and delivered the 1,200-odd pages of orchestrated score to the Opéra-Comique in the summer of 1874. He seemed to realize that he had fulfilled his genius at last. "They make out that I am obscure, complicated, tedious, and more fettered by technical skill than lighted by inspiration," he said to a friend. "Well, this time I have written a work that is all clarity and vivacity, full of color and melody."

The first performance was given on the evening of March 3, 1875, a historical date in the annals of opera. At first, it seemed to be the same old story. When the final curtain fell, there were only "three or four faithful and sincere friends" around the composer. The words are those of Ludovic Halévy. "They had reassuring phrases on their lips but sadness in their eyes," he continued. "**Carmen** had failed."

It is often said now that **Carmen** was really not a failure at first. The fact is, it was. It had forty-eight performances during its first two years, true. But, as the French say, it was a *Succès de scandale*—the audience found it vulgarly shocking, more than a little obscene, and therefore, sensational. Carmen is murdered by Don José just before the final curtain, and Carmen is a seamy character, not a sweet and innocent maiden. All this was in violent contrast to operatic tradition.

After the first six performances, **Carmen** played to half-empty houses. Toward the end the management flooded Paris with passes.

The critics were almost wholly and vehemently hostile. To read their views today is to appreciate the perils of music criticism. Bizet's friends considered the opera a failure; Bizet himself considered it one.

Less than three weeks after **Carmen** opened, its composer had a severe attack of angina. Since early adulthood he had suffered periodic attacks of irradiating pain in the chest and throat. Between attacks, he was as strong as a horse and worked like one. But this time he did not recover quickly. He was discouraged and depressed, completely unaware he was on the threshold of immortality. Geneviève took him to their little house in the country, hoping he would convalesce better there.

On the night of June 2, 1875, Marie Célestine Galli-Marié was singing the title role of **Carmen** for the thirty-first time. During the scene in which Carmen reads her own death in the cards, Galli-Marié was seized with a terrible premonition. When the curtain fell, she fainted. It was all she could do to get through the final act, and then she broke into uncontrollable weeping.

She had been very much impressed by the composer. She knew full well that Carmen was one of the great heroines of opera, and she played the role precisely as the composer wished; her interpretation influences the better Carmens of today. Whether by coincidence or not, the moment of her premonition was around the moment of Bizet's death. The next morning a telegram arrived from Halévy. It read: "Our poor Bizet died last night."

Bizet's father survived him by eleven years, long enough to witness his posthumous fame. His mother had been dead since 1861. Eleven years after his death, Geneviève married Emile Straus, a Paris lawyer, and this second marriage was no less successful than the first had been. She died in 1926, fifty-one years after Bizet and four years after their son, Jacques, who achieved some prominence as a writer and journalist.

Tchaikovsky, who was in one of the first audiences to hear **Carmen**, predicted that within ten years it would be the world's most popular opera. Some twenty years later, the Opéra-Comique gave its three hundredth performance and is now well past its three thousandth. And this is only one opera company. By now the total number of performances all over the world is beyond counting.

25

Johann Strauss, Jr.

JOHANN STRAUSS, Senior, was a waltz king. He would have been *the* waltz king if Johann Strauss, Junior, hadn't felt and acted upon a ferocious desire to overthrow and supplant him. What Senior did, Junior made himself do very much better. Son now looms over father as a giant looms over a pygmy.

To become a waltz king isn't much for a musician to strive for. Music is all but without limit, a world; and the waltz is three-four time, a pin's head in that world. One of Junior's first teachers pointed this out to him because Junior was so singularly concentrated. Get off that pin's head, the teacher said in effect, and you can be another Beethoven.

Junior insisted upon his musical strait jacket, and because he was a genius, he managed to express the world in waltz time. To call him *the* waltz king is to appreciate him not nearly enough; his proper associates are the greatest composers. One of the greats acknowledged this with a flourish. In autographing a lady's fan, he put down the principal theme of **The Beautiful Blue Danube** and wrote under it: "Unfortunately, *not* by Johannes Brahms."

Most waltzes merely are music to dance by; the music itself is secondary. Some of Junior's waltzes, however, can produce an emotional impact akin to that of a Beethoven sonata, although of a different kind, of course. They are bittersweet. They create an aura of man rising over sorrow—dancing with a broken heart. They're gay on the surface but melancholy beneath, filled with yearnings for ends much desired yet impossible to attain.

The creator of this music, from early childhood, was always driving to put his father in the shade. In more than the usual genetic sense, he stemmed from his father, who was the son of poor Viennese innkeepers. Born on March 14, 1804, Senior was attracted to the dance musicians who played in the parental inn. His mother and stepfather wished something better for him and apprenticed him to a bookbinder. But when he rebelled, they made no great fuss about it. By fifteen, he was fiddle player in a band.

If he had been just an ordinary fiddle player, they would have been right. Dance music for the masses was crude and sweaty stuff then, and the musicians who played it were, in the main, tramps. But there wasn't anything ordinary about Johann Senior. At twenty-one, he had his own band of eleven players. By the time he was twenty-six, he employed some two hundred musicians, divided into several bands.

He elevated the waltz from a folkish dance of Austrian peasants to the point where it was a pleasure for anyone to dance to. He did it by composing waltzes which were increasingly distinguished for their fire, drama, melody, and variety. He did it by playing waltzes with musicianly breadth and depth and helping his musicianship along with a brilliant flair for showmanship. As a performer, his dress was always exquisite. He conducted with the bow of his fiddle; his facial expression was volcanically emotional. Now and then, he'd take over the melody, making it laugh and sob with dramatic bowings, while the orchestra played behind him.

Largely by his efforts, waltz madness swept Vienna and then the world. Poor Franz Schubert was hungry and unknown in this same city while this popular musician was skyrocketing to fame and fortune. He had married and his personal life was miserable. He had met Anna Streim, an aggressively strong-minded young woman, who, liking his looks, set her cap for him. This was unfortunate, in a way, although it was to result in the birth of Johann Junior, on October 25, 1825, there in the city where Beethoven died two years later.

It was unfortunate in that it resulted in unceasing unhappiness for both of them. Johann Senior was no less strong-minded than Anna and, perhaps, even more unyielding. He had a hot temper; she was a meddler. He was autocratic in outlook, and she knew full well that her way—whatever way it was and regardless of any opposition—had to be the right way, even in matters of music and the orchestra. The stress between the two was intensified by the arrival of their first-born.

Almost from the beginning, the boy was acutely interested in the source of his father's power. Mother thought the smoke-filled dance rooms of inns and coffeehouses, where Father held forth, were the most wonderful places in the world, and she told the child so. Father, who knew of the sordid goings on behind the scenes, knew also that, for each success like his own, there were a hundred failures. He wanted better odds in life for his son and so tried to put his foot down. He prohibited young Johann being taken to hear him and his orchestra.

But when the boy was six, Mother slipped him into the murkiest corner of the coffeehouse where he could see and hear his father without being too visible from the bandstand. Going there was the boy's idea, and his mother aided him. So, at a quite tender age, we have a clear view of Junior taking Senior's measure.

He and Mother were as thick as conspirators usually are. Meanwhile, other children had come or were coming—Joseph in 1827, two years after Junior; then Nelli in 1829; Therese in 1831; Ferdinand in 1834 (he died at the age of two); and finally Eduard in 1835.

Father had no difficulty with these children or with Mother concerning them. The difficulty was with Junior and his determination to beat Father at Father's game. Since Father was both a man with a hot temper and a man with a harassing career on his hands, we shouldn't wonder that he was irked frequently.

He was irked not so much by young Johann learning music as by his concentration on dance-hall music and an exceedingly theatrical manner of playing the violin, appropriate for only one place—the dance hall. Much of this was going on behind Senior's back, and he'd run across it by chance. Living in an age when the rod was highly regarded, he got down his rod often and went to work on Junior.

He couldn't win. He found it more and more pleasant to go on foreign tours with his orchestra and, when he was in Vienna, less and less pleasant to go home. When he did go home, he found it expedient to retire to his study and stay there. Junior, by now, was in command on the home grounds, since he commanded Mother. At last, in 1841, when Junior was sixteen, Senior stopped going home altogether. He was licked; he knew it and resigned the field.

This, however, was little more than a prelude to Senior's troubles. Before and after the family breakup, Junior had been instructed by some of the top men from Senior's orchestra, men who knew by heart every one of Father's tricks. Mother had arranged that; it was supposed to be secret; but the men were intimates of Father's, and it seems plausible that he must have known. What he didn't know was where all this conspiring was going to lead—that was so implausible, it probably didn't occur to him.

In 1844, Vienna was plastered with notices that the nineteen-year-old son and namesake of its most popular dance-band leader and dance composer was making his debut at the head of his own orchestra and would play his own compositions. We living today love sensations; the Viennese of that day were no different.

What made Junior's debut so sensational were the rumors preceding it: that Junior was compelled by his native bent to do what he was doing, despite the objections of his father; that his father had known for years Junior was much more gifted than he was and had made desperate efforts to suppress a dangerous rival; that this boy genius would have been martyrized by his father if it hadn't been for his understanding and loving mother.

Junior's public attitude—and Mother's, too—was one of martyrdom. Butter wouldn't have melted in their mouths. Junior was forever sending letters to Senior, asking for a reconciliation—and letting the public know what he had done. Junior made a point of including Father's waltzes in his programs and making sure that no one was unaware that Senior never included any of Junior's waltzes in his programs.

No one can doubt that Senior's position was exceedingly difficult. He tried to maintain a dignified silence; he tried to ignore the existence of a Johann Strauss, Junior. Junior made that next to impossible. Father conducted a military band. One of Junior's earliest intrigues was to get the conductorship of another military band. The two bands now and then played in the same park, before huge crowds of sensation-hungry Viennese. In the presence of these onlookers, Junior, on his podium, bowed reverently toward the distant podium where his father stood. Senior never returned the compliment. Not only was he being badgered by his own son; he was a world-famous musician and his son was a callow upstart trading on his father's reputation and name and professional techniques.

At this period, the waltzes the younger Strauss composed were all but indistinguishable from Senior's except for their lesser quality. His methods of conducting were father's methods to a T: He conducted with a bow, he swayed his body with the beat of the music, he executed little dance steps, he bowed his fiddle with theatrical intensity and emotion. If you had known Senior as composer and conductor, you wouldn't have had the slightest doubt that Junior was his slavish imitator.

But this was only Junior's beginning; his drive was not only to do what Father did, but to do it better.

It wasn't long before he was better in the conducting department. He was tall, straight, beautifully mannered, exquisitely tailored, even more exquisitely barbered—his waxed long black mustache, combined with his big dreamy eyes, excited the female heart—and, being much younger than his father, he also was much more supple and handsome.

After five years of rivalry between the two, Junior was the acknowledged top conductor in the Viennese dance halls, and his fame had spread beyond Austria. Senior contracted scarlet fever. He was only forty-five years old, but he was worn out by his labors and by his emotions, too, probably. His body offered little resistance to disease, and so he died on September 25, 1849.

He was hardly in his grave before Junior and Mother moved in and took over his orchestra, despite the objections of some of the musicians.

All this time Junior had had his fanatically devoted mother at his elbow. No woman could have been more consecrated to a son—or to any man, for that matter. He commanded her, but she also commanded him. She was in charge of his money, and he was earning huge sums. Through her, he exercised what amounted to paternal authority over the younger children. He had taken over from Senior even here, and only one thing remained. Senior still was the Waltz King.

The son thus needed time to compose, but he couldn't turn over the orchestra—or, rather, orchestras, since the Johann Strauss Orchestra was divided into a number of units—to just anybody. He needed another Strauss, and he turned to his brother, Joseph. Preferring the music of Beethoven and Mozart, Joseph hadn't objected at all to Father's ban on dance-hall music. He'd been educated as an architect and was not eager to become a dance-band conductor. But big paternalistic brother spoke to Mother, and the two of them finally had their way with Joseph. Later, Eduard, who was ten years younger than Johann, also was pressed into service.

By 1862, Johann, now thirty-seven years old, was filled with riches and fame but discontented. Only once, as far as is known, had a woman other than Mother challenged his heart. This one had been a lovely Russian, but Mother had pointed out her defects. Now he met Henrietta Treffz, opera singer who had had the honor of a dedication from Mendelssohn and had arrived at the melancholy estate of faded prima donna. But she was a strong-minded woman, considerably older than Johann, with definite ideas and the ability to realize them. Before Mother quite knew what was happening, Henrietta and Johann were deeply in love and were married.

Mother surrendered gracefully. At once, she delivered to the bride the fortune her son had earned and placed in her care, assuming that the woman closest to him would, of course, be his proprietor. If she had hoped to retain some little part of her former domain, she was disappointed. Johann hardly ever came to see her.

Meanwhile, Henrietta was establishing a personal kingdom for her king—a villa near where the emperor summered and a palace, no less, in the most fashionable section of Vienna. There were luxurious studies in which he could create music, lovely gardens where he could meditate, servants who bowed and scraped to the master, adoring admirers who appeared as if by magic at dinners and receptions—and disappeared as magically when he might weary of them. Above all, there was exquisite finery to adorn his person.

Henrietta, whom he called "Jetti," was in charge for sixteen years—until she died suddenly, in 1878, from a heart attack. During these sixteen years, Johann created some of his most wonderful compositions and became, beyond the slightest quibble, the Waltz King—not only that, but also one of music's imperishable names. To Henrietta's regime belong **The Beautiful Blue Danube, Tales from the Vienna Woods, Artists' Life, Wine, Woman and Song, Thousand and One Nights, Vienna Blood,** and, above all, **Die Fledermaus (The Bat),** the prototype of all Viennese operettas, and which actually is opera rather than operetta—Opera with a capital O.

Mother had died in 1870 and so had Joseph, only five months later. Johann was stunned by each shock. There can be no question about the genuineness of his grief, but more conspicuous at the time was his terrifying fear of death. He couldn't force himself to attend either funeral—the idea of someone close to him being confined to the earth was unendurable. So, when Henrietta died, he fled with all possible speed to Italy.

When he returned to Vienna he was so changed he might have been another man. No longer was he the perfectly poised, suavely sophisticated man of the world who gave the impression he had seen and felt everything. After Henrietta's departure, he was in bits and tatters emotionally until Angelika Diettrich came along.

She was only twenty—and he was fifty-three. But she was a strong-minded woman, and before he knew it he was married to her, within months of Henrietta's death. It lasted only a few years. She evidently thought the Waltz King was like his music: effervescent, gay and sad by turns, filled with life and love. Actually, he preferred his study and gardens to ballrooms and cafés, was a poor dancer although the greatest composer of dance music, and was accessible only to a comparative few whom he found congenial.

After his divorce from Angelika, he still was in need of a strong-minded woman and who would function as one for his benefit. He found her in Adele Deutsch, whom he had known since childhood and who was a widow now.

They were married in 1883, and once more serene orderliness returned to his villa and palace, and in the sanctity of his study, immortal music began to show again—**Voices of Spring, The Emperor Waltz,** and the operetta, **The Gypsy Baron,** which contains the

Treasure Waltz. Since Adele survived him, the remainder of his years were serene and productive.

During his lifetime he was among the most famous men in the world. An example of his fame in our country is that on his only visit, in 1872, he received a fee of $100,000 for fourteen concerts at a Boston exposition. The fee brought him—he disliked leaving Vienna and his life there. That city worshipped him. Emperor Franz Josef said to him ironically, "You're an emperor, too." And he was.

As he grew older, he dyed his graying hair and took meticulous care to preserve the youthful lines of his body. It was a matter of intense pride to stay young, since the fear of death haunted him. In 1899, when he was seventy-four, he caught a cold while conducting the overture to **Die Fledermaus.** It led to pneumonia, and death came on June 3, mercifully while he was unconscious. His admirer Brahms had died in Vienna two years before.

Eduard carried on with the Johann Strauss Orchestra for only two years longer—he had been its principal conductor for most of his adult life. He took it on a tour of 81 United States cities in 1900; and, after playing for a ball in New York on February 12, 1901, formally disbanded it. Then he went into retirement, and died in 1916.

The great Strauss composed a few more than five hundred pieces for dancing, mainly waltzes, and sixteen operas or operettas—and nothing else.

As for the other Strausses: Strauss, Senior, got his opus numbers up into the hundreds, too; but today he is mainly a historic figure. His second son, Joseph, composed almost three hundred waltzes, polkas, and quadrilles. Their interest now is chiefly in their being by the brother of Johann. Eduard composed, too, but not very consistently. His works are almost forgotten.

26

Foster

WHERE is the American who has never heard and been moved by **Old Black Joe** and **Old Folks at Home?** This American doesn't exist, probably, and there is the proof of the power that was Stephen Foster's. It's something to marvel over, this power. No other musical genius exerted so much over so many for so long.

Yet, Foster is never mentioned in the same breath with those we call "the great composers." If the worth of music is measurable by what it does to and for millions of people, this omission is neither just nor accurate.

But it's understandable. His power is like **Jeanie with the Light Brown Hair** because it is a nebulous, indefinable substance "floating like a vapor on the soft summer air." Technically, the music is in the musical kindergarten. From his scores, you might infer that their composer was barely a musician. Intellectually and emotionally, the verses he wrote for the music (or vice versa—no one can be sure which came first) are on the level of a twelve-year-old. You might infer from them that their author never really became an adult.

On the other hand, you can infer quite the opposite—that the author reduced all musical, intellectual, and emotional profundities to their elemental base and so, working with ultimate simplicities equally meaningful to twelve-year-olds and mature sophisticates, manipulated them at will in order to stir such human beings as you and me.

Stephen Foster was born July 4, 1826 (a year before the death of Beethoven), in what was then Lawrenceville, Pennsylvania, a village which now is part of the city of Pittsburgh. His mother, Eliza, had had, by then, much experience with childbearing and child rearing, for Stephen was her ninth. We can get an idea about her from these sentences in a letter she wrote to her stepson, William Junior: ". . . Indeed I am but a dependent being in every respect, being too timid to contradict one so cute as your father, for if I made a divided house and led off to something of my own invention, he would be sure to overthrow it all, so that I will ever and anon train myself into the first great necessary lesson of resignation, and raise my thoughts morning and evening to Jehova for my daily bread and to forgive me my trespasses as I forgive those who trespass against me."

Her husband's sense of his own importance and worth was well developed. Resignation? Humility? Not for him. He was the kind of man who would maintain a lost lawsuit in the courts for years, and he did. He was a promoter, and his promotions were marked with daring and imagination. As a politician, he served in the Pennsylvania legislature and as mayor of Lawrenceville, and held several minor appointive offices from time to time. He was a devoted father, but domineering, a strutter, and not a man who could unbend—for a child or anyone else.

When Stephen was around three years old—which was around the time his affectionate and exuberant twenty-year-old sister was dying and his younger brother was being born and then dying—he began to show an interest in music. This wasn't surprising, since the family was by no means unmusical. But no one had much time for music. Things were going badly for the home.

Stephy was six when Father lost the home due to foreclosure. Thereafter, the number of Foster homes were many, and sometimes the family boarded. What with business depressions and Father overreaching himself in his promotions and Mother's resignation to fate, the atmosphere in the home was hardly less than hectic and was rarely, if ever, reassuring. And Father was away from home a great deal of the time, seeking political favors or holding political office or for his business promotions.

It is worth noting these details and others, for our genius was going to grow up into an artistic creator obsessed with creating homes —**My Old Kentucky Home, Old Folks at Home**—and typically homes which had been lost, somehow, homes which were "far, far away" and unobtainable. He was obsessed, too, with creating love, but love which wasn't realized or even realizable or had been irretrievably lost —**Come Where My Love Lies Dreaming, Jeanie with the Light Brown Hair, Beautiful Dreamer.**

During this time, Eliza wrote a relative that her six-year-old was forever whistling **Auld Lang Syne.** She was a shrewd observer. "There still remains something perfectly original about him," she remarked. By the time he was ten he was reminding his absent father, in a letter, that he had been promised "a comic songster." And when he was fifteen, his father wrote a relative that Stephy's "leisure hours are all devoted to music, for which he possesses a strange talent."

At fourteen, he had been sent off to boarding school, where he was homesick. Many years after his death, a schoolmate recalled him as he was then: "His was a generous nature to a fault, with a soul attuned to harmony. His love of music was an all-absorbing passion, and his execution on the flute was the very genius of melody."

Up to this point he had been a most teachable boy. Now his schoolwork was poor and getting poorer. He didn't seem able to concentrate; he was acquiring a reputation as "a dreamer." It became evident, in due course, that he was uneducable, which caused much alarm among his relatives. The family was accomplished and prominent. Step-brother William was achieving means and reputation as an engineer and was to become a vice-president of the Pennsylvania Railroad. Sister Ann Eliza married Edward Buchanan, whose brother, James, was going to be the fifteenth president of the United States.

But Stephen idled away his time, improvising on the family piano, singing songs at parties with his teen-age friends, writing poetry and setting it to music. He also was seeing something of the theater and of the river front, and boats that went along the Ohio into the Mississippi and thence all the way down to New Orleans. At the time, the minstrel show was the most popular kind of theatrical entertainment. White men blacked their faces with burnt cork and burlesqued the Southern Negro slave in both comic and pathetic aspects.

The youth soon was to become the mighty genius of this form of theatrical entertainment, and many people have considered it remarkable that a man who never saw the South wrote such moving Southern songs. So it should be pointed out that he wrote not Southern songs but human songs with simple, elemental sentiments that are true of human beings and stab at the sentimental hearts of human beings of any position, nativity, or color.

As Stephen grew into manhood, the family's despair for his future grew, too, and a brother in business in Cincinnati was prevailed upon to hire the twenty-year-old dreamer as bookkeeper. Stephen's interest in business was nil. Besides playing around with music and verses, he liked going to parties and being a loving friend to as many young people as he could manage. He exuded love and kindness, the qualities he valued the very most, to everyone, and his tender concern concentrated upon the downtrodden, the abused, and the victimized.

No one had the least inkling of the power he would attain. True, he had sent a song to a New York newspaper when he was eighteen, and it had been printed. It was **Open Thy Lattice, Love** and is good enough to have survived. But there had been no fee, and no one had given it much mind. Now, in Cincinnati, he took several of his songs to a publisher who was very happy to publish them and to pay royalties to boot, which we living today can understand perfectly because one was **Oh! Susanna** and another **Old Uncle Ned. Oh! Susanna** swept the country.

The Fosters were amazed but delighted and proud. Their dreamer had made himself famous with breath-taking speed. He now appeared capable of being a credit to his family. In 1849, when he was twenty-three, he signed an advantageous contract with a leading national publisher. It looked then as though nothing could stop him.

Back in Pittsburgh, he took up again with an old friend, Jane Denny McDowell, daughter of a physician. They were married in July of 1850. There is just about no doubt that she was Jeanie of the light brown hair.

He took her to the home of his mother and father, such as it was and it wasn't too much, although he now could finance his own home. Evidently, he was so very attached to his parents there was no breaking away even a little. Things were troubled from the beginning. Father, who had been known to take a drink now and then, was by this time a teetotaler and temperance preacher. Stephen challenged him by taking drinks regularly, although not yet excessively.

As regards the women, what followed is a story too familiar to need detailing. Two women exercising their holds upon one man at the same time is one too many, even if one is his mother. It is enough to say their married years were years of strain and unhappiness for Jane. But, as a provider, Stephen began them in peerless fashion. Three of his songs of 1850 were **Camptown Races, Nelly Bly,** and **Oh! Lemuel.** Any minstrel man would tell you that they were designed for the minstrel stage with exquisite perfection. And this was recognized and rewarded at once.

One idea of his cleverness: Publishing a song under a pseudonym—**I Would Not Die in Spring Time.** That was to set the stage, to build interest for an "answer" song which came out under his own name: **I Would Not Die in Summer Time.** Everyone seemed entranced with this dueling with sticky sentimentalities, until a journalistic wit punctured it all by versifying satirically—*I Would Not Die at All.*

Another shrewd move: E. P. Christy was the number-one minstrel of the day. Foster made a deal with him—for a fee, he could sing the new Foster songs first, in advance of their publication. The sheet music, when it came out, bore the notation "as sung by the Christy Minstrels." That helped the sales and advanced the interests of the composer, since Christy was then more famous than Foster.

The Christy Minstrels were the first performers of such masterpieces as **Massa's in de Cold, Cold Ground, Old Dog Tray,** and **Oh! Boys, Carry Me 'Long.** Man of the theater that he was, Christy knew smash-hit material. Whatever Foster proposed, he accepted. So when Foster wrote that, for an additional fee, he could put his own name on the next Foster song as its composer, he accepted that. At the time, it wasn't unusual for famous performers to get credit for the work of ghost composers. Foster's own reasoning was that he was tired of his reputation as a composer of "Ethiopian" songs and wanted to detach his name from the field. It was the sheerest chance that this song was one of his best, if not his very best. It was **Old Folks at Home,** often called **Swanee River.** It bore Christy's name for years, although he never once asserted proprietorship and never collected a penny in royalties. The canny composer was getting the royalties and letting everyone know he was the real author.

By 1854, Foster's publishers could boast that they had sold over 130,000 copies of this song, 90,000 of **My Old Kentucky Home,** 74,000 of **Massa's in de Cold, Cold Ground,** and 48,000 of **Old Dog Tray.** Those were phenomenal sales; Foster, as a composer, was at the very top.

But, by then, his marriage was on the rocks and he, as a human being, was on the way down. The year before, Jane had taken her baby and left her husband to his mother's exclusive care. Foster reacted by running away to New York, where he created **Jeanie with the Light Brown Hair.** Jeanie, you will recall, was lost beyond recall. She was but a memory:

> I sigh for Jeanie,
>   but her light form strayed
> Far from the fond hearts
>   round her native glade;
> Her smiles have vanished
>   and her sweet songs flown,
> Flitting like the dreams
>   that have cheered us and gone.
> Now the nodding wild flowers
>   may wither on the shore
> While her gentle fingers
>   will cull them no more;
> Oh! I sigh for Jeanie
>   with the light brown hair,
> Floating like a vapor
>   on the soft summer air.

Whatever was the state of Jeanie, Jane was readily attainable. She loved her husband. Some reassurances, especially a home for her apart from his mother's, would have brought her back instantly. But he returned to Pittsburgh—and to Mother. Mother died in January of 1855, and Father died about six months later. Late that summer, Foster reclaimed Jane, and they set up a home of their own.

Now he was really drinking. The result was that he overdrew his royalties accounts again and again. To bring them into balance, he sold the copyrights of old songs outright, retaining the copyrights only of the new. But it wouldn't be long before he had to sell those copyrights in order to settle new debts. Jane had to get a job. She was clinging tenaciously to her duties as the woman-in-charge and did so for just as long as it was possible.

In 1860, he went to New York again, perhaps to get away from his drinking life in Pittsburgh. Jane couldn't go along because he was incapable now of supporting her and their child.

When he'd married Jane ten years before, he'd bought a 200-page bound book of blank pages in which to work out his verses. All his best songs and many of his minor ones are in the book, worked out with great care. Up to 1860, just about every song was to his own words. The last pages of the book contain the working out of **Old Black Joe**, published in 1860.

But, in New York, he had no manuscript book because he no longer wrote his own verses. He set to music whatever was brought to him— by singers, by young poets, by any who wanted to couple their names with that of a famous composer. The music was, for the most part, no less hack work than were the verses. The little he got for it he spent on drink.

It wasn't long before his reputation as an alcoholic exceeded his reputation as a composer. He lived in a flophouse and spent his days in a saloon behind a grocery store.

But there is only pain in lingering here. Let's hurry along. In January, 1864, he was taken to New York's big charity hospital, Bellevue. He had fallen over a water pitcher. It broke and a fragment cut his throat. He died of this wound on January 13. If he had lived until July 4, he would have been thirty-eight years old. In his ragged purse were thirty-eight cents and a scrap of paper on which he had written, "Dear Friends and Gentle Hearts." An idea for a song title, doubtless. But take off the plurals, and you have an ideal epitaph. He was a dear friend and a gentle heart.

Many years later, when Jeanie with the light brown hair was seventy years old, or thereabouts, her granddaughter said "Granny, tell me about Grandfather." Without hesitation and without the slightest quibble, the aged woman said he was the most wonderful man who ever lived.

27

Tchaikovsky

IF EVER a man needed a rudder, it was Peter Ilich Tchaikovsky. As a child he had been "brittle as porcelain." As a man he was no less fragile. Yet no woman could have been his rudder merely because she was a woman—since womanliness frightened him out of his wits. Nadejda von Meck evidently realized this. At least she respected it, and—working entirely through letters—preserved him for the thirteen critical years that put him among the great composers.

Like Chopin's, Tchaikovsky's very first reactions to music were of pain. The young child wept hysterically, crying to his governess, "Oh, this music, this music! Save me from it! It is here, here." And he held his hands against his head.

He was born May 7, 1840, into an unmusical family. His father was a well-to-do mine inspector, and the Tchaikovskys were of the substantial middle class of Czarist Russia.

His governess, Fanny Duerbach, a Frenchwoman, said of the child, "His sensibility was extreme; therefore, I had to be very careful how I treated him. A trifle wounded him deeply. He was brittle as porcelain." Conspicuous during his childhood was his concentrated and dependent love for his mother.

She died of cholera when he was fourteen. His sense of loss was extreme. For a time it seemed he wouldn't recover. Finally, he turned from his grief to mothering his younger brothers—the twins, Anatol and Modeste—and he clucked over them as long as he lived.

Because it was cultural, the unmusical Tchaikovskys exposed their children to music and music lessons, Peter learned to play the piano passably well, but no one suspected he was talented.

His choice for a career was the law. At nineteen, he left law school and became a clerk in the Ministry of Justice in St. Petersburg. He was dandified, effeminate, poetical, aesthetic. Little was expected of such a young man, and he seemed to expect little of himself.

Then something exploded inside his complicated inner workings.

Now twenty-one, he sought instruction in music technique. Five years later he was a master of harmony, theory, and counterpoint and a technical musician of the topmost rank.

This was nothing less than a miracle. No one ever came to music so late and went so far. After being graduated from the St. Petersburg Conservatory, he became professor of theory at the Moscow Conservatory and soon wrote a text on harmony that is still meaningful and influenced many composers. He was composing, too. These early works display brilliant means that, most often, were directed toward empty ends. Either he had nothing to say or couldn't say what he wanted to.

Although he was no longer concealing his prodigious talent, he felt compelled to conceal himself from others. He suffered from the tormenting guilt of his homosexuality—and the fear of exposure and disgrace. Even in company he was alone with himself. When he conducted before an audience, he held onto his head with one hand, for he was convinced it was about to fall off.

Such was his condition when, in 1876, Nadejda came into his life. He was thirty-six, she nine years older, enormously wealthy, a widow, and mother of twelve children, whom she tyrannized. She lived like a hermit, protected by retainers and servants in one or another of her mansions, accessible to only a few outsiders.

One of these was Nicholas Rubinstein, director of the Moscow Conservatory and (like his brother, Anton, who composed the familiar **Melody in F**) an eminent pianist. He was granted this privilege because he was a musician. Nadejda loved music as much as she loved her children—perhaps more, as she came in time to suspect, at frightful cost to her conscience.

Rubinstein played for her a piano transcription of **The Tempest**, a symphonic fantasy, hoping to interest her in its poor, struggling composer. She responded as so many millions have to Tchaikovsky's music—with shortened breath and moistened eyes.

She commissioned a work and paid for it generously. Then she commissioned another and another. These led to an annuity. You may wonder if she was gingerly feeling her way, lest she went too far too quickly. The money wasn't important. She knew it. Money has never yet created a genius or made a genius fruitful. Whether intended or not, she was using her money to involve Tchaikovsky in efforts to explain and justify his most complicated emotional aspects. But entirely by mail! She gave him a womanly confessional without there being a woman in it.

Did she know the absence of the physical woman was an indispensable condition? No one will ever know if she knew what she was doing. If she didn't, then we must accept a remarkable example of feminine intuition. In what piled up into a mountainous correspondence, the lady often seems to be exploring. For instance: "There was a time when I wanted to meet you. But the more charmed I am, the more I fear meeting you. I could not talk to you. If somewhere, accidentally, we should meet, I could not look upon you as I would a stranger. I should give you my hand but only to press yours wordlessly. At present I prefer to think about you at a distance, to hear you in your music and in your music to feel with you."

Note the "at present" and the hints that if they should meet she wouldn't harm him. He had these covert invitations to persuade her to see him in the flesh. Over the thirteen years of their ever-increasing intimacy—by mail—they were frequently in Moscow at the same time. Her servants carried her letters to him and returned his to her. Once he even lived in one of her big houses for a while, when she was in residence at another. It is all incredible. You would find it hard to believe it could happen if it hadn't. Yet Nadejda displayed sensitive intuitiveness for another musician of note—Claude Debussy. You have to accept that she was capable of knowing what she did and doing it most deliberately.

By correspondence, she stabilized his mind. She was a haven in all his emotional crises (and there were many), as accessible as his writing desk. He was in constant spasm from brooding, self-pitying emotion. Until she provided relaxing sedatives which released the emotion into music, it was bottled within him. Only a few months after she heard The Tempest she was already relaxing him.

"Let me confess that I am incapable of separating the musician from the man, and in him, servant of such a great art, more than in other people, I look for these human qualities I revere," she wrote. "My ideal man is a musician, but only when character equals talent does he make a deep and true impression. . . . I am happy that in you, musician and man unite so beautifully, so harmoniously, that one can give oneself to the full charm of your music. It expresses fineness and truth."

But take the matter of his wife. It hardly seems necessary to say she was a most unfortunate girl. A student at the Conservatory, she had taken it into her head to pursue him. With feminine wiles, she soon had him entrapped. Like many another sufferer from his specific emotional disease, he thought marriage might prove a cure. It didn't. After the formalization, he fled in the wildest kind of panic, thought of suicide, found he lacked the courage, and so waded up to his waist into the cold waters of a river, hoping to get pneumonia and die of it. All this he told Nadejda, but without telling her the real reason why the bride was so frightening.

"I knew suddenly that I felt for her not even simple friendship, but that she was abhorrent to me in the full sense of the word," he wrote. ". . . My wife is in no way guilty. . . . I wished terribly to die. Death seemed the only way. But death by my own hand was out of the question. . . . Death wouldn't come to me on her own accord. I shall not and cannot go to her. What remains?"

Considering everything, Nadejda's reply hardly could have been more strengthening. "I am not an optimist," she replied. "I do not lay false colors upon the evil things in life. But there are conditions to which one must *se résigner*, or, more exactly in Russian, at which one must wave one's hand, make peace with, and grow accustomed to."

By now it must be clear to what extent music is indebted to this woman for preserving a badly mixed-up genius. His fourth symphony was dedicated to her, with this inscription: "To my Best Friend." It is the symphonic milestone that marks the point at which he unreservedly began expressing his hidden emotions. They called it "our symphony." He wrote her, "to you alone I want to tell—and can tell—its meaning."

The fifth symphony also belongs to the years of their intimacy. Also the violin concerto, **Francesca da Rimini, Hamlet,** and **Manfred** symphonic poems, six operas, including **Eugen Onegin** and **Pique Dame, The Sleeping Beauty** ballet music, **Marche Slav,** the Italian **Caprice,** and the 1812 **Overture,** besides scores of songs, piano works, choruses, and a considerable miscellany. He also revised the piano part of the **B-flat Minor Piano Concerto** and the **Romeo and Juliet** overture-fantasie, composed the **2nd Piano Concerto,** and started **The Nutcracker** ballet score.

They were busy and fruitful years, during which he also taught and traveled. He forgot his fear of his head falling off and conducted his own works whenever he was invited, which was frequently, because he was becoming famous. He was even venturing into society and enjoying people.

Then, in September, 1890, came a letter from Nadejda that closed this period with the abruptness of a slammed door. The letter was cold. She told him she had lost her fortune, which was an outright falsehood, and his pension was at an end. This didn't matter to a composer who was receiving royalties from all over the world. At the end of the letter she warmed slightly, saying she hoped he would "think of me sometimes." This sounded like a final farewell, which it was.

But he didn't believe it, and wrote her:

"Is it possible you think me capable of remembering you only when I use your money? Could I forget even for a second all you have done for me and all that I owe you? Without exaggerating I can say you saved me. I would surely have gone mad and perished had you not come forward with your friendship and sympathy.

"No, my dear friend, be assured I shall remember and bless you to my last breath. . . . I kiss your hands with all the warmth my heart contains, beseeching you to realize once and for all that no one has greater sympathy for you, no one feels himself more truly part of your troubles or shares them more than I."

There was no reply. He never had an explanation. It was months before he found out she hadn't lost her fortune. Then he couldn't imagine why she had dismissed him. Nor is there an entirely authentic explanation even now. We do know that her favorite son, Vladimir, was dying by inches of cancer and she herself was ill of tuberculosis. It is surmised she asked herself if she had neglected this son during the years she devoted to a composer she had never met, and if she was to blame for her son's doom. It is surmised further that her own sense of guilt drove her to abandon her "best friend."

But Tchaikovsky was clinging to an increasingly faint hope that she would relent. In 1891 he came to America and conducted four concerts in New York and one each in Baltimore and Philadelphia. He saw Washington and Niagara Falls, was entertained lavishly by Andrew Carnegie and other multimillionaires, liked the Americans, and had a good time.

In June, he was back in Russia. Nadejda had never left his mind. He told a friend he understood now that her friendship had been "a commonplace and meaningless farce which fills me with humiliation and disgust." But he didn't mean it, of course. The Nutcracker was finished. Feverishly he traveled around Europe, accepting every professional engagement offered him, pursued by his old personal devils.

In February, 1893, he began composing his 6th Symphony (the Pathétique). His brother Modeste said that in the composing "Peter Ilich cast out all the black spirits which had possessed him for so long."

Tchaikovsky considered the Pathétique his greatest work. He said it had a program, but it would "remain an enigma to all." Nevertheless, he continued, "The program is indeed permeated with subjectiveness, so much so that not once but often, while composing it in my mind during my journey [from Russia to Paris] I shed tears."

On October 28, 1893, it was given its first performance, in St. Petersburg, the composer conducting. On November 2, he drew a glass of water from the tap and drank it. November was the peak of the cholera season, and no one in his right mind drank tap water unless it had been boiled. Tchaikovsky knew this, and it has been said he drank it deliberately.

On the other hand, he had seemed cheerful for weeks. There was no unusual tension, and he may have been careless or thoughtless. But he did contract cholera, the disease that had killed his mother, a fact he mentioned as he lay dying. In his delirium he cried, again and again, "Nadejda! Nadejda!" And on November 6 he died, aged fifty-three years and six months, less one day.

As a master of the big orchestra, Tchaikovsky is second to none. Listen to how he exploits its every resource, with imagination and an infallible sense of drama and color. What a technician! As a symphonist, he ranks as one of the three supreme masters of the nineteenth century—first Beethoven, then Tchaikovsky and Brahms—or, if you're a Brahmsian, Brahms and Tchaikovsky.

28

Rimsky-Korsakoff

NICHOLAS ANDREIEVICH RIMSKY-KORSAKOFF achieved within himself a triumph of mind over heart. He was minutely honest and carefully self-regulated. This mind of Nicholas Andreievich still is a force in music. We are indebted to it not only for his own musical substance but, in considerable measure, for that of his friends and "children," Modeste Moussorgsky and Alexander Borodin.

He came into this world well placed. His mother's family had blood connections with princes and counts of the old Russian nobility. His father had been a high government official. The Rimsky-Korsakoffs were decidedly upper crust. His father's brother, for instance, was an admiral, commandant of marines, and a favorite of the czar; his own brother reached flag rank in the navy. At the time he was born, on March 18, 1844, in the town of Tikhvin, his father was sixty-one years old and had lost much but not all of his means by having been a man of the heart, and a soft heart at that.

Although he was the only finished musician in his family, the source of his musical talent was obvious, he told us in his autobiography: both his parents had musical ability and there had been musical ability among their relatives. But as a small child he wasn't interested in music. He sang, he thumped a drum, he had some piano lessons, for no particular reason. He did those things well, but there wasn't the least thought he'd ever be a musician. The Rimsky-Korsakoffs were dedicated to the navy and government service.

His mind was excellent right from the start, he said. "Reading was child's play to me. I learned to read without being taught. My memory was splendid. . . . Arithmetic I began to grasp very quickly. It cannot be said I was fond of music at that time. I endured it and took barely sufficient pains with my studies."

He said so—so that was how it was. This autobiography of his, *Chronicle of My Musical Life*, which he began writing during his middle years but which wasn't published until after his death, is remarkable for the accuracy with which he saw people and events and the honesty with which he looked at himself. There have been a number of efforts to find flaws in his own picture of himself. But these efforts have only confirmed it.

When he was twelve his father deposited him in the government school at St. Petersburg where the sons of gentlemen were prepared for careers as naval officers. No place for hypersensitivity, that school. At the end of each week the boys were assembled in the dining room. Those with high marks were given apples; those with low marks were flogged then and there. Each class was tyrannized by older boys whose Neanderthal intelligence hadn't permitted them to keep up with boys of their own ages.

His mind calculated precisely how much it needed to put out to avoid floggings, which was necessary because his mind was never interested enough in the courses to earn apples. As for the bully-boys, although as a man he spoke of violence and bloodletting with tut-tutting disapproval, he taught them to respect him by knocking out their teeth before they could knock his out.

Sundays and holidays he visited in the homes of relatives and family friends. There he heard amateurs sing and play musical instruments and now and then he was taken to orchestral concerts and the opera. He began thinking music was rather nice, and arranged for some more piano lessons. Nothing very strenuous, he assured us, but he didn't have much time. Summers, he was on ships. Once he fell off a yardarm, but he fell into the sea rather than onto the deck. A mere incident, that, according to his way of thinking and feeling.

Still, his interest in music was growing, however slowly. It became, he said, "a passion." His piano teacher showed him some things about composing and arranging. He was interested and began sketching a symphony. The teacher took him to a musical soirée at which held forth Mily Alexeievitch Balakireff, a musical screwball who was then only twenty-four. His was a powerfully pervasive and insistent personality.

Balakireff gave soirées because he liked being the master with disciples sitting at his feet. He played the piano better than the seventeen-year-old Rimsky-Korsakof had ever heard it played. He knew the practicalities of other instruments and of the orchestra, and he was an established composer and professional musician. Futhermore, he was a man of very forceful opinions, who dismissed Bach and Mozart as worthless and had no use for formal counterpoint, formal harmony, and other formal tools of his trade. He depended upon instinct and insisted that anyone with real talent could do likewise.

The youth was overwhelmed. He showed Balakireff his halting

efforts to compose and Balakireff accepted him as a pupil and told him to go right ahead and compose a symphony and never mind his ridiculous idea that he didn't know how. Their relations as master and pupil became close. Rimsky-Korsakoff was at Balakireff's home every Sunday for months. Then he was graduated from the naval school and was off for three years of sea duty which he had to have if he was going to be commissioned. Balakireff was enraged that music was by no means the most important one thing in the life of this eighteen-year-old.

The duty was aboard a sailing ship which took him to England, to New York, to Rio de Janeiro, to the Mediterranean. He told us that "music had been wholly forgotten and my inclination toward artistic activity had been stifled." He hadn't quite yet attained to the formidable reserve and dignity which were to be his bulwark later, and so he was able to join the sailor carousals when the ship was in port, although tentatively. When he got around to the telling in his autobiography, he characterized some of their aspects thus: "How base and dirty!"

Returned from the sea, he was commissioned and with his pull got a soft job in the St. Petersburg naval establishment, which left him with much time on his hands. He took up with Balakireff and Balakireff's "circle" again. In the circle were: César Cui, full-time engineer and part-time composer; Borodin, a doctor of medicine and a musical genius; and Moussorgsky, who was on his way to becoming a hopeless alcoholic but happened to be a musical genius, too.

Rimsky-Korsakoff made a fifth. He and the others were going to found the Russian School of Composition, a school so very Russian it couldn't be anything else; as "the five" they were going to make a very large splash with their harmonic daring and innovations and their uses of Russian folk themes. Up to this point Russia had produced very little music. Tchaikovsky was a young man with his major works before him, but these works were going to be in the main stream of the art. Anyway, his life centered in Moscow and "the Five" flourished in St. Petersburg.

Balakireff was the artistic "father," and an intolerant and arbitrary one. Cui went along with his dictates. Moussorgsky's efforts to go along never quite panned out, and Balakireff thought him "weak in the head." Borodin was much too busy with science to listen to "Father" with more than half an ear. That left only Rimsky-Korsakoff to contend with Balakireff.

He completed his symphony under Balakireff's tutelage; when it was performed, there was applause for the young composer. He composed two longish symphonic pieces, **Antar** and **Sadko**, orchestral overtures and fantasies, and a number of songs; these also were performed and published. Almost with each passing day, he knew more about what he was doing than he had known the day before. He was discovering "the rules" and "the laws."

Balakireff's unease increased. His "disciple" was moving away from heart and instinct toward complete dependence on mind. Six years passed and "one fine day," as Rimsky-Korsakoff put it, the St. Petersburg Conservatory of Music asked him to become its professor of practical composition and instrumentation, and professor of the orchestra class. On the St. Petersburg scale it was as if Harvard were offering a professorship in astronomy to a self-educated astronomer.

"Had I ever studied at all, had I possessed a fraction more of knowledge than I actually did, it would have been obvious to me that I could not and should not accept the proffered appointment, that it was foolish and dishonest of me to become a professor," Rimsky-Korsakoff told us. "I was a dilettante and knew nothing. This I frankly confess before the world. I was young and self-confident. My self-confidence was encouraged by others, and I joined the Conservatory."

He was only twenty-seven. When he described it, he was elderly and loaded with honors and fame. He looked back on it as other men look back on escapades of their heedless youth. Why, he said, he had been totally ignorant of counterpoint! And "I had hardly any notion of the structure of a fugue." Worse, perhaps, he hadn't known the names of the intervals and chords. Then, in an effort to see the other side, he acknowledged that the mere existence of **Antar** and **Sadko** proved that these things, so far as he was concerned, weren't important. It was more important, he granted, to "hear and recognize an interval or a chord" than to know their names.

Actually, he knew what he needed to know. What remained was to classify his knowledge and label it. As he described it: "At first none of my pupils could imagine that I knew nothing, and by the time they had learned enough to begin to see through me, I had learned something myself. . . . Thus having been undeservedly accepted at the Conservatory as a professor, I soon became one of its best and possibly its very best pupil—judged by the quantity and value of the information it gave me."

He remained an officer of the navy but with only nominal duties until he was established securely at the Conservatory. He gave up his commission then, but the Rimsky-Korsakoffs had influence, and he got the well-paid civilian post of inspector of naval bands (which some years later was abolished as useless). He worked at it. He wanted the bands to play better and to play better music, and he also wanted to know all the ins and outs of wind instruments. He took them home, and taught himself to play them; he found out precisely what they could and couldn't do.

At the same time he was studying stringed instruments. Within three years after his appointment he was conducting formal classes at the Conservatory in counterpoint and harmony. Within ten years or so he was one of the most learned technical musicians in the world and bringing great honor to the Conservatory. He held his professorship for thirty-seven years, until his death, and shaped generations of conductors and composers, including Alexander Glazunoff, Serge Prokofieff, Igor Stravinsky, and many others. Of his textbooks, *The Foundation of Instrumentation* still is in use.

His life had been one of complete orderliness up to the time he found his academic niche, and it remained undeviatingly so as long as he drew breath. He married the correct girl in that she was musical and came of a family that was on a par with the Rimsky-Korsakoffs. They lived together in most orderly fashion, becoming parents of seven children who were brought up according to the established ways. Winters in St. Petersburg, summers in the country—that was the pattern. He was a director of that, a trustee of this, a member of this and that committee—and she was unfailingly pleased to be Madame Rimsky-Korsakoff.

It would be easy to dismiss him as a stuffed shirt, which is frequently done. But that isn't fair. For instance, there was his devotion to the irresponsible Moussorgsky, who as a personality was his exact opposite. Before his marriage, they lived together. When Balakireff considered Moussorgsky an "empty head," Rimsky-Korsakoff knew he was a great genius. While Moussorgsky lived, Rimsky-Korsakoff was his confidant, musically and personally; when he died, Rimsky-Korsakoff took over his messy mass of manuscripts and labored diligently for years to make his music playable. He smoothed out many a turn which he considered rough, polished many a phrase which he thought crude. For that he has been bitterly criticized. Nevertheless, thanks mainly to Rimsky-Korsakoff's labors, Moussorgsky is known to the world.

His autobiography tells how conscientiously he worked and how he was always asking himself, Was this Moussorgsky's intention? When he had finished, he deposited all Moussorgsky's original manuscripts in a St. Petersburg library so that if anyone wished to go over the same ground and have a try at judging the composer's intentions better than he had, the material would be easily accessible. He would have done as much for Borodin if Borodin had required it. While Borodin lived, Rimsky-Korsakoff was after him to slow down a bit on the medicine and chemistry and make the time to work on his music. When Borodin died, Rimsky-Korsakoff took over a hodgepodge of notes, sketches, and fragments of the opera **Prince Igor** and completed it.

During all the years he was teaching, conducting, editing, arranging, and being a pillar of academic society, he also was busy composing his own works. Opera was his specialty and he composed fifteen. Then came orchestral pieces and then songs. We can only take his word for the crudity of his early works because as his skills grew he revised them and so everything of his has the high polish of the master technician. A most consistent characteristic of all his works is an exceedingly orderly building with bright and contrasting colors in the manner of a painter. There is very little emotion expressed— no emotion at all in the way Tchaikovsky made music the carrier of emotional torrents. There is very little drama, and no drama in the way Moussorgsky's music is dramatic. His music is lyrical and often tuneful, but not for the purpose of touching our hearts; rather, its aim is to charm our minds.

Whatever emotion he felt he kept largely to himself. In recounting the death of his daughter, Masha, at the age of six, he went no further than to refer to her as "my poor little girl." He told us that on the second anniversary of the death of Borodin he and his wife and other intimates gathered in Borodin's old apartment, where they played Borodin's music on the piano, "in order to spend a few hours together in memory of the dear man." On a matter of principle, he was like a rock. His friends he loved with steadfast loyalty while being aware of their faults. Rarely did any of them see a really emotional expression in him. The few recorded were all connected with music. An example: the Russian singer and actor, Feodor Chaliapin, and Rimsky-Korsakoff heard Richard Strauss' then ultra-modern opera **Salome** together in Paris. Chaliapin recalled that after the opera they went into a café and his companion was "literally ill. 'What filth it is!' he burst out. 'It's absolutely revolting!'" Rimsky-Korsakoff's own preferences in material for operas and for music generally were fairy tales.

He died in St. Petersburg of heart disease complicated by asthma on June 21, 1908, at the age of sixty-four.

What has kept and will continue to keep his memory green are such orchestral pieces as **Spanish Caprice, Scheherazade, Russian Easter Overture, Antar,** and orchestral suites taken from his various operas, especially **Le Coq d'Or;** his operas as such are all dead outside Russia.

Rimsky-Korsakoff

29

Borodin

WITH Alexander Borodin, whose place among major composers is unchallenged and secure, it is reasonable to wonder what he might have accomplished in music if he hadn't been so deeply interested in chemistry, in medicine, and in advancing the intellectual and social rights of the female sex.

It is just as reasonable to wonder what heights he might have reached in science and feminism if he hadn't bothered so much with music. But our point of view is Borodin the music master and we have to be astonished that his claim to our attention is based only on two symphonies, two quartets, an opera, and a dozen or so lesser works.

Sir Henry Hadow, the English musicologist, remarked that "no musician has ever claimed immortality with so slender an offering." Borodin could and did offer his excuses. We're lucky to have that little, he'd say, because he was only "a Sunday musician." Weekdays he was a professor of medicine and an analytical chemist engaged in the experimentations which earned him an enduring reputation in that field.

Much of this well-assorted work was accomplished in a home which usually reverberated to a bustle like a railroad station waiting room. It was presided over by a wife who insisted upon the right of her cats to walk about on the table during dinner and to curl themselves around his neck while he ate. Furthermore, her nocturnal attacks of asthma were always cutting down on his sleep. Not only did he have infinite capacity for work and for people—he had the sweet, tireless patience of an angel.

Of the group of Russian nationalistic composers called "the Five," Borodin was one of the three who earned immortality. The others were Modeste Moussorgsky and Rimsky-Korsakoff. In pure musicality he was by no means the lesser. In some ways he was the major. Moussorgsky used music to convey drama and delirious emotions. Rimsky-Korsakoff painted with tones as a painter uses a brush.

Borodin's music largely is for music's sake alone, for all of its very Russian quality. He was the symphonist of "the Five," and the dealer in musical abstractions. As in chemistry and medicine, he always knew precisely what he was doing and why.

His father was a descendant of the kings of an ancient kingdom in the Caucasus which was absorbed into the Russian Empire, and for that reason he ranked as a prince of the empire. However, Borodin was not a prince because his mother was his father's mistress rather than his wife. When he was born, in St. Petersburg on November 12, 1833, Prince Luke Ghedeanoff was sixty-one years old and the mother, Eudoxia Antonova, of the cultured and moneyed middle class, was twenty-four. The babe was given the family name of one of his father's serfs, one Porphyry Borodin.

When the prince died, six years later, he provided generously for both the mother and the child. Nevertheless, Eudoxia's position was ambiguous, to describe it mildly, and it is not difficult to see the roots of Borodin's lifelong crusade for the equality of women, particularly in education and in the social scales. When this child became a man he founded, with great expenditures of energy, a school of medicine for women, and any woman seeking to lift herself from traditional bondage had only to ask for it to get his help.

The household of his early childhood was feminine—his mother, his nurse, and his cousin, Mary, who was his playmate and grew up with him. Science appealed to him enormously, and languages too. In childhood he mastered French, German, and English and in his teens learned Italian. This child had a first-class brain. Around the age of six he heard a military band play and from then on he attended every band concert and made friends with the players. His driving curiosity was why sounds came out of their instruments, and how.

At nine he composed a polka because he had fallen in love with a friend of his mother's and understood that when one had a lady fair one needed something to dedicate to her. Eudoxia hadn't realized he was that interested in music, since he was so busy with the chemical laboratory he had set up in his room, where he was manufacturing fireworks and noxious gases. She got a teacher who taught him the flute and another who instructed him in the piano. (Later he was going to teach himself to play the cello.) But he wasn't taught music really, except what he taught himself. Nevertheless, he was composing.

As a side interest, of course. He also was dabbling with sculpture and painting. He was seventeen when he entered medical school and studied botany and chemistry in addition to anatomy, the natures of diseases, bodily functions, and other medical subjects. From all this it should be apparent he was anything but a "normal" boy. His chemistry professor was a renowned scientist. This youth appealed to him. "Mr. Borodin!" he shouted. "Stop thinking about ballads! Here I believe in you and I'm training you to be my successor. You can't hunt two rabbits at the same time." The young man replied gently he hadn't been thinking about ballads—he had been thinking about the fugue.

The year before he was graduated as a doctor of medicine, at the age of twenty-five, he served as physician in a military hospital where one of the officers in charge was a dandified product of a military school, Modeste Moussorgsky, who also was an amateur musician. They became close friends, but at the time Borodin was busy with medical work which included dressing the backs of serfs which had been cut into ribbons by the lash. That made a profound impression on a man of his sensitivity. He became an academic scientist rather than a practicing physician.

After graduation and after a few years in German universities adding to his scientific education, he joined Moussorgsky as a pupil of Mily Alexeievich Balakireff. Teacher was amazed that one of his musical talents and interests had "given no importance to the impulse that drove him toward musical composition." Balakireff corrected that with his usual roughness. He made the amiable scholar understand "composition was his real business"—at least for a few months while he composed the first movement of his first, **E-flat Major**, symphony. But the university term rolled around. Despite Balakireff's rage, he accepted appointment as assistant professor of organic chemistry.

The students loved Borodin, then and always. One of them left a glowing account of him as a teacher of science. "When working in his laboratory we [students] felt like we were in our own homes," he said. Around this time this friend of the female sex at large married the one woman peculiarly suited for him. She was Catherine Protopopova, who was sickly and so needed a great deal of looking after, and selfishly eccentric, which required no end of loving forbearance. She also was musical, playing the piano quite well, and loved him deeply in her own way.

Nor was this wife all his broad back could carry in addition to music and to science. As a professor and also as the son of a prince, even though illegitimate, he had social standing and society ladies were constantly inveigling him into serving on all manner of artistic, social, and philanthropic committees. To be sure, he was using the ladies, to help him with organizing financial and other support for his projected medical school for women.

Within two years he rose to the rank of full professor and wherever he bustled about, giving off cheerfulness as a hot stove gives off heat, he hummed and whistled and sang—music always was in his mind. The symphony was completed and performed and won much acclaim. He began composing his first quartet and was giving thought to his second, the **B Minor**, symphony. He was an irregular attender at Balakireff's parlor, to the latter's annoyance and frustration, but there he met Rimsky-Korsakoff, who had just returned from the long-sea-duty tour that completed his training for a naval commission.

Although only twenty-one, a mere stripling musically and otherwise (Borodin by now was thirty-two), Rimsky-Korsakoff joined Balakireff in being outraged that a man who was a musical genius wasn't devoting his full time to it. But Borodin's humor and good nature were as inexhaustible as his energy. "I'm never able to concentrate upon composition except during my summer holiday or when some ailment compels me to keep to my rooms," he said. "My musical friends don't say to me, 'I hope you've been well.' They say, 'I hope you've been ill.'"

Rimsky-Korsakoff was powerfully attracted and soon became Borodin's most intimate friend—his most intimate musical friend, that is. In each of his fields Borodin had intimates who spoke that field's highly specialized language, and the friends of any one field were incomprehensible to the friends of the others. Rimsky-Korsakoff, as supervisor of naval bands, brought band instruments around to the university for Borodin to toy with, which he did with great gusto, to the distress of other inhabitants of academic halls. He had loved those band instruments as a small boy and now he weighed portions of his new symphony with so much brassy orchestration that those portions were unplayable until he corrected them.

"Anybody entered his house at any time whatever and took him away from his dinner or his tea," Rimsky-Korsakoff told us in his autobiography, which always sparkles with love and admiration when Borodin is the subject. "Dear old Borodin would get up with his meal or his drink half-tasted, would listen to all kinds of requests and complaints and would promise to 'look into it.' People would hang on him with unintelligible explanations of their business, gabble and chatter by the hour, while he himself constantly wore a hurried look, having this or that still to do."

The home life of Borodin and his wife was "one unending disorder."

"Once I came to their house at 11 in the evening and found them at dinner. Leaving out of account the girls, their protégées, of whom their house never had any lack, their apartment was often used as a shelter or a night's lodging by various poor or 'visiting' relations who picked their place to fall ill or even lose their minds. Borodin had his hands full of them, doctored them, took them to hospitals, and then visited them there.

"In the four rooms of his apartment there often slept several strange persons of this sort. Sofas and floors were turned into beds. Frequently it proved impossible to play the piano because some one lay asleep in the adjoining room."

At dinner or tea the visitor became most sharply aware of the cats which "paraded across the dinner table, sticking their noses into plates, unceremoniously leaping to the diners' backs. These tom-cats basked in Catherine Sergeyevna's protection. . . . You might sit at their tea table, and behold! Tommy marches along the board and makes for your plate. You shoo him off but Catherine Sergeyevna invariably takes his part and tells some incident from his biography. Meantime, zip! and another cat has bounded at Alexander Porphyrevich's neck and, twining himself about it, has fallen to warming that neck without pity. 'Listen, dear Sir, this is too much of a good thing,' says Borodin, but without stirring, and the cat lolls blissfully on."

Rimsky-Korsakoff was often beside himself, knowing that Borodin was composing by bits and drabs his one opera **Prince Igor**, and having seen some of the bits which convinced him it would be a masterpiece of genius if it were ever completed. He was constantly after Borodin, arguing, cajoling, persuading. Borodin merely kidded him along.

Rimsky-Korsakoff described it thus: "When asked if he had written anything he would reply, 'I have,' but what he had actually done was to write a batch of letters. 'Have you transposed such and such a number?' I inquired one day. 'I have, indeed,' he replied with perfect gravity. 'I have transposed it from the piano to my writing table.'"

On this same writing table he was composing also the complex papers describing his chemistry investigations. He published twenty of these, in Russian, German, and Italian. His academic duties grew rather than lessened. The chemistry departments were being reorganized and he felt it necessary to study the setups of several German universities for ideas. Meanwhile, he completed his second symphony and, after three years of working on it a little bit at a time, finished his quartet. A friend wrote and asked how he was coming along with **Prince Igor**.

"Whenever I have to mention this opera I cannot help laughing at my own self," he replied. "I feel rather like the old wizard who wrapt in his love for Naina does not realize that time is flying, and starts acting only after he and his beloved one are stricken in years.

So far I have felt shy of letting it be known that I am engaged on an opera. My real business, after all, is scientific work and I feared lest by concentrating too much on music I discredited that work. But now, everybody knows. And I am, so to speak, in the same position as a girl who having thrown her cap over the mill, has secured a certain amount of freedom."

Seventeen years after it was started, **Prince Igor** still was unfinished. Borodin was in his fifty-fourth year, in his full vigor. The evening of February 16, 1887, the university professors were hosts for a dance. Borodin wore a Russian national costume and he couldn't have felt gayer. One instant he was the life of the party and the next instant was dead. His main heart artery burst. He went out like a light.

The news got around rather slowly. Early the next morning, the critic, V. V. Stassoff roused Rimsky-Korsakoff. "I shall not say what a blow this death was to myself and all his other intimates," Rimsky-Korsakoff told us with his characteristic restraint. But his immediate action also was characteristic—he knew his obligation to the art of music. He and Stassoff went at once to Borodin's apartment, gathered up all his musical manuscripts, and carried them back to Rimsky-Korsakoff's home.

He and his young student, Alexander Glazunoff, sorted the manuscripts. Glazunoff also had heard Borodin's half-written and unwritten ideas for **Prince Igor** many times. Rimsky-Korsakoff reported: "Glazunoff and I settled the matter as follows between us: he was to fill in all the gaps in act three and write down from memory the overture played so often by the composer, while I was to orchestrate, finish composing and systematize all the rest that had been left unfinished and unorchestrated by Borodin."

And so they did. There also was manuscript of two movements of a third symphony. Glazunoff had heard Borodin play the themes he had in mind for one of the missing movements, and he wrote them out from memory. And there were scraps of notes for the other missing movement. So this major work and several smaller ones were patched together.

30

Moussorgsky

M ODESTE MOUSSORGSKY'S place now is among the great masters. Far below him are the eminent composers of his day who condescended to him, who berated him, and who failed to understand either the man or his art. Very probably we, too, would have judged him the same way had we been in their places. They were not villains but only well-intentioned people, and there is no one to blame not even Moussorgsky.

His drive was to be original. He owed little to others and musically he is all but without ancestors. Listen to him reciting his guiding principle: "To new shores! Fearlessly, through tempest and inner shoals and sunken reefs, to new shores!"

Also listen to Vladimir Stassoff, a Moussorgsky intimate and his first biographer, giving his first impressions: "I have no use for Moussorgsky. . . . I have never heard him express an intelligent idea. All in him is flabby and dull. He seems to me to be a complete idiot."

It was easy to be mistaken about him. There was his "nervous disorder," as he called his efforts to drown himself in a sea of alcohol. There was his craven fear of women. And there was his apparent compulsion to appear trivial and superficial.

The Moussorgsky whom Borodin met the first time was, Borodin said, "a very elegant, dapper little officer in a brand-new close-fitting uniform." He had "shapely feet, delicate, altogether aristocratic hands, elegant, aristocratic manners" and was "very modest, unusually polite and cultured." His conversation was "somewhat through his teeth—rather affected." When "the ladies made a fuss" over him, this foppish youth "sat at the piano and, coquettishly throwing up his hands, played excerpts from Il Trovatore, La Traviata, and so forth, very pleasantly and gracefully, while the circle around him murmured charmant, délicieux, and so on."

Moussorgsky was then seventeen years old and had been in military service since he was thirteen. He was born in March, 1839, in the

Russian village of Karevo (which has since been renamed Moussorgsky), about three hundred miles south of St. Petersburg. His parents were of the aristocracy and owned some forty square miles of land along with hundreds of people—serfs, who went with land.

His mother, Julia, was nervous, poetic, sentimental, and an amateur pianist, who gave him his first music lessons. According to Moussorgsky, his father, Peter, "worshiped music," and he delighted his parents by "extemporizing music before knowing even the most elementary rules of piano playing." Yet, neither parent thought of providing this lad with a musical education.

Instead, he was packed off to the cadets' school in St. Petersburg to be trained as an army officer, one of the few careers considered proper for an aristocrat. The commandant of this school was proud of his charges when they drank too much champagne but shocked if they drank any vodka, because vodka was the common drink of the common people.

A military school was hardly ideal for a supersensitive, delicately balanced boy. But we should keep in mind that neither exposure to drinking nor even encouragement to drink will necessarily create an alcoholic. Alcoholism is a disease and has a much deeper basis than that.

Moussorgsky had just been commissioned when Borodin met him. His father was dead, and he was living with his mother and his older brother in St. Petersburg. The brother, incidentally, had been through the same school and was also an army officer but was neither an alcoholic nor a genius. Nor did he ever get into trouble.

The genius was already getting into trouble. He suggested serfs were not unlike aristocrats and army officers and were, in fact, human beings. He was showing a taste for the company of common people. And he was drinking. At the age of nineteen, he had to take "a cure" for his "nervous disorder" and resigned from the army, probably by request.

While still in the army, he was admitted to the circle around Alexander Dargomyzsky, a then-famous composer in Russia. There he met the leading musicians of the day and heard the newest music played and discussed. He seemed overwhelmed by revelation; now he knew what he wanted to do, he said—he wanted to compose music.

He already played the piano brilliantly. His friends said he could have been one of the foremost pianists of his age if he had worked at it. He also sang well. All this was his musical talent. His formal training and teaching had been slight. In the techniques of composition, he was illiterate. And he was eighteen years old.

Balakireff, the master to whom Moussorgsky applied for lessons, was only twenty and still in the process of teaching himself the techniques of composing. He was more than just a teacher. He was also friend, caustic musical and personal critic, and confessor.

The really unusual features of Moussorgsky were buried deeply. On the surface were only their pathetic manifestations. A few sentences taken from his letters to Balakireff indicate the unknown and perhaps unknowable substances:

"I was tormented by a cruel disease, mysticism."

"I suffered terribly and became morbidly sensitive. Then, perhaps because I found distractions or perhaps because I indulged in fantastic dreams, this mysticism decreased and my brains, having reverted to normal working order, I took measures to extirpate it altogether."

"Thank God, I am getting better after cruel, very cruel sufferings. . . . My soul has killed my body. . . . Dear Mily, strive to curb me, help me to keep myself in hand."

He fought this inner battle not only then, in his youth, but to his very last breath, and he fought its manifestations, the saddest of which was his compulsion to destroy himself with drink. What the force was that caused these terrifying battles, we can't know; but we do know his fear of women, his horror of even the idea of marriage, and that the original title of his **Songs and Dances of Death** was **She—Death Personified.** We also know his morbid preoccupation with the idea of witches and their doings. This was the basis of his **Night on Bald Mountain,** which is a concentration of horror and terror.

Until 1861, when he was twenty-two, he lived the easy life of a wealthy landlord. In that year an imperial decree freed the serfs, which ruined the Moussorgskys. From then on, his life was one of severe poverty, since he had no more capacity for managing money than for managing himself. His source of livelihood was a miserably paid civil service clerkship, a livelihood always thinned by his drinking and now and then threatened by his extended bouts.

His mother's death, when he was twenty-six, plunged him into the alcoholic sea; he was morbid in his attachment to her. He lived first with his brother, then with friends, then in furnished rooms, then with friends again. He never had, as an adult, what we would call a home, and a heart-wringing picture is of him standing in the gutter with his few possessions around him. He had just been evicted from a room for not paying the rent.

While living this sordid outer life, he was formulating in his inner life a great and original musical art which has influenced composers of all lands right up to the present day. "You know how soft I am," he wrote Balakireff, but in any matter of his basic art he was anything but soft. He was rewriting the laws of harmony, which were considered by most, if not all, of his friends to be at least semi-sacred; he was insisting that music had to have the reality of life itself; he was denying that beauty for beauty's sake alone was worthwhile. This only suggests the nature of his originality. Views like these caused Stassoff to call him "a complete idiot."

Moussorgsky's letters to Balakireff about his music show his strength as a creator. An example: "My spleen . . . was an author's spleen. I'm ashamed to have to confess it, but it is the truth. I was embittered by your attitude in the matter of my witches. I considered, consider, and shall continue to consider my work satisfactory. . . . Dear friend, whether you agree to perform my witches or not, and whether I hear them or not . . . I shall alter neither the general plan nor the treatment. . . . Every author remembers the mood in which he worked, and that feeling or memory helps him to abide by his own standards!"

Rimsky-Korsakoff wrote him out of shock and dismay, having caught him dead to rights violating the laws of harmony. Moussorgsky replied: "Let me tell you, dear Korsinka, the act of creating carries in itself the laws of beauty, whose tale is told by inner criticism, not outer, and whose consequences are determined by the artist's instinct. Where either of these two elements is lacking, there can be no artistic creation. Artistic creation implies both and the artist is a law unto himself."

For a while he kept showing his output to these critical friends. When he sent Rimsky-Korsakoff the first act of his projected setting of a popular play, The Marriage, he accompanied it with a little note: "I willingly deliver myself into my tormentor's hands." This act was given a private performance. Rimsky-Korsakoff said "everybody was delighted with his skillful characterizations . . . but baffled by many peculiarities of the harmony." Borodin said it was "an extraordinarily curious, paradoxical achievement . . . but, as a whole, a failure." Balakireff thought it a curiosity. Dargomyzsky said Moussorgsky had gone too far. It was that evening that Stassoff realized the author was no "idiot." Rather, he was a stupendous genius.

From then on, Stassoff acted as if he had been appointed by God to protect, encourage, and cherish one of His most unfortunate yet most gifted creatures. It was Stassoff who rescued Moussorgsky from the drinking dives; and it was to Stassoff that Moussorgsky confided his artistic plans and dreams—to Stassoff and to a few women. He feared women, yet a few managed somehow to be sympathetic and helpful to him.

Secretively, in a little more than a year, he composed **Boris Godounoff**, which ranks among the best operas of all times. It was submitted to the Imperial Theater in 1870, when he was thirty-one. The committee of judges was shocked, and we can't wonder. The opera was all choruses and dialogue. It had no love element; there was no big part for a woman nor for a tenor. "The people," collectively, were a principal character.

Moussorgsky accepted these objections of a practical nature readily enough, since they did not touch on his artistic principles, and prepared to revise Boris. He showed the manuscript to all his friends and let them make suggestions. But his revised version also was rejected. The friends got singers and players together and staged three of the scenes in the Marinsky Theater in February, 1873.

"The success was enormous and complete," wrote one critic. "Never within my memory had such ovations been given a composer at the Marinsky." Another critic, who had been and was going to continue to be hostile to the composer, wrote that he was "astonished by the unexpected beauties of those three scenes. A lack of skill and knowledge is perceptible in them, but the spiritual power . . . outweighs the defects."

Eight months later, the Imperial Theater announced it was going to stage the whole opera, despite the view of the committee of judges. A woman was behind the decision. Although there was no big part in it for her, Julia Platonova, the reigning prima donna of St. Petersburg, had informed the management that unless it produced Boris she would not renew her expiring contract. When Boris finally was unveiled in its entirety early in 1874, the public enthusiasm was boundless, despite hypercritical critics.

Moussorgsky read one of his critics and commented: "Fools have little of that humility which has never deserted me, nor ever will so long as I have brains in my head." He was now thirty-five and for some time had been at work on an even bigger and more complex opera, **Khovanshchina**. "My head feels like a boiler with a roaring fire underneath it," he told his faithful Stassoff. In gratitude for the sympathy and understanding Stassoff was supplying, he dedicated the opera to him.

"There is nothing absurd in my saying, 'I dedicate to you my own self and the whole period of my life during which **Khovanshchina** will be composed,' " he wrote Stassoff. "I vividly remember living Boris, in Boris. And in my brain, the time I lived in Boris has left precious, indestructible landmarks. Now a new work, your work, is seething, and I am beginning to live it. How many invaluable impressions, how many new lands to discover. Wonderful! So I pray you accept the essence of my tumultuous self, with the dedication of **Khovanshchina**—a dedication which you begot together with the work itself."

We can be doubly touched, because the opera was never finished—by its creator. His inner enemy interferred. He had more bouts of delirium tremens and at least one of alcoholic dementia. In this condition, he undertook composing another opera, **Sorochintsy Fair**, and tried to compose the two simultaneously. The result was that he repeatedly bogged down and never finished either.

Ilya Repin, a painter who attained notoriety by making a portrait of the alcohol-ruined Moussorgsky in his last days, told how it was with the composer and his self-appointed guardian. "Vladimir Stassoff, returning to St. Petersburg after a journey, had been compelled to rescue his friend from the utmost depths," Repin wrote. "It is incredible how this well-bred, cultured, witty, polished officer of the Guards as soon as he was without Stassoff would break down, sell his furniture and clothes, and go haunting the lowest taverns. How often Stassoff, upon coming home, had to spend long hours hunting for him in one disreputable den after another."

The tragedy was rushing toward its inevitable end. But there were interludes when creative genius was fruitfully at work. **Songs and Dances of Death** belong to this period; also **Pictures at an Exhibition**, composed to commemorate the life of his friend, V. A. Hartmann, a painter and architect, whose death had plunged the composer into more than his normal gloom. Another woman intervened—the singer, Darya Leonova, who, in 1878, took him off on a concert tour to serve as her accompanist and collaborating artist. She hoped travel and change would do him good, and it did for a while.

Three years later he appeared at her flat in St. Petersburg. "He was in an appalling state of perturbation," she said. "He said he was done for, helpless, and nothing remained for him but to beg in the streets. I assured him that what I had I would always share."

That night he slept in a chair in her parlor.

"He came to breakfast looking quite cheerful," she continued. "Then he collapsed. I summoned a doctor and his friends. We decided he should be sent to a hospital."

In the hospital, the doctors slowly brought him out of delirium. They kept him, after he recovered, to make sure he had nothing to drink for a while and to build back his strength with proper diet. He was a charmer; the hospital staff became devoted to him. His birthday was approaching. An attendant thought it wouldn't harm him to celebrate in the way he wished—with a little brandy—and gave him a full bottle.

That was on March 27, 1881. At five o'clock the following morning, the dawn of his forty-second birthday, a nurse heard him cry out in terror, "It's the end. I am lost." When she got to him, he was dead.

31

Dvořák

IF Antonin Dvořák had had the choice, he would have been a maker of locomotives instead of the maker of such symphonies as the one he called **From the New World** and composed in our country. In his opinion, God had had the choice. This made him contented —with his life and with himself.

Of all wonderful sights, he preferred those of flowers blooming, of trees coming into leaf, of green fields and deep forests. The songs of birds he loved; he especially enjoyed talking to pigeons.

He remained close to the earth and its fruits—unworldly but shrewd in matters of people and money, unpolished but endowed with the simple virtues: thrift, industry, and perserverance. His was the solidity and balance of the earth itself.

Of course, geniuses can be anything. This one was the eldest of eight children of Anna and Franz Dvořák. Franz, like his father before him, kept the inn and was the village butcher in Nelahozeves (or Mühlhausen, by its German name) in Bohemia, which is a province of the Czech branch of the Slavic race.

Antonin, who was born September 8, 1841, should have grown up to be an innkeeper and butcher. The cards were stacked that way. He was eight before he was sent to school and then only to learn to read and write and to do arithmetic, as any innkeeper must.

The teacher happened to be a musician. From him, the boy picked up violin playing incidentally, with little effort. No one was particularly impressed. Native musicality is not unusual among the Czechs.

When he was fourteen, he was sent to nearby Zlonice to learn German from one Anton Liehmann. To keep an inn in Bohemia one had to know German, since it was then part of the German-speaking Austrian Empire. Liehmann also happened to be a musician. Very quickly, he suspected his new pupil of having at least a touch of musical genius because Dvořák took to the viola, the piano, and the organ the instant he was exposed to them and also because harmony seemed more a matter of instinct to him than of learning.

Liehmann spoke to the father, but Franz had his peasant frugality and common sense—he was not going to waste money on music lessons for a future butcher. But finally an uncle came forward and said he would pay for music lessons. The country boy, now sixteen, was sent to the big city, Prague, and to its Organ School.

The uncle reneged. Antonin was cheerful about it; all his life he was cheerful. Always the enterpriser, he had found a way to earn a little, by playing the violin in an orchestra. Now he found a few pupils, and this provided the little more his frugal nature needed to carry him over the two-year course.

At eighteen, he was through with formal education, but he would never be through with education. His next fourteen years form one of the most remarkable records of self-education in the annals of self-made men. He learned by doing—he became a composer by composing. He composed trios, quartets, quintets, songs, symphonies, and even complete operas, taking the libretto for one out of an almanac.

When he composed something, he usually destroyed it. He had learned; he was content. "I always have paper to start my fires," he remarked cheerfully. Along toward the end of this period, he began writing "Thanks to God" at the end of every manuscript, which he continued to do the rest of his life. His progress caused him to feel he had found out for sure what God had intended for him.

All this while he had a living to make. He made it by playing in an orchestra almost every evening and often in the afternoon. The orchestra, which played in restaurants as well as for dances and in the opera house, was an education in composing, too. He heard the instruments at close range through many an hour, and he played the strings. As a composer, he was going to be weakish in counterpoint and fugue but very strong in orchestration and instrumentation.

He also had piano pupils. Among them were Josefa and Anna Cermak, daughters of a goldsmith. He liked Josefa—she had dash. He liked Anna, too, and as Josefa wasn't much interested in him, he formed a firm attachment for Anna. But his was a hardheaded practicality; there could be no marriage until he could afford a wife.

Fortunately, the time came before Anna lost patience. In one day, on March 9, 1873, when he was thirty-one years old, he ceased being an unknown fiddle drudge and became a Czech composer of renown, on the threshold of world fame. On that day, a chorus and orchestra performed his newest composition, **Hymnus**, based on a poem, *The Heirs of White Mountain*. In a battle on that mountain the Czech people had lost their freedom in the seventeenth century. Stubbornly, thereafter, they maintained their language, their customs, and their identity as a submerged nation. But it had been and still was hard going. Now, through all of Czech land, people responded to the emotional encouragement and consecration of Dvořák's hymn.

The same year his first published work, a song, appeared in a local music journal. In November, he and Anna were married. The next year he was awarded a money prize by the Austrian State Music Committee, of which Brahms, living in Vienna, was a member. Dvořák didn't then and never did suspect the slightest inconsistency between his fervent artistic and personal devotion to Czech traditions and the acceptance of subsidies and honors from the Czechs' masters, the Austrians.

Now he could give his full energies to composing and to being a good husband and father. Within three years, he and Anna became the parents of three children but, within four years, lost all three. He gave support to Anna with his resigned fortitude and reliance upon the will of God and to himself by composing his somber **Stabat Mater** and a string quartet, colored with suffering.

Meanwhile, his fame was spreading quickly from Bohemia on through Germany and Austria to England and to America, the New World. Brahms, after three consecutive years of awarding the Austrian state prize to this Czech whom he had never seen, wrote his now-famous letter to his publisher.

"Dear Simrock," Brahms wrote. "For several years past, in awarding the Austrian state prize, I have been delighted with the pieces of Anton Dvořák, pronounced Dvorshak, of Prague. This year, he submits, among other things, a cycle of ten duets for two sopranos, with pianoforte; they seem to me so perfectly charming they should be a practical publishing venture."

Simrock published the duets and the next year received from his new composer the first set of **Slavonic Dances**, which ravished the whole world of music, made a fortune for the publisher (but not for the composer, who received a pittance), and remain universal favorites. But the composer was no innocent in money matters. Like a peasant in the market place with a flock of fat geese, he knew how to haggle and how long to haggle. In the long run, he fared all right.

After these **Slavonic Dances**, he had world stature. We, living today, hardly can comprehend how very famous he was. For over twenty years, his contemporaries regarded him as one of the supreme masters. Orchestras, quartets, famous virtuosos, choral societies were all scrambling for his newest compositions. Vienna wanted him. Berlin wanted him. London was demanding him.

He disliked leaving family and familiar surroundings. Yet, he kept going on tours—the fees were irresistible. In all, he visited England nine times and Austria and Germany innumerable times. He kept right on educating himself in matters that interested him —like the English language.

His family was expanding. In all, there were six more children and all were to reach maturity and outlive their father. In 1891, he became professor of composition at the Prague Conservatory, which soon absorbed the Organ School. He held this post the rest of his life and was the school's director in his last years. During all this time his pattern of living varied only to the extent that passing circumstances compelled.

He was up and about very early every morning, never later than six o'clock. First thing was his walk. In Prague, he walked in the park, spying on the birds, looking at the trees and flowers, or he walked around the fringes of the railroad yard, studying the locomotives which he knew as well as he knew his children.

Then, Mass; after Mass, breakfast and to the Conservatory. Then, composing and lunch and more composing, a visit to his favorite workingman's café to read the newspapers and to talk with common people. Perhaps there would be more composing before dinner; and after dinner, some evenings, another café visit—and then to bed, rarely later than nine o'clock.

In Prague, this large family lived in a three-room apartment. His growing means never tempted him to move into a larger one. But the moment he could afford it, he acquired land and a small house in the country, in the village of Vysoká, in the mineral-rich hills near the Bohemian Forest. There he spent his summers, and there his morning walks usually ended in the village church, where one of the world's most celebrated musicians sat down at the organ and played to the rude miners and peasants before the six-o'clock Mass.

Vysoká was especially delightful because he could keep pigeons. He spent hours with these friends, and many an admirer overheard him talking to them.

The villagers adored him. On his name day, they usually paraded around his house, serenading him with their folk songs and shouting, "Long live Dvořák." This went on in Prague, too—to all Czechs he was an object of vast pride.

His pupils adored him. To them, this aging man seemed one of them; he could descend to their youthful level without the least effort. His classes at the Conservatory often went several hours overtime. On one memorable occasion, after he had listened to a student composition, he shouted at the youth, "That's miserable stuff. You're a donkey!" The student slunk out, but the master ran after him, shouting, "Come back, come back. You're not a donkey."

One of his many foreign students, arriving in Prague for the first time, wrote a letter asking for instruction. He waited two weeks. There was no answer; he was despairing. One morning, at seven o'clock, there was a brusque knocking on the door. It was the master. Hurry, he said—they were going to Vysoká. And they did, on a train departing a few hours later. In Vysoká, the foreign stranger became a member of the family, receiving his lessons in Dvořák's workroom. The children romped and tore through the place, shouting and shrieking. Only occasionally did they irk their father. Then, in shouts, he'd scold them; they paid little heed—they knew him.

As a celebrity, Dvořák was always meeting and mingling with the great of the world. They were struck by how much he disliked formality and ceremony, by how taciturn these things could make him. He was awed by no one, be he the Emperor of Austria-Hungary or King of England. He had his strong personal dignity and his unwavering sense of his own worth. He objected to people de-Czeching his Czech name, Antonin, into Anton. But he had his heroes. Brahms, who became his good friend, he worshiped. Yet Brahms puzzled him. "Such a great man, such a great soul, and he believes in nothing!" he said.

His adventures in the United States resulted from the persistence of Mrs. Jeanette M. Thurber, who founded the National Conservatory in New York. She had resolved to have it headed by a musician of world reputation—her choice was Dvořák. He declined several times. Each time he did, the bid went up—until it reached $15,000 a year for eight months of work and four months of vacation. With his sense of monetary values, he couldn't refuse such a fortune.

Granted a leave of absence from the Prague Conservatory, he arrived in New York in September, 1892, with Anna and their two youngest children—the others were left in school in Bohemia, under the care of relatives. He lived just as he had lived at home—getting up early, walking in Central Park, visiting the railroad yards to keep tabs on the locomotives—and also going to the docks to keep tabs on the ships, which were of intense interest to a peasant who was living in a seaport for the first time. He taught in the way that was his, and he was in bed by nine o'clock. But almost everything attracted him. He learned much more about Americans and their ways than the Americans learned about him.

For instance: Among his pupils were Negroes, including Harry Thacker Burleigh, a fine musician and singer who was to have a big part in popularizing Negro spirituals throughout the world. What Dvořák learned from Burleigh and the others can be heard in the symphony he composed at the time, his last, to which, with his gift for language that is poetic in its simplicity, he gave the subtitle: **From the New World.**

To Americans, it has to be his masterpiece; in America, it still is among the most beloved of all symphonies. You can't wonder, because its largo movement is the very essence of the Negro spiritual and the plantation songs of Stephen Foster. It does not quote any of them directly—it reminds you of a dozen spirituals, yet it isn't one. Such synthesizing is genius, and Dvořák had already done this to the folk music of the Czechs. The **Slavonic Dances** aren't quotations, either; they're the essences of musically expressed common emotions, fabricated by an exceedingly sensitive intelligence.

The **Symphony in E Minor—New World**—his opus 95, was his fifth, if you don't count the four self-educating ones, two of which were published after his death. He composed it between January and May of 1893 while living his plain and busy life in America, relaxing, occasionally, by playing cards with Czech cronies and angrily hurling his cards into the air when he lost too many hands consecutively. On the last page of the manuscript, he wrote, as usual, "Thanks to God," to which he added: "The children have arrived in Southampton. We received a cable at 1:33 this afternoon."

He often wrote little personal notes like that on his scores. This one referred to the four children who had been left behind. They were coming to America; Papa had decided to see more of this new world. That summer he was going to adventure out in the glamorous West.

Spillville, a tiny town in northeast Iowa, largely inhabited by immigrant Czechs, was the point of attraction. The eight Dvořáks had a wonderful summer there. Papa took his morning walks in the fields and woods, and he played the organ for early morning Mass in the town church. They visited St. Paul and Omaha and, on the way back to New York, gave Chicago a closer look, stopped by to look at Niagara Falls, and came down the Hudson by steamer.

The following summer he returned to Bohemia, but came back to New York in the fall. He spent three winters and one summer in America and talked about it for the rest of his life. Things were right in America, he would say—for example, the millionaire and the porter called one another "mister." But, when he went home in the spring of 1895, it was understood he would stay. He loved Bohemia too much.

He resumed his professorship and became the Conservatory director in 1901. He didn't do much directing, letting his assistant do that and even asking his assistant's leave when he wished to go to Vienna for a few days or to Vysoká before the term ended. The emperor made him a member of the Austrian House of Lords. He attended one session and was thoroughly bored.

The afflictions of old age were creeping upon him, among them hardening of the arteries. On May 1, 1904, a cerebral artery burst, and he was dead in a flash, not yet sixty-three years old.

Dvořák left 115 works with opus numbers, as well as a considerable body without. He is a composer of melody and inventiveness; his lyrical resources seem inexhaustible. He was an important song writer as well as a symphonist. Important, too, and always pleasant to hear are his chamber works, such as the **E-flat Quintet**, which was composed in America and contains some so-called "Indian" themes, the lighthearted **Piano Quintet in A Major** and the **F Major Quartet**, called **American** because it, too, was composed in our country.

32

Grieg

Edvard Grieg liked to wrap himself in husks of self-disparagement. His urge was to demote himself in life, both as a person and as a creator. Since he earned world renown, it will sound strange to suggest he succeeded.

The child was brilliant musically (but in no other way), and so he was given an excellent musical education. This resulted in a most musical young man who so excited people they thought of him as "the Chopin of the North."

His promise deluded contemporaries as long as he lived. They mistook promise for fulfillment. Now he is considered only a minor master. We cherish his **Piano Concerto**, his **Peer Gynt** music, and a few songs and little piano pieces. They are much greater as promises than as fulfillments.

Grieg could never quite let his incipient greatness become reality. In his middle life he wrote a young friend: "In you I see myself in my younger days. And I say to you, get steel into you, steel, steel! If you ask how do you get it, there is only one terrible answer: 'Buy it with your heart's blood.' God knows I speak from experience. Believe me, my friend, I don't know that I'd ask steel for you. It costs so much."

He was born in Bergen, Norway, on June 15, 1843. Although he was to come to idolize the peasants of his native land, his father, Alexander, was a prominent and prosperous merchant and his mother, Gesine Judith Hagerup, came of a wealthy and high-placed family keenly aware of social position.

Her musical education had gone beyond that customarily given young ladies, and she devoted herself to amateur musicales and improving the cultural tone of social life. She was a power, and her husband learned to tread lightly. What this meant to her children we can never know except that all were musical. Four turned out to be average people. Edvard, the self-disparaging genius, was altogether exceptional.

189

He was strongly attracted to the piano, the instrument his mother played, before he was five. When he was six she began teaching him, and a stern teacher she was. In his words: "My mother was strict—inexorable." Yet he was disinclined to accept the learning she had to give him. He hated the exercises and the routine practicing, preferring to brood vaguely over the keyboard. Almost at once, he was composing. What he composed was childish, but the urge was there.

The best musicians of Norway were social familiars in his home. One was Ole Bull, a folkish violinist who had acquired a world-wide reputation. After he listened to the boy, fifteen by this time, play the piano, things happened.

According to Grieg, his future was decided in a conference between Bull and his parents in which he had no say. The first he knew of it was when Bull "came over to me, shook me in his own fashion, and said: 'You are going to Leipzig and become a musician.'"

From fifteen to nineteen he was a student in the Leipzig Conservatory, which was one of the world's finest. He would have us believe he was out of sympathy with his teachers and they with him, and that he was a dull pupil who barely squeezed by. The truth was that he conformed precisely to his teachers, who considered him brilliant, that he had no difficulty in learning, and his marks were so good he was graduated with honor.

He was now educated, but he still felt unprepared for his career. When his father showed signs of unease over his apparent inability to get started, the young man went off to Copenhagen where a new Scandinavian musical art was stirring. There was at least a place for him there.

He fell under the spell of the remarkable personality of Rikard Nordraak, who was only a little older but who referred to himself as *the great* Rikard Nordraak, and quite rightly. He died in his early twenties, but on the basis of only a few compositions, including the Norwegian national anthem, many still regard him as the greatest musical genius ever to come out of the northland.

Whether by coincidence or not, Grieg suddenly began composing with ease and in abundance, and very creditable stuff, too—small scale, but intense and lyrical and distinctively original. By now he had matured into a small, robust man (although he had the use of only one lung, the other having collapsed permanently during a severe attack of pleurisy when he was sixteen), with much blond hair, blue eyes, and an oversize mustache. He was earnest and deadly serious, and his attitude suggested he had resigned himself to fate. But he impressed people; they liked him.

Among those who liked him very much was his first cousin, Nina

Hagerup, daughter of a Danish actress and his mother's brother. She
was two years younger than he, possessed a naturally beautiful and
well-trained voice, which she loved to exercise with his songs.

Back home in Bergen, Grieg's father was displaying less and less
patience with his son's lack of concentration on becoming a thoroughly
independent man. There was no objection, of course, to his being
a musician, but there was a strong feeling that he should start to
make it pay. Thus goaded, Edvard arranged to return to Leipzig to
give some concerts.

Before leaving Copenhagen, he and Nina startled and upset their
parents by announcing they had been secretly engaged for a year
and now wanted the betrothal publicized and a date set for the
wedding. Then he was off to Leipzig by way of Berlin, where Nordraak was living for a time. He was disappointed to find him bed-
ridden with "inflammation of the lungs," because he'd been planning
a "broadening" sojourn in Italy with money borrowed from his father
and Nordraak was to have gone with him.

Nordraak was strengthened to have his friend with him. Grieg had
to go on to Leipzig but promised to return before going to Rome.
Nordraak got steadily worse and counted the days. By now it was
evident he was on his deathbed. A few letters came from Grieg,
describing his successes. Then the final letter—Grieg had picked up
another companion and was proceeding directly to Rome. Nordraak
replied with embittered disillusion and enraged denunciations.

He died, and Grieg had no chance to make amends. His ultimate
reaction is very interesting. "I know what I had to suffer in forsaking
him, my best friend, on his sickbed, in seeing love and solicitude
misunderstood."

Despite the objections of their parents, he and Nina were married
in June, 1867, when he was twenty-four. Although there was only one
child, a sickly babe who died in infancy, it was a most successful
marriage and endured until his death forty years later.

At the time of his marriage he was settled in Norway's capital,
Christiania, now called Oslo, endeavoring to earn a livelihood as a
musician. In 1868 he composed the piece by which he is likely to be
remembered for as long as music remains what it is now: his **Piano
Concerto in A Minor**. Although it is of the Schumannesque and Leipzig type, the infusions of supernationalism in art, which he had had
from Nordraak, had taken hold. Grieg was irked by his fellow
Norse who preferred the music of the great masters to the folk
music of the Norwegian peasants. This was to grow with the years.
Peasant virtue, like any virtue, is admirable. Grieg carried his admiration to the point of absurdity.

After the concerto, however, it became increasingly difficult for him to compose, whether on a basis of folklore or from his own pure substance. He thought he had to work so hard in order to earn a living—conducting, running musical groups, piano playing, and giving piano lessons—there was no energy left over for composing. Then the Norwegian government awarded him a pension which relieved him of routine work and gave him freedom to compose. He abandoned Christiania at once, and thereafter his native Bergen and its environs were his home base.

It was no go. He became less fruitful rather than more. The blank periods became progressively longer, and eventually two and even three years would pass without his putting notes on paper. But he tried, he never gave up trying, and it became a fixed obsession that he couldn't possibly compose if there was even a chance of his being overheard while he worked out his musical thoughts on the piano. He had several small huts built, which were placed out of piano earshot of the nearest habitation and so removed from paths and roads there could be no passers-by.

Almost every year he went off on a concert tour, as conductor and pianist. His fame as a performing musician was considerable, and there hardly was a European capital which did not hear and see him regularly. During his travels he longed for Norway and for the comforting warmth and strength of his beloved peasants. But when he was touring, no one could expect him to compose. He couldn't even expect himself to compose, since there was no chance of finding secure hideaways in foreign places.

For his failures to compose while in one of his huts, he blamed the Leipzig Conservatory, since he no longer could plead that he had to earn a livelihood and had no leisure. The Conservatory had left him as stupid as he had been before he entered it, he said: It had failed miserably to teach him the technique with which to compose the big music he had within him.

Yet he made no effort to learn the technique he claimed he lacked. In fairness to Leipzig, it must be said that the works he did compose do not suffer from technical flaws, and no other of the Conservatory's graduates, who included many celebrated musicians, made the same complaint. Then, as he grew older, Grieg began blaming failing health. That can't be taken very seriously as an excuse either, because he went mountain climbing into his sixties and was undertaking long concert tours up to the very day of his death.

Now and then, the creative fire broke through the thick, high barriers—whatever they were—he himself had erected. Almost always a short piece resulted—the barriers could not be penetrated for long.

His longest sustained effort is a symphony, composed in his youth. Next longest is the piano concerto. There are five sonatas, all exercises in the form which he learned well at the Conservatory but couldn't use effectively. There are also a string quartet, now rarely performed, 66 **Lyric Pieces** for the piano, some 150 songs, and some 200 adaptations of Norwegian folk tunes for dancing, singing, and for concertizing with piano and even with symphony orchestra.

He also composed several orchestral suites, including the magnificent **From Holberg's Time,** and incidental music to Henrik Ibsen's play, *Peer Gynt,* and two works by Björnstjerne Björnson, *Olav Trygvason* and *Sigurd Jorsalfar.* All are products of his late twenties or thirties, all are episodic, and all took months and cost him spiritual agonies—"heart's blood," as he said.

From youth to old age, Grieg's habitual attitude was sadness mingled with an air of helplessness. He enjoyed an earthy joke, especially if it were told by a peasant, a game of whist, a serving of oysters, a glass of wine. He had a satirical wit which cut like a knife and usually was directed at himself. In his twenties he said he was "the recipient of a rain of undeserved compliments." When he was sixty he remarked: "So many creative spirits far more important than I, do not get the sympathy I meet everywhere." He was consistent.

His heart gave out suddenly. He was about to leave Bergen to conduct in England. Reading the face of his physician quite accurately, he said: "So this is the end." Nina came to his bedside and he said: "It must be so." He died as he had lived—resigned. It was early in the morning of September 4, 1907, and he was sixty-four years old.

33

Gilbert and Sullivan

THE names Gilbert and Sullivan are unbreakably locked together. It makes sense. Without Gilbert, Sullivan would be remembered mainly as the composer of **Onward, Christian Soldiers**. Without Sullivan, Gilbert might not be remembered at all. Each set the other on fire and gave the other enduring brilliance.

Neither Gilbert nor Sullivan knew that. Each man thought himself an independent genius. Sullivan fancied his work with Gilbert was unworthy of him. Gilbert imagined his genius was other than what it was. Neither man liked the other. To make money, they put up with each other long enough to create fourteen operas together.

Now, let's look at Gilbert and Sullivan separately. First, William Schwenck Gilbert. He was born in London on November 18, 1836, the son of a retired naval surgeon who was writing dreary novels and biographies which he considered of golden merit. In fact, he was eager to beat up anyone who suggested they were otherwise. His mind ran to violence. He was stiff, stuffy, and tyrannical.

His son shared the household with three sisters and a mother, whom Father operated like puppets. Only the boy found a way to avoid being a puppet. At a very early age he was constructing, peopling, and detailing a world of his own with words—he was writing fantasies in plays and in verse. Like Father, he was operating puppets.

What he did as a boy, he did as a man, with a furious and ruthless drive which made him countless enemies, and also made him rich and famous. We can see he was self-compelled. Two efforts, in early manhood, to do other things—he became a government clerk and a lawyer—suggest he did not altogether approve the course he was pursuing.

But he was "irresistibly" (the usual and quite superficial word) attracted to the stage which is, fundamentally, a world of puppetry, but not with any desire to become an actor or puppet. His all-consuming passion was to manipulate actors—to put words into their mouths and to dictate their every action, even to the wiggling of their eyebrows. By the time he was thirty his personality was well known—though not agreeably—in London theatrical circles.

His skin was tissue-paper thin: the least slight made him bitterly vindicative. His temper was hair-triggered and volcanic, and when aroused, his impulse was to use his fists. His favorite form of humor was the cruel practical joke. Although self-righteous and moralistic to the extreme, he was not religious, accepting no authority but his own.

There were contradictions, of course. Now and then he would assume the sweet humility of a child, although, to be sure, not for long. Or he would follow a devastating practical joke with a gesture of pure kindness. Occasionally, he would display generosity. And he loved children—he loved them with a singular concentration of affection that was all the more notable because he displayed love for no one else. We have to assume he loved his wife, since he married her. But she was completely dominated by him. They had no children.

From early childhood until death, he incessantly wrote plays he regarded as masterpieces. He was thirty when first a play of his was performed on a professional stage. By then he had written more than twenty, and before he was through the total passed seventy. He considered himself a great dramatist, "greater," he said, "than Shakespeare." Posterity's judgment of his plays has been that they're unworthy of further attention.

At thirty he also was the author of miles of verses he thought humorous. Many of them had been published in magazines, and now are enbalmed in the *Bab Ballads*. If it weren't that they contain many of the characters (in embryonic form) and much of the raw material of the Gilbert and Sullivan operas, they, like his plays, might be forgotten. They are replete with goblins and fairies and torment and torture. Indeed, there is a streak of bald cruelty through them, which, although humorously presented, doesn't seem very funny.

All this made up the Gilbert who in 1870 met Arthur Seymour Sullivan. Gilbert at thirty-four was an established, though far from the leading, playwright of the day. He had acquired a command of words and writing techniques that was amazing. We must not forget Gilbert was one of the cleverest manipulators ever of the English language. Now let's go back and pick up Sullivan.

Sullivan was born in London, May 13, 1842, and so was almost six years younger than Gilbert. He was the son of an Irish musician who barely earned a livelihood playing a clarinet in a theater orchestra and doing what teaching and music copying that came his way.

Gilbert's home had been one of financial substance and little or no love. Sullivan's home was one of poverty and much, much love.

Nature had given him a beautiful singing voice. At twelve he was admitted to the choir of the Chapel Royal. Two years later he began getting a series of scholarships which kept him in the Royal Academy of Music for two years, and then in the Leipzig Conservatory, where Grieg also was a student, for almost three.

The result was that he entered adult life a first-class musician. He played the piano almost, if not quite, on the virtuoso level and he was expert in all technical aspects of composing. He became at once a fashionable composer and conductor. His preference then and always was not to work too hard at composing, but rather to play socially with "the well-connected," to use a Gilbertian phrase. Soon he was on intimate terms with earls and dukes, royal princes, even with an exiled emperor and empress, Napoleon III and Eugénie of France.

He was composing songs, hymns, a symphony, cantatas, an oratorio, a ballet score, overtures, and two comic operas. His serious music roused much enthusiasm among his friends, who thought it the outpourings of a creative genius destined to rank with the greatest. He was going to compose much more in the same vein, and add grand opera. We, his posterity, know he was neither creative nor a genius apart from the Gilbert and Sullivan operas because we hear in his "serious" music the music from which it was derived—echoes of Mendelssohn and Schumann and others of the Leipzig school. With the exception of **Onward Christian Soldiers** and **The Lost Chord,** which stirs memories in the minds of older generations, all this mass of music is no less dead than Gilbert's plays.

Sullivan was twenty-eight years old in 1870 when he was introduced to Gilbert. He was a young man in perfect harmony with the institutions, convictions, attitudes, and foibles of Victorian England. He knew his place and was deferential to his social superiors and condescendingly kind to his social inferiors. He saw nothing whatever wrong with his world. On the other hand, Gilbert was a loner, which he would have been in any other place or time. He acknowledged no one as a superior. He had neither faith in nor love for people. His bent was raw destructiveness.

The story of the greatness of Gilbert and Sullivan has to be the story of how their personalities interlocked and powered each other and gave them a coupled immortality. Their first meeting was casual. So was their first collaboration, **Thespis,** an inconsequential operatic "extravaganza" which was produced in 1871 and was a failure. Since each man was innately incompatible to the other, there would have been no further collaboration if it hadn't been for Richard D'Oyly

Carte, impresario and speculator, known to theatrical people as "Oily" Carte.

In a truly wondrous burst of inspiration and intuition, his shrewd mind saw that those two could as artistic partners make fortunes for themselves (and for Carte, too, of course). In 1875 he brought them together again. Gilbert happened to have a libretto and this one happened to be pure farce unmarred by sadistic, supernatural or destructive quirks which would have offended Sullivan. The genial composer relished fun and he thought it funny. In only two weeks he set it to music. This was **Trial By Jury**, a one-acter which Carte presented as an afterpiece to a short opera by Offenbach. For months customers crowded the theater to hear it rather than the main attraction.

Their next was **The Sorcerer**, which contains the first signs of what Sullivan's personality was doing to Gilbert's attitudes toward his own puppets. A principal character is a young clergyman. In the **Bab Ballads** clergymen are torn apart. But this young clergyman merely is pretentious and silly. Sullivan, who would have been offended by a downright attack on such a sacred institution as the clergy, could only think this young clergyman funny.

H.M.S. Pinafore followed. Its Captain Corcoran had been Captain Reece in **Bab Ballads**. Captain Corcoran would do almost anything to make his sailors contented except marry his daughter to one of them. Captain Reece married not only his daughter but his sisters, cousins, aunts, and nieces to sailors and himself married his boatswain's widowed mother. Corcoran is human and believable even if something of a fool, while Reece is dehumanized and an unrelieved fool. One is funny. The other isn't.

Plots, characters, and attitudes of all the operas were Gilbert's. He originated everything and Sullivan could accept or reject. Gilbert the creator while in the act of creating was bound to have had the viewpoints of Sullivan, his potential censor, well in mind. He was bound to have been well aware of what would get by, what wouldn't, and how to get something passed by presenting it in a particular way which wouldn't pass if presented in any other.

Sullivan's personality, then, disciplined Gilbert's genius-with-words, by keeping the targets plausible and real and by keeping the genius directed squarely at the targets. You read the **Bab Ballads** and the plays and marvel that Gilbert, for all his cleverness with words and rhythms, knew so little about human beings. You read his librettos for the Gilbert and Sullivan operas and marvel that he knew so much.

Gilbert the wordsmith gave direction to Sullivan the composer. The flow and rhythms of his verses were so distinct and so individualistic that Sullivan in setting them was relieved of his uncertainties and self-consciousness. He was presented with a series of problems. They were concrete, and he could deal with the tangible. He solved these problems with some of the most admirable music-to-words ever composed. In the best examples it is uncanny how music precisely fits both the sense and the shape of words, how music adds to and accents the meanings of words.

H.M.S. Pinafore was an enormous success. Gilbert, Sullivan, and Carte now all had vested interests in the collaboration. It had proven a gold mine which seemed inexhaustible—if the collaboration continued. Sullivan had pressing need for money, since he was immersed in high life with his high society friends. He was fond of frequenting the fashionable resorts of the Continent, of dropping a few hundred pounds at the tables of Monte Carlo, of giving dinner parties for thirty or forty.

Gilbert was quite fond of money, too, but he had less use for it. To be sure, he had a mansion and eventually an estate. Yet his real pleasure was to rule others with absolute and unquestionable power and now he was able, for the first time, to exercise this pleasure without let. Carte built a theater, the Savoy, for the operas. Over the artistic side of this theater, Gilbert was dictator.

He formed the company whose direct, unbroken line of descent leads to the D'Oyly Carte Opera Company of the present day. To belong to this company, a player had to sacrifice even a semblance of individuality. He couldn't even dream of thinking for himself about anything pertaining to the stage. Every inflection, every gesture, every step, every facial expression was Gilbert's, and if any player even suggested an objection he was lashed on the spot with Gilbert's cruelly cutting tongue, and perhaps fired in the bargain.

Thus Gilbert not only wrote the librettos. He prescribed how the operas were sung and played. Sullivan usually got back from the Continent for the dress rehearsal of each new piece; if not, he was sure to be in the theater to conduct the opening performance. His attitude was that this composing was beneath him, and he was doing it with his left hand because it was profitable. His friends kept telling him that he was being untrue to his genius which was suited for something more formidable, like grand opera.

H.M.S. Pinafore was succeeded by **The Pirates of Penzance**, which contains the tune to which every American at one time or another has sung "Hail, Hail, the Gang's All Here." It also contains some of Gilbert's blatant disrespect for royalty which somehow didn't gag Sullivan, probably because it is funny. For instance, the "king" of the pirates sings:

But many a king on a first-class throne
If he wants to call his crown his own,
Must manage somehow to get through
More dirty work than ever I do.

Three years later, Sullivan was knighted. Gilbert was not. Queen
Victoria, naturally, made no statement but a number of times she
made a point of recognizing Sullivan and snubbing Gilbert. Victoria
would never have believed that Gilbert didn't care a rap. From his
viewpoint, he was a much greater dramatist than she was a queen.

The Pirates was followed by Patience (1881), Iolanthe (1882),
Princess Ida (1884), The Mikado (1885), Ruddigore (1887), The
Yeomen of the Guard (1888), and The Gondoliers (1889). The pro-
cedure was simple. When the popularity of one opera seemed to be
diminishing and there was a threat, therefore, to the Savoy box office,
the collaborators got busy on a successor.

Between the first night of Trial by Jury and the first night of The
Gondoliers were more than fourteen years. In that time the collaborators had traveled no farther toward a personal intimacy than to drop
the "mister" and call each other simply "Sullivan" or "Gilbert." Their
business was transacted partly by mail—Sullivan was abroad so much
—and they always begged to remain, "Yours very truly," or merely,
"Yours truly." A number of times they had been on the verge of
quarrels. Sullivan complained that no librettist was entitled to equality
with a composer—there was no precedent for it. Gilbert said they'd
collaborate as equals or not at all.

After The Gondoliers, Carte endeavored to charge the collaborators
for a new carpet for the Savoy. This was theater maintenance and,
therefore, should have come out of his share of the proceeds. Sweet,
good-natured Sullivan didn't object. He was getting enough money.
But no one put anything over on Gilbert if he knew it. He exploded
in violent expletives. Sullivan was wishy-washy for a while, then sided
with Carte. Carte said, in effect, that Sullivan was the genius anyway,
and Gilbert merely a librettist. The world was full of librettists, Carte
indicated with Sullivan's agreement. Gilbert couldn't excuse that.

So Sullivan composed his grand opera, at last, and Carte built a
theater especially for it. Gilbert wrote librettos for other composers.
This went on for four years, until all parties involved were compelled
to realize that Gilbert without Sullivan and Sullivan without Gilbert
were not going to set any worlds on fire. Carte had been hurt where
he could hurt the most—the purse. He managed to patch things and
two more operas resulted: Utopia, Limited (1893) and The Grand

Duke (1896). But Gilbert and Sullivan no longer struck sparks against each other. Posterity has all but forgotten that those two operas exist.

Sullivan never married. For years he was a most devoted friend to a highborn lady who had stopped living with her husband. In Victorian England a divorce simply was out of the question. Sullivan always maintained a discreet veil over this friendship, which we should respect. He died suddenly of a heart attack, on November 22, 1900. Two years earlier he had seen Gilbert for the last time, at a revival of **The Sorcerer**. The audience demanded the collaborators. They went onto the stage from opposite sides, without so much as a nod or even a glance for each other, took their bows, and left the theater separately without exchanging one word.

Gilbert lived on for almost eleven years. He softened somewhat, and now and then became frankly benevolent. Strangely, he sought reconciliations with some of his old enemies. An actor whom he had cut dead for thirty years received a letter from him proposing that they become friends. In 1907, he accepted a knighthood from Victoria's son, Edward VII. He accepted it reluctantly, explaining he knew it was a bauble but he took it because it gave prestige to the theater.

In his old age, he had formed a great fondness for the society of young women, but all was quite fatherly and most proper. He drowned while swimming in the pool of his estate with two girls on May 29, 1911, a few months short of his seventy-fifth birthday.

34

Elgar

A STRIKING thing—how the composer of the celebrated **Enigma Variations** struggled with a private and very personal enigma all his life. He never solved it.

This man was Sir Edward Elgar, Bart., the outstanding English composer of modern times. Not only his **Enigma Variations** but much of his music confronts us with enigmatic qualities. That may be why it keeps on appealing to us.

The wonder of Elgar the creative artist is how close he came to attaining the overwhelming power of a very great master. Often his music seems about to burst into tremendous light and revelation. But it never does. In a single line it can be both startlingly original and rather commonplace. His musical speech is hasty-sounding, with a let's-get-it-over-with bluntness.

As a man, he had the qualities of his music. When he spoke, his sentences often faded into ambiguity. He combined the mien of a strait-laced Victorian with quirky humor and petty eccentricities. Behind an oversized mustache, his mouth was well obscured. It was hard to tell whether its corners were up in a smile or down in sorrow.

According to him, his musical genius stemmed from his mother's voice. She read poetry, and as a little boy of three or four he tried never to let her stop. Not until he was a few years older was he sharply aware that his father, his father's brother, and his father's closest friends were all musicians. Music had been a regular part of his home life from the time of his birth, June 2, 1857, yet he wasn't attracted to it directly, but by way of the liquidly flowing voice of his mother. When he appreciated that music flowed, just as words did, he resolved to be a great musician.

He went about achieving this ambition in an indirect way. Instead of seeking instruction where it was most easily available, he went outside his home to learn the rudiments. Thereafter, he was mainly self-taught, which is learning the hard way.

His father and uncle operated a music shop in Worcester and played violins in amateur musical societies. In due course, Edward was playing a violin on equal terms with them. He was a poor student in school because he wasn't interested. His interest was concentrated on the solitary hours he spent in the shop's storeroom, struggling with technical books.

All this would approach the incredible if we didn't have Elgar's word for it, plus the knowledge that he had very little formal instruction in the piano and the violin, and none whatever in counterpoint, canon, fugue, and harmony. He listed the books he mastered alone as a child, and each is difficult enough for an adult mind which is being guided by a competent instructor.

Of course, he must have picked up useful musical knowledge from his father but he gave Father no credit and always made a point of having been self-taught. He was proud that at fourteen he was able to replace his father now and then at the church organ over which he presided. He was very proud that at twenty-two he was a conductor of an amateur orchestra, with Father among the musicians.

During this period, he was in the grip of a fantastic dream of becoming one of the foremost violin virtuosos in the world. He had to give up that idea and be content with making himself the dominant figure in Worcester's musical activities. In addition to teaching the violin and the piano to a number of pupils, he became the conductor of a second amateur orchestra and organized, trained, and conducted a third among the employees of the county insane asylum. He had to learn the rudiments of playing the oboe, clarinet, and various brasses in order to teach the would-be musicians how to play them. All three of his orchestras were shaky on technique and ill-assorted as to instruments. He had to make special arrangements of music, eliminating the parts for instruments he didn't have, simplifying the parts of those he did have. You can find technical eccentricities in Elgar's mature compositions, but you can't miss the fact that he was a master of instrumentation, orchestration, and harmony.

He was so involved in this grinding routine of teaching and leading amateurs, and finding money to keep himself and their hobbies going, you would have predicted with the utmost confidence that he would live all his life and die in obscurity in his little corner of the world. But you wouldn't have taken his inner drive into consideration. From early childhood he had been composing, although by fits and starts. When finally he was forced to give up the idea of astounding the world as a violinist, he switched to creating the music itself. Almost at once he had the evidence that he was capable of creating music which meant something to an audience. The first composition of his performed by a professional orchestra was enthusiastically received. This was in 1883, when he was twenty-six.

With all possible zeal he set himself to composing. Yet when his father retired as organist in St. George's Catholic Church, after thirty-seven years, the son eagerly took his place—and played music which his father never played and of which he disapproved, and also music of his own creation. Several years earlier he had moved out of the home of his parents and began living with a married sister.

His livelihood was coming from teaching the violin. One of his pupils was the daughter of a knighted major general of distinguished and moneyed ancestry. This Caroline Alice Roberts all but overflowed with sympathy and understanding. She and Elgar were married, and for the rest of her life she was a loving, understanding wife, mother, manager, and major-domo of their almost innumerable establishments.

At this point it is necessary to mention that the English are devoted to singing—and to listening to singing. Then (as now) there were many choral societies, made up of amateurs and guided by one or more professionals. Worcester was a center for these enthusiasts, and Elgar entered their service, first as a conductor, then as a composer. The Worcesterites learned to all but worship him, for he provided music they sang more easily and effectively than any they had sung before. It made them sound, to their own ears, like professionals.

Some seven years passed before this fame seeped outside Worcestershire and the neighboring counties. Then he wrote an inconsequential but pretty melody, **Salut d'Amour** (which some began calling Sally Dammer). Within a few years he was famous the length and breadth of the isle.

From his middle thirties on, his public life was one of ever-growing fame, worship, and honors. At forty-three, the self-taught master got resounding academic recognition, an honorary doctorate of music from Cambridge University. It was the first of a long string of doctorates, including one from Yale. He was knighted at forty-seven, an early age at that time for such an honor. In his last years he was created a baronet.

Elgar's private and creative lives were indistinguishable. Composing was a very personal matter surrounded with obstacles which had to be overcome before he could compose at all. The process was acutely depressing and it was very fortunate for him that he had his Caroline Alice. Once he was over the obstacles, the music flowed onto paper, and his output was quite large although, in the United States where choral singing has no mass support, relatively little of it is well known.

But he also composed extensively for orchestra and among these works are two symphonies, a concerto for the violin, and one for the cello.

Before and after the throes of composing he was rarely still. He shuttled incessantly, the faithful Caroline Alice in attendance, from his native Malvern Hills in Worcestershire to London and back again. From house to house, in town and country, they moved, and each house in turn palled in time. And there were many trips to the Continent. His restless mind turned now and then to diversions like chemistry and the study of microorganisms, as though trying to escape from something.

He endeavored to give the appearance of a hail fellow. In spells, he would attend the several gentlemen's clubs which had honored him with memberships and haw-haw over the most dismal joke. But he was too forbidding in his reticences to succeed. One of his intimate friends waited almost thirty years before he mustered the courage to ask him the meaning of the theme of the **Enigma Variations.** Elgar looked him in the eye and said: "That would be telling." This friend gave this as his appraisal of the man: "He was himself the enigma, and remained so to the end of his life."

Victorian England adored him. Students of the English remark on their loving tolerance of the eccentricities of the great. If some of his remarks seemed impossible to classify as humor, they were classified as whimsy and he actually was whimsical. His only child was a daughter, born in 1890. He took the first syllable and the last syllable of her mother's two names, Caroline Alice, and named her Carice. Another time he took syllables out of his own, his wife's, and his daughter's names and put them together into a word with which he named a house.

He was for all practical purposes the royal composer. He composed for occasions honoring the aging Victoria and dedicated a major work to her. He composed a coronation ode and other works in honor of her son and successor, Edward VII, and composed for Edward's great-grandchildren, the present Queen Elizabeth and her sister, Princess Margaret Rose, when they were in their nursery. But **Pomp and Circumstance** was not composed for any royal or state pageant. His plan was for a set of six marches, all glorifying pomp and circumstance, and the idea came from inside him without any known prompting from the outside. He completed only three.

Caroline Alice died in 1920, when he was sixty-three years old. He was in a state of collapse for two days but soon after the funeral was off to fulfill his conductorial engagements. Caroline Alice had trained her daughter in her duties, and Carice, even after her marriage, was at hand to provide sympathy, understanding, and excellent management for the rest of his days. In his last months he was working on a third symphony, seeking an operatic libretto from George Bernard Shaw, and still conducting. By now he was a doddering old man with his eyes focused into the past, and he died quietly on February 23, 1934, at the age of seventy-seven.

Among his oratorios and cantatas, **The Dream of Gerontius** is now generally considered to be the masterpiece. Indeed, it probably is the finest of all his works. Among the orchestra works, the **Enigma Variations** maintain their popularity and high repute among musicians. The **Concerto for Cello** is part of the repertoire of every cello virtuoso. It isn't what is called easy listening. Yet attention to it can be rewarding.

35

Puccini

GIACOMO PUCCINI was the son of a dominating mother and the husband of a dominating wife. It is interesting, although not necessarily significant, that the women he created in imagination— Manon of **Manon Lescaut**, Mimi of **La Bohème**, Cio-Cio-San of **Madame Butterfly**, and Floria of **Tosca**—toy with dangerous situations and are destroyed.

Albina Puccini, his mother, dominated over misfortune. "The world is not for cowards," she said. At thirty-three, she became a widow with six children and a seventh on the way. The first four were girls, the eldest thirteen. Then came Giacomo, who was five; then another girl; and finally, the posthumous son of her late husband.

Mama Puccini had married a man eighteen years older than herself and one who was a prominent citizen. Michele Puccini was the official music master of Lucca, an old town not far from Pisa in northern Italy. His Puccini forebears, in an unbroken line of father-son succession, had been the Lucca town musicians for more than a hundred years.

The town authorities promised Mama that when her little boy was old enough he could have his father's job. They believed the Italian proverb: "The children of cats catch mice." They also gave Mama a tiny pension and left her to feed, clothe, and educate her brood and to preserve the prestige and traditions of the Puccinis as best she could.

This was back in the 1860's. The one genius among the Puccini musicians was born December 22, 1858. Of Mama's many trials, he was among the most difficult. He was silent, sullen, withdrawn. Worse, he gave every indication of having no musical talent whatever.

To Mama, that was unthinkable. One music teacher said the lad was hopeless. She hired another and admonished him to work hard and not to despair. But Giacomo idled away his time. In school, his marks were dismal. Catching birds was the only endeavor he enjoyed.

Then, very suddenly, his resistance to Mama collapsed. Almost overnight, it seemed, he became a proficient musician. At fourteen, he was playing the organ in several churches and the piano at dances. And he showed a modicum of ambition—he thought he'd like to compose operas.

His essential aloofness and indolence remained unchanged. He began showing a taste for practical jokes, the unhumorous and cruel kind. He continued to learn very slowly, was twenty-one when he finished at the Lucca academy.

Mama was not discouraged. She "begged"—as she said—from relatives and wheedled a scholarship out of Queen Margherita. As a result, Puccini entered the Royal Conservatory in Milan, where one of his principal professors was Amilcare Ponchielli, composer of **La Gioconda.**

Ponchielli understood the sad, tense young man—at least enough to recognize his operatic bent. When Puccini finished the three-year course and received the degree of master—maestro—Ponchielli was instrumental in launching him on his first opera, **Le Villi,** which now is almost forgotten. Puccini composed it quickly and easily. Its first performance was a big success. He telegraphed Mama he had answered eighteen curtain calls.

At this time he was sharing a poor room with another debt-ridden young man, Pietro Mascagni, who was later to distinguish himself by composing **Cavalleria Rusticana.** The future operatic celebrities had only one bowl between them. After they had eaten their beans out of it, they'd wash it and fill it with water to wash their faces.

Le Villi freed Puccini from the bowl. It paid his debts, and it attracted the attention of Giulio Ricordi, head of a music-publishing house that held a virtual monopoly on Italian operas by controlling the output of all the major composers. Ricordi put Puccini under contract and undertook to support him while he worked on a new opera.

At this point, Mama Puccini died. Her son all but fell apart. Once he had written these revealing words to her: "If occasionally I give you cause for anger, it is not because I do not love you dearly but because I am a beast and a rogue." While he was in the pit of his grief for her, he met the woman who was going to dominate him in her turn.

She was Elvira, wife of Giuseppe Gemignani, a schoolmate of Puccini. Tall, straight, beautiful, and tense, Elvira was twenty-four, two years younger than Puccini, when she met him. Her husband, it was said, could call no part of himself his own. Not long after meeting Puccini, she left this husband and became Puccini's wife—his informal wife, since Italian law and custom did not permit divorce.

It was a solid, enduring marriage, based upon the affinity of their needs. She endeavored to own him in every particular. He spent the years slyly frustrating her endeavors and, even more slyly, making her more miserable than she ever could have made herself. Gemignani, it should be added, never complained publicly over losing her. When he died, nineteen years later, her marriage to Puccini was formalized.

When the marriage began, he was working on his second opera, **Edgar**. To hurry him along, Elvira would lock him in a room with his piano. Verdi composed **Il Trovatore** in less than a month, she shrieked at him. "And you're going to take five years to compose **Edgar**. You are a good-for-nothing!" It did take him five years, and **Edgar** was so poor a success it could almost be called a failure.

The future looked bleak to the now 31-year-old Puccini in that year, 1889. But Ricordi's patience was matched by his faith in his own intuition. He had supported Puccini for five years; he kept right on supporting him. Few gambles have been so richly rewarded. In the next fourteen years Puccini was to create four operatic masterpieces, make himself world-famous, and earn millions for himself and his publisher.

This was the point where he began creating *the woman* in his imagination. Her first guise was that of Manon. Then she became Mimi, then Floria, then Cio-Cio-San. But her pattern was always the same. Her way of living was wrong. Nevertheless, it gave her both pleasure and happiness. This was temporary, alas. Suffering and unhappiness followed, and then her pitiful death. Puccini always assured his admirers he was in love with her—or, rather, with her four counterparts. He sounded utterly sincere. He was.

What he was doing is clear from the way he worked and the results he obtained, although the chances are he himself didn't know it, at least consciously. **Le Villi** and **Edgar** were stories presented to him by their librettist, which he accepted without question. He merely set them to music. After **Edgar**, he formed and shaped the stories of his operas himself, self-tormented all the way with doubts and fears.

He didn't actually write the librettos. Of that he was incapable. He exhausted the poets who did write them. He was a merciless driver of poet slaves, according to Luigi Illica, one of the six who had a hand in preparing **Manon Lescaut** and, with Giuseppe Giacosa, the coauthor of record of the librettos of **La Bohème, Tosca,** and **Madame Butterfly.** The work of the poets became a series of "slaughters," Illica said. "Entire acts were cut to pieces. Ideas judged beautiful one moment were banished the next, setting at naught in one minute the long, heavy labor of months."

Some of the poets resigned. Illica and Giacosa stuck, since they were riding to fame along with the composer. But their labors were monumental. Each libretto took two to three years. Puccini never could say what he wanted or what he liked, only what he didn't want and didn't like. His instincts, rather than his mind, were guiding him —painfully, slowly, with much backtracking. During protracted sessions with his poets, he always chewed his nails down to his fingertips, Illica said.

Puccini spotted the form of *the woman* in various places; once he had seen her, all this painful work was to shape her to his hidden ideal. Manon was discovered in the novel from which Jules Massenet had only recently taken his highly successful opera, **Manon.** For his opera, Puccini merely gave the girl her full name, **Manon Lescaut.**

Mimi he spotted in the Paris Latin Quarter tales of Henri Murger in which she is only a minor character and quite different from the one she became under Puccini's guidance. His friend, Ruggerio Leoncavallo, who wrote **Pagliacci,** was composing a **La Bohème** at the time. That made no difference to Puccini, and Leoncavallo called him a thief and was, thereafter, his enemy.

Floria Tosca he found in Victorien Sardou's play, *La Tosca.* Alberto Franchetti, then a popular opera composer and once a pupil of Puccini's father, owned a libretto of the story and was working on it. He was hoodwinked out of it in ruthless fashion. And Cio-Cio-San, Puccini found in a hit play by John Luther Long and David Belasco, the American playwright, a play called, like the opera, *Madame Butterfly.*

During the agonies over **Manon Lescaut,** the Puccinis began living in Torre del Lago, a hamlet of some one hundred inhabitants, on the bank of a shallow and dismal lake near Pisa; and this became their permanent home. It suited him well. As he grew older, he was always seeking out even wilder and gloomier retreats which, one way or another, Elvira spoiled for him.

Torre del Lago should have suited her, too. She liked people even less than he did. She was in "continuous black," he said. But he didn't object, really. After all, he spent his life "in a sack of melancholy," to use his words. At Torre del Lago, he was again preoccupied with catching birds, as he had been during his boyhood; but now he caught them by shooting them.

Elvira objected, because it kept him away from his work. He hired a youth to slip into the house in the early morning, while she was still abed upstairs, and bang some of his themes over and over again on the piano to make her think he was working when he was really out on the lake, banging at ducks. The work on **La Bohème** went so slowly she often shrieked, "Bohème will be finished on judgment day!" She blamed his "tramp friends" and made the house too inhospitable for them to enter.

These friends were a group of painters, sportsmen, and local idlers. In honor of Puccini's labors, they made an abandoned shack into a "Club Bohème," where they played cards, drank, and vied with one another in practical jokes and horseplay. Puccini played with them enough to keep Elvira in constant foment. However, the composer of **La Bohème** was anything but a Bohemian, since artistic Bohemianism requires, first of all, unselfishness.

It was remarkable how he managed to keep Elvira in foment. He must have realized her jealousy was without limit and possessiveness made her a fury. Yet, in one way or another, he chose to let her know that he was not only extremely attractive to women but also susceptible to them. Once, Elvira attacked a young woman with an umbrella. Another time, she attacked Puccini with her nails, scratching his face. Understand, Puccini was more often guilty than not. The question is why he kept offering evidence against himself.

Manon Lescaut, which had its première in February, 1893, made Puccini famous. **La Bohème**, first performed with Arturo Toscanini conducting, in February, 1896, gave him a world fame of the kind enjoyed by a movie star today. **Tosca's** first performance was in January, 1900, and that of **Madame Butterfly** in February, 1904. Through these years, he was in constant demand to go here and there to supervise his operas and make personal appearances. He accepted many of these invitations, although he never seemed to enjoy going, and when away, he wrote Elvira long letters telling her how much he missed her, and also dropping hints of the attractive women he was meeting.

In due course, she began accompanying him wherever he went, the better to guard her property. In 1905, she grimly accompanied him to Buenos Aires and, in 1907, to New York, where he was lionized by the Metropolitan Opera and its supporters. While Puccini attended the functions, she secluded herself at their hotel.

After their return to Torre del Lago came the climax to the emotional game he had been playing for so many years. Doria Manfredi was a young maid in the Puccini home. Elvira suddenly accused her of being her husband's secret love. She discharged her; she told the girl's mother and relatives and the entire village and asked the priest to have the sinful girl driven from the village.

Puccini tried to stop Elvira. Nothing could. She stormed on and on. There was only one way for poor Doria to escape. Three months after the original accusation, she took it—she committed suicide. Puccini instantly left Elvira, fled to Rome, told friends it was "forever."

Doria's family brought suit in criminal court, charging defamation of character, threat of bodily harm, and libel. At the trial they proved beyond question that Doria had been innocent. Elvira was found guilty and sentenced to prison. While her appeal was pending, the family withdrew its action. Puccini's lawyers had made a financial settlement.

It wasn't long before Puccini took Elvira back. Their son, Antonio (their only child), who now was grown, acted as conciliator. Puccini had discovered he couldn't live without his Elvira. She was chastened. They resumed their old life, but on a much less hectic basis.

This tragedy interrupted his work of making an opera of another Belasco play, **The Girl of the Golden West,** in Italian **La Fanciulla del West.** It is about cowboys, gold miners, and Indians in California during the Gold Rush. The heroine, Minnie, is not even related to *the woman.* Puccini finished it with even greater difficulty than he had had with the others, and the work reflects this. Worse operas have been composed, but never by an operatic genius of Puccini's caliber. **The Girl** was first given in December, 1910, at the Metropolitan Opera. It has been moribund ever since.

Puccini now was finished as a creative genius. We can only guess —we will never know—why. He was still frantically seeking *the woman* in literature and plays. Now he couldn't find her. His publisher, friend, and unfailing guide, Giulio Ricordi, died in 1912. The patiently suffering poet, Giacosa, had died in 1906; and Puccini quarreled with and arbitrarily dismissed Illica during the preparation of **The Girl.** Elvira, contrite, gave him no trouble any more.

La Rondine, his next piece, was no better, and maybe worse, than **The Girl.** It was composed during World War I to fulfill a prewar contract with an Austrian publisher. Puccini's clumsy way of handling the matter made him appear much less than an Italian patriot, which got him into trouble. As a matter of fact, his world was too centered in Puccini for him to have been a patriot.

He tried to regain his powers with three one-act operas, to be presented on the same program under the title **Il Trittico—The Triptych.** They were **Il Tabarro, Suor Angelica,** and **Gianni Schicchi.** Only the last one, a comic opera and quite funny to people who understand Italian, survives in a state of health. The others are very sick; it is the name of their creator that keeps them alive. **Il Trittico** had its world première at the Metropolitan in December, 1918.

Puccini was trying to enjoy being several times a millionaire, with his yacht, his fancy motorcars, his elegant tailoring. But not too hard. As he said himself, he "enjoyed" melancholy more than anything else. And he was suffering because his years were mounting; he hated growing old and kept the grayness of his hair hidden by systematic dyeing. Then, in 1920, when he was sixty-two years old, his life suddenly brightened—he thought he had found *the woman* once more. She was Liù, a slave girl in a play by Carlo Gozzi, called *Turandot*. He subjected new poets to the agonies Illica and Giacosa had suffered when he was at the height of his powers.

By 1924, when he was found to have cancer of the throat, the opera was finished save for the last part of the last act. Knowing he was going to die, he mourned only for the unfinished state of Liù. He hated the idea that Turandot would be performed and someone would have to say, "Here the composer died." When it was performed, in Milan in April, 1926, Toscanini put down his baton with Puccini's last note and said to the audience: "Here the master laid down his pen." Puccini had died November 29, 1924.

36

Debussy

EMILE RÉTY, official of the Paris Conservatoire, said scornfully to a trouble maker among the pupils, "So! You think dissonant chords don't have to be resolved! What is your rule?"

The brash youth, Achille Claude Debussy, wasn't devastated; he replied, "My pleasure."

This was Debussy's rule in living his life as well as in creating his music. In the former, his pleasure caused him constant unease and gave him no happiness. In the latter, his pleasure gave the musical art fresh and fruitful paths away from worn-out forms and made him a highly original genius.

A woman, relying largely on her intuition, since she didn't know him very well, said his air was like a "Do Not Enter" sign. She thought the sign meant "Do Not Hurt Me."

Nadejda von Meck, intuitive patron of Tchaikovsky, hired Debussy for a while as her private pianist. She, too, noted this quality. She thought his playing "brilliant, but he lacks any personal expression." Intuition—feminine or poetic, or both—is as good a rod as any for measuring such a man as Debussy.

The saddest story is of another woman, who, having been his wife for five years, knew him well. Twenty-three years after he abandoned her, causing her to shoot herself in despair, she was quietly attending lectures on Debussy at the University of Paris. Evidently she was still trying to understand him—and carried the riddle to her grave.

He was a riddle to all. His sister, Adèle, said that when he was a child he "would spend days sitting in a chair, thinking; no one knew of what." He was born on August 22, 1862, in a dingy flat above his father's china shop at 38 Rue au Pain, Saint-Germain-en-Laye, a suburb of Paris. Neither his father, Manuel Achille, nor his mother, Victorine, was in any way distinguished, either in person, attainments, or ancestry.

Soon after Adèle's arrival, two years later, the china business failed altogether. The family moved into Paris where, as a petty clerk, Manuel Achille continued earning a miserable livelihood. Adèle was sent to live with relatives; so were three younger brothers, as they were born. Victorine clung to her eldest. She was passionately fond of him, it was said, and extremely emotional. She wouldn't even let him go to school.

Manuel Achille's sister and her lover, Achille Antoine Arosa, a banker, had been the lad's godparents. They hired a piano teacher for him. A few years later, Antoinette Flore Mauté de Fleurville, who had been a pupil of Chopin, heard him play. Manuel Achille said the boy was going into the navy when he was old enough. Madame Mauté was outraged. "This boy *must* be a musician," she said. She taught him herself, and so well that he was admitted to the Conservatoire at the age of eleven.

He was not a brilliant student, but he was a challenging one. His aversion to rules made him a thorn to the faculty. He formed a lasting dislike for the music of Beethoven, because, he said, a teacher fitted the words "O Mother of anguished suffering" to the rondo of the **Pathétique** piano sonata. It was his pleasure to "abuse" the laws of harmony and counterpoint; to him, a feast for the ears was to scramble the "correct" (or textbook) relations of chords and keys. Many a pupil was expelled for much less. Clearly, he impressed his teachers while shocking them.

Antoine François Marmontel, the piano master, indicated their bewilderment when he said the boy "doesn't like the piano, but he does like music." Debussy was no personal favorite of his; yet, when a Russian multimillionairess asked him to send her a pianist for the summer, he sent Debussy. Nadejda von Meck was vacationing in Switzerland and Italy. She wrote Tchaikovsky about the somber youth of eighteen, who plastered his hair down on his forehead to minimize a huge, bulging brow.

Debussy taught her daughters and accompanied their singing. He played in her private trio. He played piano duets with her. He also proposed marriage to one of the girls and was refused. The summer ended; he had to return to the Conservatoire.

Back in Paris, his emotions attached themselves to another older woman, though considerably younger than Nadejda. The attachment was doomed for several reasons. For one, the lady had a husband, who treated Debussy with the utmost kindness. The culture Debussy lacked he acquired in this home. With Parisian sophistication, the husband thought the young man's infatuation with his wife could cause no real harm. It didn't.

At the Conservatoire, Debussy was trying to win the Prix de Rome.

He placed second in 1883, when he was twenty-one; whereupon his composition teacher, Ernest Guiraud, who was orthodox but tolerant, reminded him that the judges were all believers in traditional harmony and he would do better if he kept this in mind.

The next year he submitted the cantata **L'Enfant prodigue** and won the first place. Now Debussy had his prize and, instantly, didn't want it. From Rome he wrote the most dejected letters. He even threatened suicide. (Suicide talk often recurred in his life.) Three years in Rome were more than he could stand. He returned to Paris after two and became one of the artistic Bohemians whose haunts were the cafés of Montmartre.

His living, such as it was, came from teaching and arranging music for piano, accompanying singers, and a little musical journalism now and then. No one could have known, nor was he aware himself, that he was absorbing the materials for a new musical art. From having spent two summers in Russia with the von Meck family, he had heard Russian music, particularly Moussorgsky's. At the Paris Exposition Universelle in 1889 he had heard Oriental timbres and rhythms. Twice he had gone to Bayreuth, the Wagnerian paradise, to hear that master at the fountainhead. He was getting materials from other arts—the light and color of the Impressionist painters; some of the aesthetics of the Symbolist poets, who were trying to "take back from music what poetry gave it."

Unconsciously he was synthesizing the materials he had been absorbing into a material wholly his own. He had already composed the cantata **The Blessed Damozel** and had set to music five poems by Baudelaire, which were harbingers. In 1894, when he was thirty-two, he completed **The Afternoon of a Faun**, which, in addition to being a masterpiece, is one of the landmarks of music. With it the main stream of musical composition reached a turning point.

Meanwhile, he was at work on another masterpiece, his opera **Pelléas et Mélisande**. Its creation was to trouble him for ten years, during which time Gabrielle Dupont played her part in his art. His friends testified she was as beautiful as she was blonde. He was devoted to the color green. She had green eyes. He loved cats. Gaby, according to a friend, "looked at you as resolutely as a cat."

Now he was struggling to create a woman in music, that ethereally innocent and unworldly woman, Mélisande. Gaby, the real woman, couldn't have been further removed from the woman of his imagination. In the fifth year of his struggle, he wrote his friend, Pierre Louÿs, the poet: "Gaby with her steely eyes [note: they're no longer green] found a letter in my pocket . . . with all the romantic trappings to move the most hardened heart. Whereupon—tears, drama, a real revolver, and a report in *Petit Journal.* . . ."

Gaby's successor was Rosalie Texier, a simple, good girl from the country, who worked in a Parisian dressmaker's shop. Debussy called her "Lily-Lilo." They were married October 19, 1899. He gave a piano lesson that morning to finance it and spent his last sou on the wedding festivities, because he wanted to begin married life penniless. Some fourteen months later, he wrote on the score of his orchestral **Noc-turnes**: "This manuscript belongs to my little Lily-Lilo. All rights reserved. It is proof of the deep and passionate joy I have in being her husband. Claude Debussy. At the peep of January, 1901."

Pelléas et Mélisande was performed for the first time at L'Opéra-Comique the following year, with Mary Garden as Mélisande. There was critical bewilderment—the work was unique and astonishing. But it was an instant success and made its composer famous almost overnight. Its core was the otherworld woman, Mélisande. Like many another character created by art, she was more real than real. Now that she existed, there was nothing more her creator could do with her or for her.

Less than two years later—in the summer of 1904—Debussy abandoned his little Lily-Lilo and took up with Emma Bardac. She was a prominent singer, who sang his songs in a manner most pleasing to him, and the wife of a financier. Debussy's friends were astonished. They had noticed no strain whatever in the Debussy household. Lily-Lilo, shocked and distressed, aimed a revolver bullet at her heart, missed it, and recovered. Paris was rocked. A number of Debussy's friends would have nothing further to do with him. Practically all his friends subscribed—some anonymously—to a fund for Lily-Lilo.

Debussy expressed himself in a letter: "Whatever the cause, I have had many a fall and have hurt myself so much that I have felt utterly exhausted for hours afterward. There are many reasons for this, of which I will tell you someday—if I have the courage, for it is all very sad."

And again: "You should know how people have deserted me! It is enough to make one sick of everyone called a man. I shan't tell you all that I have gone through. It's ugly and tragic and ironically reminds one of a novel a *concierge* might read. Morally, I have suffered terribly. Have I some forgotten debt to pay to life? I don't know, but often I've had to smile so that no one should see that I was going to weep."

When she recovered, Lily-Lilo agreed to a divorce, after Debussy had set aside some of his royalties for her support. Madame Bardac's divorce took longer, but finally they were married. She was the mother of Debussy's only child, Claude Emma. In the joy of fatherhood, he hinted that one of Lily-Lilo's faults had been her failure to have children. **Children's Corner** was composed for his daughter and dedicated "To my dear little Chou-Chou, with her father's affectionate apologies for what follows."

During the period he was changing wives he was composing some of his most characteristic and finest music. **Estampes,** which include **Gardens in the Rain,** belong to 1903. **The Sea (La Mer),** three gorgeous symphonic sketches, was first performed during the month Chou-Chou was born—October, 1905. The first three of his piano **Images,** including **Reflections in the Water,** appeared that year, too. Children's Corner (**Jimbo's Lullaby, Serenade for the Doll, Golliwog's Cakewalk,** etc.) was composed between 1906 and 1908.

He was now one of the most famous and most controversial musicians alive. There were droves of Debussyites dogging him personally and artistically, making it difficult for him to remain strictly within himself. He shunned and distrusted them. Although he was a poor conductor, he was in demand everywhere as a conductor of his own works. For the fees—certainly not for the fame—he traveled extensively. His fame, now that he had it, he despised.

There had been a steady decline in the quality of his creations even before January, 1909, when he learned he had cancer. He, who had rebelled against established forms and rules, had his own formulas and rules, which now made it seem as though Debussy were imitating Debussy. As his disease progressed, with pain his shadowing companion, it was bound to dominate his thoughts and emotions. Development, artistic or emotional, ended; decline was inevitable.

He lived until March 25, 1918—the period during which the German "Big Bertha" was shelling Paris in the last year of World War I. He composed less and less; only occasionally did he rouse himself to painful effort. On the title page of one of these last compositions, he chose his own epitaph—Claude Debussy, musicien français—and it is cut into the stone of his monument in Paris. Little Chou-Chou died of diphtheria in 1919, aged fourteen, Lily-Lilo died in 1932, and Emma, her successor, in 1934.

To us, Debussy no longer seems a revolutionist, but more a classicist, so far have his artistic heirs carried the freedom he asserted. This freedom was mainly in harmony. Debussy harmony moves freely in space; chords resolve every which way or do not resolve at all; you can't say at any given point which key is the key. The first critics said he ignored melody, an accusation he resented, and rightly so, as he was a melodist of high order. But his melodies are hardly more than sighs and flashing and pensive smiles.

Debussy suggests; he never states. He sets forth the impressions of a picture, never the picture itself. He provides the materials for moods and for dreams, which can be whatever we make them. Like the man, Debussy's music is at least twice removed from that which it portrays or suggests.

Of his piano music, everyone should know the two sets of **Images,** and **Estampes,** and the first twelve of the twenty-four **Preludes,** among which is **The Sunken Cathedral.** Of the orchestral works, foremost are **The Afternoon of a Faun** and **La Mer. Nocturnes**—made up of **Clouds Fêtes,** and **Sirènes**—are full of charm.

With **Pelléas et Mélisande,** the music so perfectly fits the characters and action that much is lost without the stage performance—provided it is an excellent one, because no other opera can be so readily ruined by a poor performance. A most engrossing entrance into the world of Debussy songs may be had through the three **Chansons de Bilitis,** the **Ariettes oubliées,** and **Le Promenoir des deux amants.**

37

Mahler

WHILE composing his symphonies Gustav Mahler usually included a funeral march. For a while he included clanging cow bells as well. No other major composer so clearly put so much of his own hidden self into his music, willy-nilly. It's too bad we don't know why funeral marches, clanging cow bells, and many another odd or weird symphonic touch had such undeniable values in his creative processes—and what the values are.

If we knew, he would be one of the favorite symphonists of most of us, or so you are persuaded by the many instances where his music attains to an enormous power comparable to that of the supreme masters. These flashes have universal meanings, but they occur amidst symphonic meanderings which, because they don't suggest their own values and we don't know what the values are, can only seem tedious and meaningless.

Yet these passages must have been jammed with meanings for him, since he drew them out to such extravagant lengths. He said he never "experienced" except while creating music. Most of us experience through every moment of our lives. "A symphony," he said, "must be a whole world." Because of their complexities and high emotional voltages, we can't doubt his symphonies are. But by and large they're his private worlds.

He excluded us with his private language, by making his symphonies exceedingly difficult to perform, and by making them so long they're hard to fit into symphonic programs. Only amateurs and geniuses ignore practicalities, and he was a practical musician, having been a leading conductor of his day. From that you could guess he didn't care whether his music was performed or not performed. But he cared a great deal.

Furthermore, he was aware he often defeated his own ends and spent many a wearisome, worrisome hour trying to figure out why. You can see his predicament, and sympathize. There he was, burning

with the symphonic genius which put him into the direct line of
descent of the masters of the romantic symphony, from Beethoven
through Schubert and Brahms. Was he being the torch-bearer who
was extinguishing the sacred flame with his own confusions and
obscurations? That's a question to torture a genius's conscience, and
the explanation he finally settled on for one of the more inescapable
of his creative weaknesses is interesting.

This weakness is that when a Mahler symphony reaches a sublime
height of grandeur it typically breaks off into some trivial little tune.
When he was a small boy, Mahler recalled, he came into the room
where his father was berating his mother. This roused in him torrents of emotion. He couldn't endure them and ran out of the house
into the street, where an organ grinder chanced to be grinding out
a most trivial tune, **Ach du lieber Augustin**. This, Mahler decided
quite on his own, was what always afterward compelled him to follow
musical profundity with banality.

During the last year of his life, he had a four-hour conversation
with Sigmund Freud in the hope that that psychological genius
would provide him with helpful insights into himself. After listening
to Mahler's account of Mahler, Freud said he was surprised Mahler
had married a woman whose name was Alma—Freud would have
thought Mahler would have married a woman whose name was Marie
because his mother had been called Marie. Mahler was thunderstruck.
His wife's full name was Alma Maria but he called her Marie.

Marie, his mother, was the mother of twelve children. Gustav, the
genius among them, was the second in birth order yet the eldest of
the living, since the first died in infancy. He was born July 7, 1860, in
Kalist in Bohemia, which then was part of the Austro-Hungarian
Empire but now is part of Czechoslovakia. She was the daughter of a
soapmaker and had been married through a broker, in accordance
with Jewish practice, to a coachman, Bernhard Mahler, whose mother
was a street peddler.

She was sickly, walked with a limp, and complained of heart trouble.
Bernhard was industrious, ambitious, and rose eventually to the
proprietorship of a small-scale distillery. Gustav always said he was
heartless in his attitudes toward his wife, but if his brothers and sisters had such an idea they didn't talk about it and it never bothered
them.

Whatever kind of husband Bernhard was, he was a good father to
Gustav. When the very young child showed an interest in music, Bernhard got instruction for him, and Bernhard took the fifteen-year-old
boy to Vienna and got the audition for him at the Conservatory,
which resulted in his being admitted as a pupil. He plunged through

the three-year course, winning prizes, dazzling teachers.

Already he had the intense, driving personality which so many people were going to describe with the same word—"demoniacal." You can see the young Mahler was as deeply troubled as the adult Mahler, if only by his choice of friends. The three who were the most intimate, then, in his teens, including the superlative song composer, Hugo Wolf, were all going to die insane.

After his graduation, he acted for a while as though he would be a professional composer. But his creative processes then and afterward were accompanied by defensive agonies, as though creating was laden with dangers. Then in his youth he submitted a complex piece in a prize competition for which Johannes Brahms was one of the judges. Brahms was pushing fifty, a fatherly figure with a patriarchal beard. Mahler was sure that Brahms, in unmitigated meanness, deprived him of the victory.

Since Brahms then didn't know Mahler existed and since he had no meanness in him, the idea was absurd—and doubly absurd when we know that some ten years later Brahms generously helped the young man along his way. But the incident reveals Mahler's outlook, which was never going to change substantially.

After two years of agonized composing, he ostensibly gave up the role of composer, or, rather, of a musical creator who lived by and for his creations. He was only twenty when he became a conductor and until his death he was principally and primarily a conductor, which was useful for purposes other than livelihood. No one could expect him to compose, particularly himself, when he was so busy with such an exacting job, and he worked so very hard at the job it was a wonder he had any energy left for anything. With sorrow but with eagerness, he was always ready to explain he was only a "summer composer," since he was free, or could have been free, of conductorial duties during his summers.

He began as a conductor with menial tasks in fourth-rate opera houses in small towns. Eight years later he arrived at the top of the profession when he was appointed music director of the first-rate Budapest Opera. From there he went to the Hamburg Opera and when only thirty-seven arrived at Europe's topmost post, that of music director of the Vienna Opera and conductor of the Vienna Philharmonic. Without question he was one of the finest conductors of all time. He drew interpretative wonders from performing artists, both as individuals and as groups, which they hadn't known were possible, and his personal reward was that many of them, and perhaps most of them, learned to despise him.

That he earned from them, too, by being a heartless tyrant. In all musical matters and in nonmusical matters to the extent he found possible, he was a dictator and no consideration was granted anyone who presumed to understand music differently than he did. Since his teens he also had exercised what tyranny he could inside his family, to which he clung with fanatical zeal. But Bernhard was the reigning tyrant there. Bernhard died when his genius-son was twenty-eight, and only eight months later Marie, the mother, died. Mahler took over his younger sisters and brothers as much as they allowed. Sister Justine became his housekeeper at once and soon Sister Emma joined the household. Neither married until after he had married and replaced them with Marie, the wife, which was rather late in life for all.

A vivid description of Mahler the conductor is that of Guido Adler, Viennese musicologist of the time, an intimate of Brahms as well as of Mahler. "When the little man with the lively movements approaches the podium, silence falls," Adler wrote. ". . . his face speaks earnestness and holy zeal. The flashing eyes cast forth brilliant light. At mystic passages they gaze dreamily before him. The vigorous chin expresses an energetic will, as do the dilated nostrils of his sharp-cut nose and the high forehead, which makes furrows at the first rise of doubt or anger, but then there are the fine narrow lips that can smile gently. Thoughtful and superior in everything he does, he gives free rein to the movements of his body which sometimes become grotesque with nervous twitchings and tappings of the foot."

The celebrated conductor Bruno Walter was a coach under Mahler at the Hamburg Opera when Walter was eighteen and Mahler thirty-four. Walter became his lifelong friend and devoted disciple, and here is Walter's description of his first communion with the master. An opera rehearsal had been finished and Mahler invited Walter to walk with him. "I was fascinated to observe how the same intensity, the same spiritual tenseness that he had just revealed during rehearsal was now manifested in his conversation.

"The vehemence with which he objected whenever I said something unsatisfactory to him—and how timidly I said it—his sudden submersion in pensive silence, the kind glance with which he received an understanding word on my part, the unexpected, convulsive expression of secret sorrow, and added to all, the strange irregularity of his gait—a stamping of the feet, a sudden halting and rushing ahead again—everything confirmed and strengthened the impression of demoniac obsession, and I should hardly have been surprised if, after saying good-by, he had started moving faster and faster and had finally flown away from me in the shape of a vulture."

Mahler the creator was not as clearly seen. This part of him he concealed and denied as much as he could and still retain it. Between the ages of twenty and thirty he destroyed almost everything he had composed. Starting out anew, he created three song cycles and his first symphony, which structurally—but only structurally—is conventional. After his mother's death he worked fitfully on his second, which is conventional in no sense, is in five movements, and requires a soprano, contralto, a chorus, and full orchestra.

Between thirty and forty he completed it and also composed his third (six movements, soprano, contralto, chorus, orchestra) and his fourth (four movements, with solo for soprano). But between forty and fifty he composed five symphonies which he called symphonies and a sixth which he called a song but is a massively scored symphony (**Song of the Earth—Das Lied von der Erde**) and sketched out a seventh.

By lining up his creations in this way, we can see how the urge to create became more obsessive as he grew older. And more involved. The symphonies between forty and fifty are the symphonies of incessant thumpings of percussive instruments, at times to the point where it seems the roof will surely fall from the pounding vibrations, of funeral marches, of cow bells, of weird horn calls which summon, but what we can't know.

They are symphonies calling for vastly augmented orchestras and for instruments which are not standard for the symphony orchestra— the mandolin and guitar, for instance; and for great masses of singing voices, particularly women's voices. And hanging over these enormous outpourings is a strange, brooding quality tinged with black melancholy. There is a program for each. Some we know, some we don't. He was touchy and contradictory about his programs and even, at times, denied they existed. Yet it is known that he couldn't compose without a program. But those we know are of little help in understanding the music. They are couched in the cloudy thoughts which Germans of his time called "mysticism."

Mahlerites point to his "technical innovations" and suggest that they advanced the techniques of composition. Indeed, Arnold Schönberg, who was preparing a genuine musical revolution at the time, always spoke warmly of Mahler the composer. But he was under personal obligations to Mahler the man, and if Mahler's "technical innovations" were that rather than personal eccentricities they ended with Mahler and adorn only his private world.

His dictatorship in Vienna lasted ten years. To get it, he accepted baptism and became a Roman Catholic. His musical sponsors were many and included Brahms. His artistic reforms also were many and were driven through with ruthless frenzy. He lifted the opera to the heights and filled the backstage quarters with wounded sensibilities and seething resentments. At the same time he was stirring up troubles for himself as conductor of the Vienna Philharmonic. For example, what are musicians likely to think of a conductor who reorchestrates one of Mozart's last symphonies and adds to Beethoven's **Pastorale** drum effects which never occurred to Beethoven?

He had had occasional "affairs," with women older than he. At the age of forty-two he was attracted to Alma Maria Schindler, who was much younger than he, and she to him. There was a frenzied courtship and they were married within months. This Marie, the wife, was the daughter of a famous Viennese painter. In German, *mahler* means painter. Within three years they became parents of two daughters. The elder died at the age of four. When she was a baby—a flourishing, healthy baby—he had composed his very morbid song cycle, **Songs on the Death of Children—Kindertotenlieder,** and the distraught mother said he had tempted fate and this was fate's answer. This was typical of both their outlooks on life.

Since youth Mahler had been periodically ill—with illnesses which modern medical science classifies as psychosomatic, that is, due in some part to the influences of mind over body. He always felt he had a weak heart. His mother complained always of a weak heart. These illnesses were becoming more exasperating as his other troubles intensified.

The members of the Philharmonic voted to replace him as conductor. They had had enough. At the opera, dissensions finally were so out of hand he had to resign. He posted a letter of farewell to the company on the backstage bulletin board. Hardly had he walked away before someone ripped it off, tore it into shreds, and flung the shreds on the floor.

He was in much demand elsewhere, of course, and chose to accept an offer to conduct at the Metropolitan Opera in New York. But he was feeling ill much of the time and his once-abundant energy no longer was what it had been. But he was principal conductor of the New York Philharmonic for two seasons (at $30,000 per season!) and the old pattern reappeared—dissension, then resignation.

His last concert was on February 21, 1911. He was physically ill, of a blood infection. He and Alma Maria returned to Europe. Day by day he became weaker and got so weak he lacked the strength to hold even a book. By May they were back in Vienna and on May 18 he died, not yet fifty-one years old. His last words—words of delirium —were: "Mozart. Mozart."

38

Richard Strauss

As long as much of the musical world quivered with shock and horror at the things Richard Strauss did with music, his creative genius flourished. But when most of that world stopped being shocked and called him "the greatest living composer," his creative genius wilted and died.

This could have been coincidence, of course. All we know for sure is that he spent the last thirty-eight years of his long life striving unsuccessfully to regain the summit he had reached with **Der Rosenkavalier**, the finest opera composed so far in our century.

Richard Strauss placed a very high value on his artistic enemies. They made a hero of him—in his own mind. To endure them all with smiling equanimity ennobled him, in his opinion. But while his enemies were diminishing, until finally the remaining few were like frantic and empty bursts of wind, he felt a spiritual closeness to Don Quixote, who tilted not with men but with windmills.

This Strauss, who was no relation of the other Strauss, the Waltz King of Vienna, was the son of a horn player and a brewer's daughter, born in Munich, June 11, 1864. But his father, Franz, was no ordinary horn player. He was first horn in the Munich Court Opera for some fifty years, a master who was praised by Wagner, whom he despised. Nor was his mother, Josephine, the daughter of any ordinary brewer. She was a Pschorr, and Pschorrbrau has contributed no little to the high reputation of Bavarian beer. Richard Strauss was highborn then, to both position and wealth.

His father was short-tempered and temperamental, even beyond the accepted limits for artists. "Strauss," said Wagner, "is really an unbearable fellow." In music, he was against anything suggesting change. In the household, he was the presiding tyrant. Luckily, his wife, meek and sweet, never opposed him. In the traditional way of German parents, they expected a great deal of their son, especially in industry and deportment.

He was an incredibly industrious child and perfect in behavior. At four, he was playing the piano; at six, he was composing and playing the violin. By the time he was sixteen, his works were being performed by professionals. While he was absorbing the exacting education of German schools, he was absorbing musical theory, harmony, counterpoint, and orchestration with Germanic thoroughness. At twenty-one, he was established as a conductor as well as a composer—and was locally famous.

Everything in him and everything he touched were permeated with his passion for neatness and order. Six feet three inches tall, very slender and straight, he regulated himself with stern military-like discipline, whether for work or for play. A beer drinker, he drank the allotted amount and not one drop more. A cardplayer, he played an allotted number of hands, no more and no less.

From this personal position of strength, he was tolerant and loving, if somewhat condescending. To himself, there was only one important person in the world, and he was that person. Even as a child, he had been like that.

We should sympathize with his father. No tyrant was ever more frustrated. Storming and ranting against Wagner, Liszt, Berlioz, and the other innovators, he lived to see his son become a Wagnerite and an innovator. His loyalty always remained strong, however, although he was constantly shaken. He remarked of one of the son's innovations, the opera **Salome**, now considered a masterpiece: "My God! My God! This nervous music! It is as though beetles were crawling around inside your clothes!"

This "nervous music" began with the tone poem **Aus Italien.** Compared to what was to come later, it was very mildly original; but the audience at the first performance in Munich in March, 1887, broke out into boos. Old Strauss rushed to his son, intending to console and comfort.

But the young man couldn't have been happier. Those boos had delighted him. He wrote his uncle: "There was general bewilderment and rage because I'm beginning to go my own way now, creating my own forms and giving lazy people headaches. . . . The lively applause was joined with a fair amount of booing which, of course, pleased me greatly. . . . I'm on the road that I want to take and perfectly aware there was never a great artist who wasn't reckoned crazy by thousands of his fellow men."

Strauss was beginning to use music to tell a story, an idea then hateful to musical people. But even more offensive to traditionalists was that he harmonized as he pleased. To achieve a particular effect, a dissonance or even a wind machine was more useful to him than a conventional modulation or a violin. When you keep in mind that he had the brasses bleating like sheep, you can imagine how he must have made scalps creep.

Aus Italien was followed by the tone poems Don Juan, Macbeth, Death and Transfiguration, Till Eulenspiegel's Merry Pranks, Also Sprach Zarathustra, Don Quixote, Ein Heldenleben (A Hero's Life), and Sinfonia Domestica. Most of them are now played and listened to quite calmly, like the masterworks of any other musical genius. (In his old age, Strauss mourned that he began as a revolutionist and ended as "a classic.") But in the last decade of the past century and the first decade of this one, when they were fresh and new, these pieces had the power to rob some people of their reason. The composer was treated to more than boos and hisses—he was denounced as a criminal is denounced, in language that present-day writers would hesitate to use.

Strauss thrived on this treatment. Each new tone poem was more sensational than its predecessor, with effects increasingly more weird (by the standards then). But it is interesting that this violent defiance began to taper off with Don Quixote (even though this introduced the wind machine). Strauss' genius for portraying human character musically is never more manifest than here—the Don is pathetic because he is futile. You have to wonder if the Don was not Strauss himself—in Strauss' mind—especially since this work was followed by A Hero's Life in which Strauss is, most definitely, the hero.

The insight A Hero's Life gives into its creator is quite startling. Part one tells us how very noble, how very courageous, and how very great the hero is. In part two, we learn his enemies—"antagonists" they're called in the program notes—are mean, small, eaten away by envy of the hero. Next, we're told how the hero's "helpmate" scorned him at first—until she realized what a stupendous hero he was; then she became sweetly submissive. Now, the hero meets his antagonists on "the battlefield," and for a while all is clangor and strife although we hear the helpmate cheering the hero on. The antagonists are routed, the hero is triumphant. Following this is a section called "the hero's mission of peace," and we hear the hero's soul grow in superhuman nobility as his works increase. Those works are quoted—the works of Richard Strauss. Finally, there is "the hero's escape from the world" in which he contemplates a life crowded with achievements. The world scorns him still, but he is philosophical, and so his soul departs and A Hero's Life ends with impressively heroic funeral music.

It hardly seems necessary to look elsewhere for an idea of how his creative imagination worked and what it used for fuel. But very great difficulties were in the making for that imagination for one simple reason—the antagonism that so stimulated it was diminishing. The world was acclaiming Richard Strauss. More than ten years had passed since **Aus Italien,** and all varieties of eminent persons considered him the greatest living composer. As the result, perhaps, the next tone poem, **Sinfonia Domestica,** was the last and the weakest. It depicted such things as spats between the composer and his helpmate, and you hear their baby in his bath, replete with happy gurgles and splashing.

It was first performed in New York in March, 1904, the composer conducting. He was on one of his enormously successful tours—admirers by the thousands everywhere wanted to look at him.

But he wasn't through with his efforts to be a scorned and battling hero. He had turned to opera à la Wagner. In this year, 1904, he was preparing one of the mightiest shockers in the history of music—his opera **Salome,** based on Oscar Wilde's drama. Everyone must be acquainted with its insane and criminal female by now. Enough to say Strauss omitted no sensuous or bloody detail. Rather he capitalized and underscored.

Beginning with its first performance in Dresden in December, 1905, it scandalized the world, and the furious denunciations of the composer were many and bitter. The horrified directors of New York's Metropolitan Opera forced the artistic management to withdraw it after only one performance. But it so happens **Salome** is a work of genius. Strauss himself said, "A great artist is instinctively recognized by the great public as a natural genius." And **Salome** acquired supporters quite as rapidly as it acquired antagonists. The "great public" sided with the supporters by filling the opera houses where it was performed. Today it is a part of the common repertoire and considered no more shocking than **Rigoletto.**

With **Elektra,** his next opera, Strauss tried to out-Salome **Salome.** Based on the classical Greek tragedy, it tells how Elektra aids and abets her brother, Orestes, in murdering their mother. The motive: Mother had aided and abetted a lover in murdering her husband, their father. **Elektra** was first performed in Dresden in January, 1909; but after **Salome,** it shocked very few people. The composer's remaining antagonists made very hollow sounds because now they were without followings. Incidentally, as opera, **Elektra** is no great shakes.

After **Elektra,** Strauss reversed himself completely. His next opera was comic. There were no insane, depraved people in it, but only very human people—some noble, some base, all recognizable as not too different from the people all of us are. This was **Der Rosenkavalier,** his masterpiece, which was first performed in Dresden in January, 1911. That was the year of his forty-seventh birthday. He didn't know it then—perhaps he never knew it—but he was through as a creative genius.

Since the age of twenty he had been continuously employed as an orchestra conductor. Working his way up through the provincial German cities, he had arrived, by 1908, in the top post as director of the Berlin Royal Opera under the patronage of the kaiser. During all the years he was composing tone poems and opera, it had been part of his routine to rehearse an orchestra four to six hours during the day and give a performance in the evening. During off seasons and any holidays, he usually was touring somewhere as a guest conductor.

Meanwhile, he had acquired his "helpmate." She was Pauline de Ahna, a prima donna who was the heroine in his first and now all-but-forgotten opera **Guntram**. She was the daughter of a general, and to that can be added, most accurately, every inch of her. Her manner was one of command.

Because Strauss parodied her as a scolding wife in another of his inconsequential operas, **Intermezzo**, and in **Sinfonia Domestica** and because he now and then used her as an excuse for not doing what he didn't want to do anyway, a legend has grown up of the domineering wife and the henpecked husband. In truth, they were counterparts of each other. Theirs was a shared passion for management and drill sergeant's efficiency.

She was associate manager of Richard Strauss, since he was his own manager, dealing with the impresarios and concert managers himself and making them squeal with anguish over the fees he demanded for performance rights and for his personal appearances. She dealt with the personal side of their joint enterprise—Richard Strauss. His meals were scientifically put together to keep him lean and strong and energetic. The household sanitation exceeded that of first-class hospitals because germs caused sickness and sickness contaminated efficiency. She assigned one of the maidservants to kneel before every caller and wipe off his shoes before he had advanced more than a few feet beyond the threshold. That was the way germs were brought in.

She also was policewoman over her husband's daily schedule. A conferee who overstayed his allotted time was interrupted by Frau Pauline. If her husband showed any signs of lingering too long with dinner guests, she said, "Richard! Get to your composing!" All this with the utmost courtesy, of course, but also with the utmost firmness. The iron wills of the Strauss household, both male and female, were always cloaked with "civilized" amiability and a proper regard for the social amenities. Culture reigned. The leading painters, writers, and musicians were frequent guests. But they were received, entertained, and dismissed on an unvarying schedule.

Richard Strauss remained as director of the Berlin Royal Opera during all of World War I. In 1919, he became director of the Vienna State Opera and remained there until 1924, when he retired from conducting to devote himself to composing.

It is pointless to go over the compositions of the period. All are informed by technical mastery and devoid of the sparks which lift the creations of geniuses above those of craftsmen. The years passed; these compositions piled up; the Strausses grew older and older together, living their disciplined lives in austere luxury, at times in a castle in Vienna but mainly on their estate in the Bavarian Alps.

When the Nazis came to power, he accepted the high-sounding position they gave him, as president of the Reichmusikkammer, the organization that directed all musical activity in the Reich. Their motivation was clear: He was the greatest living German in the field of music. His acceptance disappointed many of his admirers. But he was a son of Imperial Germany and had no sympathy whatever with democracy as a political doctrine. On the other hand, his only child, Dr. Franz Strauss, had married a Jew and the librettists for most of his operas were Jews.

His open friendliness with the Nazis didn't last long. He resigned the post and retired to his estate, staying there throughout World War II until American occupation troops arrived. Among them were admirers of his music, and they helped him slip into Switzerland, where he lived in exile until cleared of the charge of having been a Nazi.

A genial old gentleman, he was, by that time, devoted mainly to the German card game skat, of which he was a superb master. Frau Pauline disapproved, but in matters which he regarded as important he paid no attention to her. He was stooped, now. What hair he had left was snow-white. But there was energy and interest in the clear blue eyes, shining like saucers in the fair old face. He had his appendix out when he was eighty-one. Otherwise, he was never ill seriously until his last illness, brought about by age. He died on September 8, 1949, eighty-five years old. Frau Pauline died eight months later, on May 13, 1950. She was eighty-seven.

39

Sibelius

JEAN SIBELIUS was the hermit composer. For more than fifty years
he lived in a forest near Järvenpää, about twenty miles from Helsinki, the capital of Finland. He had a wife for all those years, to be
sure, and, as they arrived, five daughters. In the fullness of his more
than ninety years, he had more than thirty grandchildren and great-
grandchildren. Nevertheless, he was and had been always a solitary.

A light often shone throughout the night in the study window
of his log house. While everyone else slept, the master was
pursuing his lonely questing within himself. When day came, he
often disappeared into the forest. No one could have shunned the
world more than he did, yet, at the same time, labored more assidu-
ously to bring the world to his doorstep.

Probably no person famous for so long ever succeeded in hiding
his essential self so thoroughly. For more than fifty years admirers of
all sorts made the pilgrimage to his remote retreat. They saw him,
all right; they talked with him. Some were asked to stay for dinner. He
chatted with them, endeavoring to be amiable. But there was an in-
visible barrier no one could cross. Sibelius was aware of this. Pointing
to himself, he cried, "Sphinx!"

All visitors remarked on his withdrawal. One wrote that he "sensed
a double personality. No host could have been more responsive, attentive, and charming, yet there was an aloofness of the spirit, as of a
cloistered monk, discussing politely for a few minutes certain necessary mundane matters, who would be glad to get back to his normal
life of prayer and contemplation."

Two things Sibelius never discussed—Sibelius and Sibelius' music.
The late Olin Downes, one of the world's best-known music critics,
once endeavored to probe into the composer's creative processes.
Downes had been a stanch friend and discerning interpreter of
Sibelius the artist. Sibelius the man, in gratitude if for no other reason,
wanted to reveal himself.

"He recognized my need, he wanted to do something for a friend, and he was the picture of misery," Downes wrote. "He mumbled incoherent words, his features worked as though he were in a nightmare, indistinct guttural exclamations struggled to come forth, until finally he shook his head and turned to me in sheer desperation. 'Ich kann nicht,' he exploded in German, and sighed deeply. He just couldn't."

This is the man who was the greatest symphonist our century has so far produced. Inarticulate though he was with words, in his seven symphonies he arranged and expressed supercharged emotions with precise orderliness. We hear a pervading melancholy and sometimes a wistful longing. But we also hear struggle and strife. Drama exists on almost every page. The culminations of his works usually are compounded of majesty and grandeur.

He was born in Hämeenlinna (Tavastehus), Finland, on December 8, 1865. His ancestry was Swedish and Finnish; his forebears were mainly of the professional class. His father, a physician, died before Sibelius was three years old. Thereafter, he lived in a principally feminine world: first, a world made up of a doting mother, doting grandmothers, doting aunts; then, a world peopled by a meek, submissive wife and five daughters—and located in a forest.

He was formally named Johan Julius Christian Sibelius and, as a boy, was called Janne, the Swedish way of saying Johnny. At that time, Finns of the educated classes often took the French form of their first names. When he became a man, he called himself Jean. An uncle who had called himself Jean had had a supply of visiting cards printed just before he died. By becoming Jean, the nephew was able to use those cards. Frugality was characteristic of the man.

The boy was given to rapidly shifting moods. One moment he would be bubbling, his hearty laughter ringing out for no compelling reason. Then he would be glum, and nothing cheered him. No one knew why—that was just Janne. But everyone knew he lived, at least part of the time, in a world of fantasy. He saw witches, goblins, and fairies in the forest and sometimes would scare himself out of his wits.

He was strikingly fond of what is called nature as though man and men, as well as sunsets and landscapes, weren't nature. His pleasure was wandering in the forest and meadows, with a butterfly net. For boyish games he cared not a whit, according to some of his schoolmates who often found him utterly engrossed with a magnificent sky and a grand horizon. Yet, he was a leader among them. They loved his jokes and gaiety—when he was in humorous mood; his strength and strangeness gave him prestige. Schoolwork didn't interest him at all; so he dreamed away the classroom hours. The teacher often said,

"Sibelius is in another world again."

Meanwhile, he was interested in music but certainly not on the child-prodigy level. There were amateur pianists among his female relatives, and he learned from them. Also, he composed a little bit. If he hadn't turned out to be a musical genius, that probably would have been forgotten.

By his own statement, music did not really "take hold" of him until he was fifteen. And then his idea was not to compose but to become a violin virtuoso. When he wandered into the forest he took his violin with him. "I gave the birds endless concerts," he said years later. "When sailing, I often stood with my violin in the bow of the boat and improvised to the sea." His schoolwork, always poor, became poorer.

The violin continued to make it poor when he entered the university at Helsinki, with the idea of becoming a lawyer. He thought his grandmothers, especially his mother's mother, wouldn't approve of him becoming a professional musician. But, according to his own recollections, he had the bow in his hand practically from dawn until dusk every day. He paid scant attention to his other studies, and it was his relatives who finally told him he'd better give up pretending to be a law student and devote himself entirely to music.

A friend of this period recalled: "He always gave the impression of having suddenly dropped from a distant planet or of having made his entry into this world in some other impossible way."

He was well into his twenties when he buckled down to learning the composer's tools. By now, he was beginning to realize he could never become one of the finest violin players in all the world. He hadn't started learning soon enough, he decided. But he could become one of the finest composers. He was well aware that he had greatness in him; the question was only one of direction.

He learned quickly and thoroughly. After a year of study in Berlin and another in Vienna, he became, at twenty-six, a teacher of theory in both the music and orchestral schools in Helsinki. At this time, too, 1892, Finns realized their race had produced a musical genius, when **Kullervo** and **En Saga**, both extended poems for orchestra, were played in Helsinki. At that time Finland was striving to shake off Russian bonds and assert itself as an independent nation. **Kullervo** expressed the Finnish mythology about the ancient lineage and integrity of the Finns as a people. **En Saga** did no less, although the reference was not as clear. Together, the two pieces made their composer the musical herald of Finnish nationalism.

In this year Sibelius married Aino Järnefelt, daughter of a lieutenant general who also was a fervent Finnish patriot; and here began a record of self-effacement to challenge that of the master himself. The world hardly knew the man who composed some of its best-loved music; it knew his wife not at all. But the world can surmise her supreme importance to him from just one incident. When all Finland celebrated the seventieth birthday of this "uncrowned king of Finland," he was inveigled to a banquet and even into making a speech. He stood up. His facial muscles worked feverishly. He was stricken dumb. His old wife had stood, apparently to aid him. In this instant of overwhelming distress, he whirled and held her in a long, long embrace.

But back in 1892 when they were young, he was struggling against the desire to retreat into the forest. His friends of that time re- membered the intensity with which he flung himself into social living —how he tried to enjoy social gatherings, how he toyed with the traditional Bohemianism of the artistic class. This was the time when the legend of his conviviality began—the fable that Sibelius, when partying, was inexhaustible. But clearly he didn't like his whirl at the gay, careless life. He couldn't yet retreat into the forest, however. He had his career to make, a livelihood to earn, as his daughters were beginning to be born.

During this period music flowed from him without seeming effort, largely music which celebrated the beauties and strengths of Fin- land. He was becoming a symbol of Finnish patriotism worth many battalions in the struggle against the Russian tyranny. From our own feelings, we, as Americans, cannot know that his music stands for Finland. All we can know is that Finns say it does and most stirringly in **Finlandia.** In 1897 the Finnish government recognized this and awarded him a pension, but it was too small to permit him to give up his income from teaching.

In 1900 his world fame began. The Helsinki Philharmonic Society made a European tour, with Sibelius as assistant conductor, and played his music, including his **First Symphony.** Now he was able to give up his two teaching posts. But he still had to keep his private pupils and so had to spend his winters in Helsinki. (Summers were spent in forests or at lakes or the seashore.) And he was undergoing a personal crisis which took a number of forms. One was the growing conviction that his ears were so badly infected he was going to end in total deafness, like Beethoven. Another was a feeling that he was not understood in the artistic circles he frequented. There was also the idea that he was too social—he accepted so many invitations that parties were interfering with his work. The upshot of it all was, when increasing royalties from his music, including the **Second Symphony,** plus his pension, permitted, he took himself and his family into the forest. This was in 1904.

There, he and his wife remained, growing prodigiously old together. Time stood still in its sameness in the magnificent spruce forest near a lake. World War I took place, and the postwar disorders which established Finland as an independent nation. The Sibeliuses hardly knew anything of what had happened. World War II disturbed the serene peace of nature only when bombing planes now and then came close and when Finland made new requirements of its most famous son, projecting him into the field of international relations or piling more honors on his apparently unwilling shoulders.

His excursions from the forest into the world outside were few and always dictated by the requirement of health or career. In 1908 he had a throat ailment, and he went to specialists in Berlin. He also visited Berlin to conduct his works. He went to Paris to receive the Legion of Honor award. He made several visits to England, beginning in 1908. He made his only visit to the United States in 1914, and was "astonished" by the large numbers and enthusiasm of his American admirers. He made a few personal appearances, conducted several times, received an honorary degree from Yale University, and as quickly as he properly could, hastened back to his forest home.

Between 1904 and 1929 he composed and so he was as much at peace with himself as his surroundings were peaceful. There was no great volume of creations when the number of years is taken into account. Five symphonies were composed, as well as the symphonic poem **Tapiola**; also a considerable number of small pieces for voice, piano, and violin, which have never been accepted as the authentic work of genius. After 1929 he produced nothing of any importance.

Sibelius lived long enough to be able to sense the verdict of posterity concerning his work. For example, the **Four Legends for Orchestra**, based on Finnish mythology and including **Lemminkäinen and the Maidens, Lemminkäinen in Tuonela, The Swan of Tuonela,** and **The Return of Lemminkäinen,** is as fresh today as when first performed—almost sixty years ago, when its creator was thirty and had not yet retired to the forest. You can wonder if Sibelius ever doubted the wisdom of his withdrawal from the world.

He thought a great deal about it, we can be sure. Through all the years he carefullly read every word written about him that he could get his hands on. After the advent of radio, he kept three sets in his log house (which had grown more spacious and more comfortable as his income increased), and whenever there was a broadcast performance of Sibelius, Sibelius tried to tune it in.

The orchestra leaders of the world he praised indiscriminately—no one can say he preferred one interpreter to another. But, as he remarked to one of his visitors, "It is better to be played badly or wrongly than not to be played at all."

His health was excellent. With the passing years, his head became balder and balder, until there was not a hair on it, and his neck seemed to become thicker, although this probably was due to the illusion created by heavier and heavier shoulders and chest. During his last twenty-five years, his face was as hard-looking as granite, from which stared quizzical and innocent blue eyes.

He still joked and evaded in the presence of admirers. One asked him who was the greatest musician of all time, and he replied: the unknown composer of ancient Egypt because he had to compose for an orchestra of two hundred harps.

Jussi Snellman, one of his sons-in-law, reported: "But beneath all his good-fellowship and joviality, there is a distinct sense of aloof dignity. In many respects, most visitors make a futile journey to Ainola [his forest home] although they seldom realize it until they have departed. They find that they have been superbly entertained, yet in some mysterious manner, the things they have sought to find have been tactfully but rigorously guarded from them. The inquisitive and curious especially find themselves foiled by the enigma that is the real Sibelius."

The **Fourth** and **Fifth Symphonies** can be mentioned without discomfort in the same breath with the symphonies of Beethoven. But the **Second Symphony** is the most accessible of the seven—it requires no effort of the listener. The **Third** and **Sixth** are difficult. The **First** is bright and absorbing. The **Seventh** is the lesser.

40

Rachmaninoff

SERGEI RACHMANINOFF was six feet three inches tall and as straight as he was lean. His face was a mask of sternness overlaying sadness and appeared to have been carved from granite. He looked so much like a soldier in his full-dress suit that many people called him "the General." He seemed hard enough, disciplined enough, unbending enough to be one.

You couldn't know that deep inside himself "the General" was like quavering jelly. He had indicted himself on a charge of criminal cowardice, and in the judgment of his private self he was guilty. He confessed, "I am afraid of everything: mice, rats, beetles, bulls, burglars. . . . I am frightened even during the day, when I am alone."

As with many another coward, cowardice made a courageous man of him. Fear rode Rachmaninoff's shoulders, a private devil, through all his years. When you know that, you can see that his years represent an awesome monument to his human greatness. This man lifted himself, by raw will, into the ranks of musical geniuses.

It becomes all the more remarkable when you realize that included —especially included—in "everything" he feared was the composing of music. As a young man, he fled in wild panic from the hall where his first symphony was being played for the first time and huddled, trembling, on a fire escape, thinking: My God! What have I done!

He played the piano for Americans for twenty-five years, traveling up and down the United States, year after year, from early October until April. His name became as familiar as those of congressmen and baseball players. He has been dead only since 1943 and many of us who saw him remember him well—as a man, even more than as an artist, since we won't easily forget his sad and stern face.

He was born on a rich estate not far from Novgorod, Russia, on April 2, 1873. It was one of the five estates which had been the dowry of his mother, Lubov, when she married his father, Vassily, a high-living officer of the czar's army. Sergei was the third of their

237

six children. By the time Sergei was nine, Vassily had run through his wife's money. All the estates had been sold; the family was ruined, and Vassily abandoned it forthwith.

But he was more a weakling than a villain. He was a charming empty-head who devoted himself to cardplaying, drinking, and chasing women; and he loved children, extravagantly. His wife was an embittered woman. It was her way to set tasks for her children to fulfill. "There's a time for everything," she told little Sergei, trying to break him in early to self-discipline. While Vassily was around, no discipline was possible. He was so tenderhearted that a trace of a tear in a child's eye melted him. After Vassily departed, his wife's mother took over the indulging of the children, especially Sergei. He was the apple of Grandmother's eye.

He was a bad little boy, embezzling pennies from his grandmother, playing hooky and haunting the skating rinks, stealing rides on the tramcars like a street urchin, falsifying his report cards, and taking advantage of the ignorance of Grandmother and her guests by playing anything on the piano that came into his head, then saying it was a work of Mozart or Chopin.

His piano playing was remarkable; it had got him a scholarship in the St. Petersburg Conservatory when he was only nine. Yet he wasn't interested in piano playing, really. The Conservatory teachers couldn't do much better toward making him attentive than his mother, who'd been his first teacher. So she looked around for a tough master for him. The choice was Nicolai Zverev, one of the professors of piano in the Moscow Conservatory. A bachelor, he lived in elegant splendor with his old-maid sister and gave the three most talented boys in his classes the privilege of living with them at his expense.

The parents and other relatives of these boys were required to give up just about all rights to them; the lads were not even allowed to go home for vacations. Zverev and his sister regulated every minute of their waking hours, required them to practice the piano three hours a day (except Sundays), and Zverev personally introduced them to the ways of the world and into "the art of living." Sergei was the property of this drill sergeant from the time he was twelve until he was sixteen.

During those four years he stopped being a spoiled and undisciplined boy—he stopped defeating his own musical gifts. The boy became the forerunner of the rigidly self-disciplined concert pianist. We don't know what changed in him during those four years or what came into his being to energize him. We do know that, as a seeming matter of desperation, he wanted to be graduated from the

Moscow Conservatory and from Zverev as quickly as possible.

Zverev "graduated" him abruptly—by renouncing him and turning him over to Vassily's sister, Madam Satin, a Moscow society woman whose home Zverev had permitted the boy to visit only twice in four years. Zverev gave no explanation. In later years, Sergei offered a lame one.

It must have been a matter of emotion. Three years after the break, when Sergei was graduated from the Conservatory—a year ahead of his class and with the gold medal that was the highest award the school could bestow on a graduate—Zverev broke down and wept, took the watch from his pocket, and pressed it upon his protégé. All his life Rachmaninoff treasured that watch.

His mother sent word for him to rejoin her in St. Petersburg. He wouldn't heed her. She had given him up to Zverev; now he gave her up with a vengeance. In his published letters and papers, she is rarely mentioned and then only in passing. Instead of returning to her, he remained with the Satins, who had two daughters a little younger than he—his first cousins, Natalie and Sophia. They were very sympathetic.

Cheerfulness never was a part of his nature, but at this time he seemed carefree, at least. His talents were impressive, as everyone around him knew—even Tchaikovsky had come to know and admire them. As part of his academic trials for his diploma, the youth composed a short opera, **Aleko**, in less than two weeks, which is interesting because of what was to happen to his creativeness later.

Aleko was produced in St. Petersburg the year after his graduation, when he was twenty, and was heralded as a work of great promise. Tchaikovsky seemed about to fall out of his box in leaning out to applaud the more enthusiastically.

He had attended the rehearsal. As the orchestra played, he whispered to the youthful composer: "Do you like that tempo?" Rachmaninoff said he didn't but he was afraid to complain. The world-famous Tchaikovsky wasn't. He said to the conductor: "Mr. Rachmaninoff and I think the tempo here might be taken a little more quickly."

You can see how all this must have set up the young man. He was composing prolifically—choruses, songs, pieces for large orchestra, short pieces for piano, and a piano concerto, and also the **Prelude in C-sharp Minor** which was to become so popular and so hackneyed that its creator came to be known to the flippant as "Mr. C-sharp Minor."

Then came disaster, his first symphony. He had no trouble composing it. It seemed to please him right up to the rehearsals for its first performance in St. Petersburg in March, 1897, shortly before his twenty-fourth birthday. But when the hall was filled with an audience and the conductor lifted his baton and the first chords sounded, the composer simply couldn't endure it. He fled to the fire escape.

Just what snapped inside Rachmaninoff—he himself said something had "snapped"—no one knows to this day, since Rachmaninoff never found out. He took to drink, he tried to teach piano in a girls' school, he dabbled with conducting, he now and then undertook a few engagements as pianist. All the while, his face was long, his eyes were moist, his self-created gloom was like a fog. Through it all, no one could have been more loving and reassuring than his cousins, Natalie and Sophia.

The girls finally got him to Dr. Nicolai Dahl. Daily, for months, the doctor put him into a hypnotic trance in a darkened room and then said to him, over and over: "You will start working on your new concerto. . . . You will work with great ease. . . . the concerto will be excellent."

This went on through the first months of 1900. Before the year was out, Rachmaninoff had the concerto, his second, almost completed. In fact, it was excellent. He dedicated it to Dr. Dahl, who had not changed him fundamentally but had taught him to live, if uneasily, with his fears and self-doubts.

In April, 1902, he married Natalie. Sophia, who had been close to him, too, remained close the rest of his years. He was to say he had three doctors: Dr. Dahl, his wife, and his wife's sister. It sounds unkind. He didn't mean it that way. He was belittling himself, which he always was doing. He loved the sisters dearly, and he was a most devoted husband to one of them.

He also was devoted to his inner self, the walled-in person that he was. Now he complained of being old, although he was barely thirty. He paid close attention to minor illnesses—his own and those of his wife and of his daughters as they were born. Death became an obsession. It was as though death was a terrifying witch from whom he always had to run.

He seemed to have a constant urge to run, to get away—from people, from situations. Yet he had the opposite urge—to place himself before people and into stressful situations. As a leading conductor in Moscow, during the early years of this century, he fled abroad or to some remote part of Russia whenever the pressure of his public grew too intense or the competition with other conductors bore down heavily. But he'd soon be showing himself to people again—if not as a conductor, then as a pianist.

If it hadn't been for a college girl, we would still be puzzling over this self-tormented man. Her name was Marietta Shaginian, and she was twenty-four years old in 1912. Rachmaninoff was thirty-nine. She was the daughter of a Moscow University professor and later became renowned in Russia as a writer.

In 1912 she was both entranced by his pianistic art and deeply distressed by his tragic aloofness and the sadness of his face. So she wrote him a fan letter and signed it "Re," for the musical note which comes after *do*. Her intuition must have guided her pen, since she touched him enough for him to answer to the "blind" address she had given him.

They corresponded for almost a year. Then they met and were friends until 1917, when he left Russia for good, after the revolution. She respected his confidences until after his death and then published fourteen of his letters to her. They were extraordinarily revealing, as a few excerpts will show.

"It was the truth, and not a lie, when someone told you that I am a most ordinary and uninteresting man."

Re was very indignant at a critic who'd called him "the troubadour of horror and tragedy." Rachmaninoff wrote her:

Deep inside me, to be honest about it, I rather prefer to believe and to listen to my heart, because there is no critic in the world who is more doubtful about me than myself.

I have two daughters, eight and four years old. Their names are Irina and Tatiana, or Bob and Tassinka. They are two disobedient, badly brought up, but charming and very interesting girls. I love them terribly. They are the dearest and brightest things in my life.

Besides my children, music and flowers, I also love you, dear Re, and your letters. I love you because you are clever, interesting, and you do not go to extremes. (This is one of the most important conditions for anyone to be attractive to me.) And I love your letters because I find in them your faith, love, and hope in me—the balm with which I cure my wounds.

Teach me to have faith in myself, dear Re, perhaps just half as much as you have in me. If I ever had faith in myself, that was a long time ago.

His "doctors," he wrote, referring to Dr. Dahl, his wife, and his wife's sister, "taught me only two things: to be brave and to have faith. Sometimes I succeeded in doing it. But my sickness sits in me firmly and with the years has developed even deeper. It will be understandable if, eventually, I decide to give up composing and become either a pianist, a conductor, or a country squire."

In 1918 he did all but give up composing. From that year on, we can count his compositions on our fingers, and have fingers left over— the **Third Symphony, Symphonic Dances, Fourth Piano Concerto, Rhapsody on a Theme of Paganini** (which is another piano concerto), an inconsequential set of **Variations on a Theme of Corelli,** and **Three Russian Songs.** These were the only output of a first-rate composer in twenty-five years! By contrast, before 1918 he had composed 62 pieces for piano solo, 69 songs, 3 operas, the early symphonies and concertos, and a considerable miscellany.

After 1918, his story is almost entirely that of a terribly gloomy pianist playing the piano as though his very life depended upon it. He played it in public—seasons of sixty and more concerts were the rule—and he played it privately. He seemed always to be at the piano, conversed with his family and his very few intimates from the piano, dictated letters while playing. Winters, he was before the public practically daily; summers, he was hidden with his family in some country retreat.

I once had a journalistic interview with him. He never saw reporters if he could avoid them. I intruded myself, as reporters do. He stared at me with his stern face, but I saw he was more scared than I was. Anyway, the ice had to be broken, if it could be.

"Why do you look so sad?" I asked, to startle him.

He lowered his eyes; his face grew infinitely sadder. "I am sad," he said.

He walked uneasily to the piano and began to play; and as he played, we talked, mainly about Beethoven. But obviously my English didn't mean too much to him, nor was his English too understandable to me—he never really mastered the language.

He was playing Beethoven's **Sonata Appassionata** or, rather, playing at it. He was taking phrases out here and putting them in there, he was reversing the order of things and toying with tempo. His playing seemed a nervous mannerism.

"Must you play *that* way?" I asked.

That he understood. Instantly the playing became ordered and concentrated upon the gathering and intensifying reverie of the second movement. This reverie breaks into a sunburst of serenity, and when it did, under his fingers, it hit me so emotionally that I gasped. He turned his head and looked at me with warm and loving eyes, and a smile shattered the sad mask of his face. Thus, I am one of the few persons, aside from his intimates, who saw Rachmaninoff smile.

In New Orleans in February of 1943, illness interrupted his last concert tour. He hastened to his home in Beverly Hills, California, a very sick man. There he died on March 28—five days before his seventieth birthday and five weeks after he became an American citizen.

As a pianist, Rachmaninoff was one of the most communicative artists of this century. You can't say that he was a great interpreter—

of Beethoven or Schumann or even of himself as a composer. But he conveyed, with an almost demoniac intensity, musical sensibilities and musical meanings which were rather personal, being his own.

As a composer, it is too soon for anyone to have a very definite opinion about his place. His compositions display his sense for melody and for rhythm. Structurally, they are conservative—he never carried anything to an extreme. There is nothing strikingly original in them, yet they bear his authentic personal stamp—they're "Rachmaninoff-esque." Rachmaninoff should also be approached through his songs, many of which are as moving as they are intimate.

41

Schönberg

ARNOLD SCHÖNBERG turned music upside down. Music's other revolutionists seem much less revolutionary when their deeds are compared to his. Beethoven, Berlioz, Wagner, Debussy and such radicals only expanded the existing means and realm of music, really. Schönberg provided the tools and blueprints with which any composer who has the will, the talent, and the nerve may be as original as he wishes to be.

His own nerve and will were absolute. We can't be sure yet about the extent of his creative talent. The passions and turmoils which enveloped him for some fifty years haven't subsided enough. At the most, he is the major prophet of the music of the future. At the least, he put a mark on musical art which it will be a very long time in losing.

Schönbergs are inevitable. For that reason they should be taken calmly although they never are. They should upset no one and, of course, do upset everyone. Look at Beethoven. When he came along with his driving need to be original, he was confronted by the perfections of Mozart and Haydn. He veered off from them and revealed byways and materials which a succession of original geniuses explored and exploited. Finally came Brahms and Wagner, who exhausted the last big possibilities.

You have to sympathize with the original geniuses who followed them. They were boxed, they couldn't veer. How to be original was anything but obvious. Some fused what existed with their personal substances and created private worlds. Others blended what existed in art with what existed in life and, because of consummate skills, got the same result. But these stratagems were wearing bare when the end-geniuses of the German musical romanticism which began with Beethoven came upon the scene.

Gustav Mahler, Richard Strauss, and Schönberg were only fourteen years apart in age, Mahler having been the oldest, Schönberg the youngest, and Strauss four years younger than Mahler. Mahler was a private world genius. Strauss was a shocker-thriller genius. Schönberg turned out to be a new musical planet genius.

He was born into a poor Jewish shopkeeping family in Vienna on September 13, 1874. His family ramifications and antecedents and his childhood circumstances are largely unknown because he would never talk about them. About all we know for sure is that he was eight when he first went to school and that when he was sixteen the death of his father ended his formal education.

Now, let's switch to Alexander von Zemlinsky. He was twenty-two, a finished, Conservatory-trained musician and scion of the upper class, when he was asked by a friend to receive a twenty-year-old amateur who was dirt-poor yet wanted a professional to criticize some compositions of his. The bored but amiable technician became very much interested as he looked through the manuscripts. They were remarkable for depth of technical sureness and understanding.

Zemlinsky asked Schönberg where he had gotten his "training." Schönberg said he was entirely self-educated, which Zemlinsky at first scarcely believed. He had had some rudimentary instruction in violin playing. Aside from that there had been no teachers, no urgings or even inspiring examples, no outside stimulation of any kind. There had been only what he always called "inner compulsion." Pushed along by it, he had absorbed a composer's techniques out of books and in solitary studies of the scores of the masters, and had taught himself to play competently on violin and cello. He still was somewhat shaky in counterpoint, he confided to Zemlinsky, who instantly and eagerly volunteered to teach him counterpoint, without fee.

Zemlinsky was attached to him for life, personally and professionally. Schönberg personally made that kind of friend; as a musician he attracted that kind of follower. It is well to realize right at the start that this archrevolutionist was at the same time an archconservative. He loved the established order of Bach, Beethoven, Mozart, and all the others with a pedantic zeal. He placed his revolution alongside it but apart from it.

He was a small man, with an alert, highly mobile face whose flesh, as he grew older, more and more resembled parchment. His characteristic attitude then and always was neutral. Rarely could anyone tell whether he was happy or unhappy. His protective armor was his mind, which also was a weapon for defense as well as offense. Never did Schönberg do anything, so far as we know, for which there weren't excellent and most persuasive reasons. He was a "let's-look-at-the-facts" man, a "let's-analyze" man.

When he was a youth and already losing his hair, he began his lifelong career as a music teacher by training groups of workingmen who enjoyed group singing and were willing to pay a little something to a "professor" who would show them how. Through Zemlinsky, he got such hack work as making piano arrangements of orchestral scores and orchestrating the piano scores of droves of Viennese operetta composers whose technical ignorance was monumental.

While living thus on the ragged edge, he was doing absolutely nothing that might be reasonably calculated to assure him of a future. Zemlinsky was busily composing the operas which gave him a transitory reputation. Schönberg was working as a "ghost" with the pretty and empty tunes which earned fame and fortune for their composers. With his melodic gifts, he could have done the same, with his left hand. But he was struggling to create a new music which couldn't possibly be popular that day or any day soon. From this we can appreciate the power of his "inner compulsion"—of his overwhelming need to be original, at whatever cost.

He was composing songs and chamber music—most notably, **Transfigured Night (Verklärte Nacht)**—which were going to be his points of departure from the old. In them you hear clearly the materials of his musical ancestors, particularly the most immediate, Wagner. In retrospect, there also are quite new elements of restless, urgent seeking. But when first performed in Vienna in the last years of the nineteenth century, they occasioned no notice outside the circle of musicians interested in the technical aspects of creation.

Schönberg was twenty-four and experiencing the distraction of love. It appears to have occurred to him rather suddenly that Zemlinsky's sister, Mathilde, had more attraction than that of being a musician who understood and sympathized musically. So they were married and were off to Berlin. Like Zemlinsky before him, Richard Strauss had recognized a potential genius and had prepared places for him there as a conductor and a teacher. But two years later they returned to Vienna. Mahler, the dictator of Viennese music, had formed an interest in Schönberg's.

We're not sure why unless Mahler had heard about the special music paper Schönberg had ordered—music paper which was twice the size of ordinary music paper, with twice the usual number of staves. Schönberg was planning to make a massive orchestration of his song cycle, **Gurre-Lieder.** That sort of thing appealed strongly to Mahler—he was using enormous orchestral and choral forces in his own symphonies. Mahler was a stanch supporter and a good friend but he didn't realize in the beginning that Schönberg now was ready to start turning music upside down.

What he was ready to do was to compose with increasing disregard for the harmonic values and structures which had been good enough for Beethoven and everyone else before and after. A particular sound either was consonant or dissonant only because of its relation to another sound or sounds—it could be either if these relationships so indicated but it couldn't be both at the same time.

These changing, fluctuating sound values—depending always on what "key" was in use—were for the sounds of the twelve musical tones which when expressed one after the other—that is, chromatically—are evenly spaced and identical in value. Schönberg was beginning to compose as though they were identical in value when not evenly spaced and regardless of the "key." In his words, he was "freeing the dissonance." The existing harmonic system said any given tone was necessarily consonant or dissonant. He said it was neither—it was just a tone and could be freely used in composition with any other or all other tones.

All this was not worked out in a day, understand. Nor was the whole of it issued at the same time. It evolved over a period of nine years, from 1903 to 1912, in a series of pieces beginning with the symphonic poem, **Pelleas and Melisande** which requires a gigantic orchestra, and culminating in settings for a string of poems, **Pierrot Lunaire**, which require only a reciting voice and five instruments. The diminution of required force is significant. Schönberg discovered he didn't need a club. By the time he finally finished the fabulous orchestration of **Gurre-Lieder** toward the end of this period, with its demand for more than four hundred players and singers, mere mass was obsolete for him.

Of all possible publics for this step-by-step revolutionary departure from the traditional, the Viennese public was the least likely to have any sympathy. Mozart, Haydn, Beethoven, and Schubert were Viennese in one degree or another and the result has been that Vienna has more musical hardheads and more musical snobs than any other place in the world. As the revolution unfolded step by step, Schönberg became a public enemy step by step.

He was subjected to such personal abuse in print and in speech as no other composer has ever had. In passing through the streets he was laughed at and hooted. There were times when he was in some danger of assault. Cliques formed to break up his concerts and prevent his music even being heard.

His accumulated notoriety was comparable only to that of a carousing, many-times-married actor. The result was that very soon no one could listen to his music with a receptive mind or even an open mind. Remnants of that still hang on. But Schönberg took it with calm good grace, then and afterward. His reactions were defensive rather than emotional. One was to form a Society for the Private Performance of Music. Only members could attend meetings. Members were pledged not to mention what they heard and neither to applaud nor to hiss. Critics were not eligible.

He was surrounded then and ever after by his pupils. We must always keep in mind he was an exceedingly gifted teacher and a teacher who enjoyed being one. He and his pupils systematized these evolved compository techniques into a formal method—the "twelve-tone method," which has rules and laws just like the traditional system. Two of his pupils now are considered to have been on the genius level—Alban Berg (1885-1935), composer of the opera **Wozzeck**, which will be very popular when the public learns to understand people as well as its music understands them, and Anton von Webern (1883-1944). The number of present-day composers who use the twelve-tone system with and without modifications is incalculable.

Schönberg never doubted "the music of the future" would be composed with his system and that, in time, his own compositions would come into great popularity. He said he always had "at least one third of the public" with him. He always had almost all, if not all, the musicians. Those who didn't like the results had to respect the sound logic of the method. At the height of the big ruckus, a foreign musician arriving in Vienna at once sought him out in order to have a look at "Satan." He found "Satan" and his pupils engrossed in an extremely pedantic performance of a Mozart quartet, something which any musician would love.

In 1923, when he was forty-nine, his good musical friend and devoted wife, Mathilde, died. By then their son and daughter were almost grown. Some years later he married a good musical friend, Gertrude Kolisch, a sister of one of his students, Rudolph Kolisch, who has become well known as a violinist, particularly as a quartet player. And in 1925 he was called to the professorship of music of the Prussian Academy of Fine Arts in Berlin, the highest position open for an academic musician in the German-speaking world.

He had ten peaceful and productive years there, until the Nazis, having come to power, dismissed him because he was a Jew. Schönberg had all but lost sight of that. He had long since given up religious observances, while philosophically concerned with religious thought. He was fond of likening the musical experience to the religious experience. Some people had come to think of him as a Christian and certainly he had become attached to Christian ideals, as can be heard in his *a cappella* chorus **Peace on Earth—Friede auf Erden**.

The Nazis recalled him to his origins. He went at once to Paris, formally re-embraced the Jewish faith and later composed a Kol Nidre. That year, 1933, he came to the United States, taught in Boston for a while, was professor of music at the University of Southern California for one year, then took the professorship of the University of California in Los Angeles where he lived the rest of his life in a white-stucco house, became an American citizen, played tennis with enthusiasm until he was seventy, and gloried in the growing up of the three children of his second marriage and all the young musical people who surrounded him on the campus and even in his home. So much the teacher, he was happy to give music appreciation courses in the public library.

When seventy, in 1944, he became professor emeritus but had his circle of pupils at home. He had also a huge correspondence with musicians everywhere, wrote extensively on music, and liked nothing better than to recall that when such a piece as, say, **Pelleas and Melisande** was performed first there had been a riot, but now people listened to it quite calmly. Once he attended a concert and heard an audience enthusiastically applaud a composition of his. "Heavens!" he exclaimed. "Am I now a popular composer?"

But he discouraged rather than encouraged performances of his own works, especially those of the last third of his active career. He felt the public wasn't ready for them; he thought it would be fifty years before it would be. Serene, philosophical, and most superior, he lived out his years and died in his stucco house July 14, 1951, in his seventy-sixth year.

In his fifty years of composing, his opus numbers totaled only 47. His works divide readily into three periods: The first was the springboard period before the revolution and the masterwork there is **Verklärte Nacht**. The second was the formative period of the twelve-tone system and **Pelleas and Melisande** and the **Chamber Symphony** are representative. The third represents the final perfection of the system, and typical works are the **Concerto for Violin and Orchestra** and **Variations on a Recitative** for organ.

But the best way to know Schönberg through his revolutionary period and afterward is in his four string quartets. The first dates from 1904, the second, 1907, the third, 1926, and the fourth, 1937. As a last word: anyone who comes to Schönberg's music expecting to be horrified or bored or mystified will be. Anyone coming to it with the ability to listen without prejudice and without fear is likely to be profoundly touched and moved. This man is a master. It may be a generation or two before that fact is recognized generally.

42

Ravel

Maurice Ravel always said he was lucky to be able to compose music. Otherwise, he wouldn't have been able to do anything. No modest self-condemnation, this—only truth. Reality seemed to bother him, since he avoided it as much as he could. To an amazing degree, he even evaded the reality of growing up.

As an adult, he resembled an impish schoolboy, entirely dependent on parents. During his last years, he still collected and played with toys. For companionship, he liked small children. Through all his sixty-two years he was almost as innocent as a child—innocent, even, of the relationships that are normal and usual among adults. Aside from his mother, whom he loved with intense devotion, he never loved a woman. Nor were there any deep, intimate friendships in his life.

Nature had helped the illusion of childishness by not letting him grow into quite adult stature; he was hardly five feet tall and frail. But most of the illusion was of his own making. It is said he worked just as hard creating Maurice Ravel as he did creating music. Because he was a creative genius, Maurice Ravel the man was a work of art.

The man preened himself endlessly, like the vainest of birds. He seemed to cultivate irresponsibility as a monk cultivates virtue. No one ever saw him at work. Composing—his one useful endeavor—he took pains to hide. Musically, of course, he was a daring innovator, an original technician, and a master with much to say.

He was born in Ciboure on the Bay of Biscay in the French Basque country, March 7, 1875. His father, Joseph, was a brilliant but erratic engineer, who created a self-propelled vehicle decades before the first practical automobile. His mother, Marie, had the gift of youth and still looked like a child when deep in adult years. (A gossip once told Maurice her true age and it all but broke his heart.)

He was taken to Paris when he was an infant; and there he grew up, in the narrow, steep streets of Montmartre, which teemed with vivid and often with raw life. In Paris he spent most of his years; he was middle-class French and Parisian. But in the dreamland in which he lived he was a Basque and a grandee, inhabiting Spanish castles and reigning over romantic Basque ports.

When he was seven, his father got him a piano teacher because he thought children should learn some music. Tiny Maurice, who had fetching bangs and a pretty girlish face, wasn't much interested. When he was twelve, he acquired a master in harmony, and then his interest picked up. Two years later he was admitted to the Conservatoire, and there he stayed for the astonishing span of sixteen years.

His parents, who were far from wealthy, pampered him. From his early twenties on, he had had more than enough musical schooling (particularly for one of his genius) to have supported himself. But he took parental support as a matter of course and spent the limited family funds lavishly for fabulous arrays of haberdashery. He insisted on being sartorially unique; his highest aspiration was to set fashions.

This obsession persisted all his life. He would spend weeks making up his mind about materials for new suits and shirts; he carried swatches and collected the opinions of his friends. He was rarely on time for anything; to be two and even three hours late was routine. His excuse, if he offered one, was that he hadn't been able to make up his mind what to wear. He was in love with himself—like Narcissus staring into the mirroring pool, enchanted by his own form.

Meanwhile, he was working away at music—in strict privacy. His piano teacher at the Conservatoire lamented that instead of being last in class he could have been first. Yet at the age of twenty he produced his first mature compositions: **Menuet antique** and **Habanera.** Four years later came **Pavane for a Dead Princess (Pavane pour une Infante défunte).** As a creative musical genius, he was fully mature at an age that is unusual in the annals of the musical art.

The year was 1899; there was a widely accepted superstition that the artist, particularly the genius, was a mysterious, aloof, disappointed, and super-romantic creature, misunderstood by a crass world and understood only by the few who made up the artistic élite. It was the age of Jules Zarembsky who, if he hadn't died at thirty-one, might have become a pianist rivaling even Liszt. While in the final throes of tuberculosis, Zarembsky had his attendants dress him in white silk shirt and black velvet jacket and carry him to a piano. There he played Chopin's **Funeral March** and died.

This was the model for a romantic fashion, and Ravel followed it wholeheartedly. He adorned his babyish face with an elegant beard, affected a monocle. Every inch a dandy, he strutted through the

salons of wealthy Parisians, who found prestige in patronizing artists
and the arts.

Suddenly, at twenty-six, he decided he wanted the Prix de Rome.
Perhaps he wanted to cut a bigger figure; perhaps he needed a reason
for extending his stay at the Conservatoire even longer; perhaps he
was under pressure to become self-supporting. Whatever the reason,
he tried for the prize in 1901 and failed, although he did place
second.

He tried again in 1902 and 1903, and failed both times. It seemed
as though he wanted to be misunderstood by the judges and to be
disappointed in their lack of appreciation. For example, the candidates
for the prize were required to compose a cantata on a religious poem.
Ravel flippantly composed his in waltz time, with mocking accents.

In 1905, he wanted to try a fourth time but wasn't permitted. The
rules said contestants had to be under thirty. Nevertheless, there was
a great outcry from the artistic salons, the Montmartre studios, and
the press led by a few music critics. Ravel pointed out that Charles
Lenepveu, one of the judges, had six of his own pupils entered.

As a result of all this uproar Lenepveu was compelled to resign
from the Conservatoire faculty; so was Théodore Dubois, the director.
Ravel gloried in the publicity. It had spread his fame as a composer
and as a misunderstood genius. Had he won the prize, it wouldn't
have gone nearly so far in "making" him.

With the hindsight of posterity, it is easily seen Ravel should have
had the Prix de Rome any time he wanted it. During the year of his
first failure, he composed **The Fountain (Jeux d'eau)**, which has to be
ranked high among modern piano compositions. The years of his
second and third failures produced his only string quartet, which
remains a staple of the repertoire, and the still-pleasing song cycle,
Shéhérazade. In the year he wasn't allowed to compete, he composed
his **Sonatine** and **Miroirs** for the piano, and began the septet **Introduction and Allegro.**

Now he was a composer greatly in demand, and the appeal of his
music made the demand greater as the years passed. A music publisher
signed him to a life contract for his total output, guaranteeing him a
fixed annual income. Thus he at last became self-supporting but kept
right on living with his parents, their indulged darling.

It is curious how his detractors divided. One set said he insulted
the heart and soul of the musical art with his "coarse" and "ugly"
innovations. Another set said he was a mere imitator of Debussy,
who was thirteen years older and, by now, accepted and greatly
admired. For a while the first performance of a new Ravel composition was good for a riot in the hall, between detractors and idolaters.

This happened to **Histoires Naturelles** and **Valses nobles et senti-mentales.**

But no one can hold out against genius very long. Jean Marnold, the musicologist, was influential in putting an end to the silly opposition. When asked by a newspaper to express himself on whether or not Ravel was just a Debussy imitator, he wrote that Ravel was the artistic heir of Debussy, in the same way that Mozart followed Gluck, Beethoven followed Mozart—each inheriting from a predecessor, yet each as individual as could be.

"One does not choose one's year of birth," he said. "If the word genius has meaning, then Maurice Ravel surely is a genius." He thanked his questioner for the chance to say this "in this spring of 1907, for the record. It is very pleasing, later, to be able to show with documentation that one was not an imbecile."

All this was Ravel's public life. Beyond providing compositions, he took only a nominal part in it. He liked to listen to fiery young poets and musicians debate the whys and wherefores of art, but he didn't say much. He liked to be seen in high society but contributed much more in mannerisms and fancy haberdashery than in substance.

He was fond of visiting the homes of friends who had children and always brought toys, which he enjoyed fully as much as the children did. The stories are many of Ravel down on his knees with six- and seven-year-olds, who treated him as one of them. To some parents, his visits were ordeals. The riotous romping went on for hours and hours.

Once Ravel's publisher happened in while he was teaching two little friends to play a piece he had written. It was so good the publisher demanded more like it. These pieces became Ravel's beloved **Mother Goose (Ma Mère l'Oye).** Strangely enough, he was working at the same time on **Gaspard de la Nuit,** a three-piece piano suite, complex in its maturity, strange in its moods, and unforgettable—particularly the weird **Le Gibet,** which depicts the criminal hanging in chains. This same year, 1908, his father died and his grief was intense.

When World War I began, Ravel was thirty-nine. Keep in mind that his country was in imminent peril, a fact clearly perceived by Frenchmen. But Ravel was curious about war; he thought it would be an adventure. After several months, he presented himself to the army recruiters, was rejected because he was underweight and undersized. He tried again and again and, at forty-one, was accepted—as a truck driver.

Under stern military discipline and the sterner necessity of playing an adult part in an adult world, he became ill in a rather short time, spent weeks in a hospital, and was returned to Paris to recover. At this point, his 76-year-old mother died.

From that day began the decline of Maurice Ravel the musical genius. No catastrophe could have shaken him more. His mother had had a long and pleasant life. But it was his contention that he had killed her by having gone into the army. Although France now was in even greater peril, he was eager to get out of service and was discharged in the spring of 1917.

Eventually he got over the palpitations and similar symptoms of nervous distress, except one—he couldn't sleep unless he was drugged or exhausted. He found it impossible even to cross the threshold of the home he had shared with his mother. For several years he lived in hotels, then bought a little house—a "toy house," his friends said—in Monfort l'Amaury, a hamlet some forty miles from Paris. He filled it with toys and little ornaments, surrounded it with miniature gardens. He liked to entertain friends there weekends, preparing odd food and drink for them with his own hands. And yet, not one of his guests—nor anyone else—really knew him deeply and intimately.

Nevertheless, he disliked being alone. Weekdays he usually spent in Paris. At night he haunted night clubs or walked the streets. To those who did not know his childlike innocence—and these included postwar American tourists and expatriates—he seemed a man of the world par excellence, the most sophisticated of the Parisian sophisticates. He had long since given up his beard. His sad face was pallid, his eyes haunted.

He was gentle, reserved, friendly. But there was a certain spitefulness in him, too. In 1920 he paid back France for having refused him the Prix de Rome by refusing to accept the Legion of Honor. This stirred a scandal, and he was forced to say he didn't feel he needed decorations. Later he admitted that pride had dictated the refusal. In 1926 he accepted the Knight's Cross of the Order of King Leopold of Belgium. A few years later he was happy to go to England to accept an honorary doctorate in music from Oxford.

His fame required more and more tours as a conductor and as a pianist, although he was no great shakes at either and knew it. He toured the United States from coast to coast in 1928, received adulation graciously. His most intense pleasure was in meeting George Gershwin and hearing Gershwin play Gershwin. He returned to France with a small fortune and many crates of household gadgets.

Now and then he produced a new work; but as the years passed the intervals became longer and longer. Le Tombeau de Couperin, his last work for piano solo—and the piano was his particular field of genius—belongs to 1917, the year his mother died. But it was well under way while she was still alive.

His best-known piece, **Boléro,** was composed in 1928 for ballet. Ravel called it "seventeen minutes of orchestra without music." It is one of the best examples of how to delay a crescendo in the literature.

In 1933 he showed the first symptoms of a brain tumor. Little by little, he sank into a stupor. He himself said, "I am going away piece by piece." At last there was an operation; and he died seventeen days later—in Paris, on December 28, 1937.

Ravel's estimation of himself was: "I have failed in my life. I am not one of the great composers. All the great have produced enormously . . . but I have written relatively little, and I did it with much difficulty. . . . I have torn all of it out of me by pieces."

43

Bartók

A LEADING candidate for the distinction of having been the greatest composer of the twentieth century was a small, frosty-eyed Hungarian, Béla Bartók. Of course, this question will not be decided by us who live in the twentieth century. Nevertheless, there is good reason for thinking Bartók may be posterity's choice.

The reason is the astonishing growing power of his music. On first hearing it is likely to sound unattractively strange, even repellent. With more hearings, you find it has somehow gotten into your very being. From the way his music sticks to you, it becomes clear he discovered very human materials and learned to manipulate them effectively.

When he died in 1945 he was little known to the big music public. Only a few performers and followers of the art fully realized the ultimate power of his music. Now, Bartók is more consistently performed than a number of masters whose immortality is proved. The fame of his music has spread quite on its own.

Its creator had neither stomach for nor skill in the art which is indispensable to twentieth-century endeavors, that being the art of self-promotion. Being shy and self-conscious, he lived behind a wall of reserve and gave the absolute minimum of his private self. Yet the inner fires burned fiercely, even though he permitted them to show only in his pride in being a Hungarian, in his scorn for hate-makers, and in his music.

He was musical almost from his first breath. But music was as important as bread in the family into which he was born in the obscure Hungarian (now Roumanian) village of Nagyszentmiklós, on March 25, 1881. His mother was an amateur pianist of superior ability. His father directed the government agricultural school, but music was both his pleasure and his obsession.

This babe was not yet two when he was demanding private piano recitals of his mother. While still in the cradle, he had listened to music with obvious interest. At three he accompanied his mother's piano accurately with a toy drum. At four he played from memory, with one finger dancing over the keyboard, the melodies of forty songs. At five his mother, Paula, gave him his first piano lessons.

Yet he was a sickly, backward child. He was slow in learning to walk and was over two before he could talk. His first years were plagued by a persistent skin eruption which tormented his mind and caused him to avoid other children. To climax these troubles, his father, whose musicianship with both piano and cello had made a tremendous impact, died when he was seven. All this influenced Bartók, although no one may say just how.

After his father's death, circumstances prevented his taking roots and closed him even more upon himself—and music. Paula also had a daughter, and so had two children to support and rear. A planner and regulator, she had the will for it. She became a teacher in the state school system, which meant a great deal of moving about among small towns. This meager income she filled out by giving private piano lessons. Béla was thirteen before she had a permanent post, in Pozsony, which now is in Czechoslovakia and called Bratislava. He was never in one place long enough to make firm friends or to become a part of anything. But he was developing a remarkable mentality as well as a remarkable musicality.

In school, after a poor start, he was getting nothing but A-pluses. Having first shunned other children out of fear of humiliation, he now shunned them for a sensible reason—they were too childish and too noisy. He collected insects and classified and studied them like a scientist. He was an incessant reader; words fascinated him, but more for their values as units of language then for their sounds and meanings.

As an adult, he playfully wrote a letter in seven languages to a friend. However, as a child, he was kept concentrated upon music by his mother. Why not? A musician, she could appreciate musical talent. When he was nine he composed his first piece quite spontaneously. She had to write it down because he couldn't, and she wrote down the subsequent pieces until he learned how. At ten he made his first public appearance as a pianist.

No one in small towns could teach him anything about music. He was a more accomplished musician than the adults around him. At eighteen, when he had finished the Hungarian equivalent of the American high school, Paula sent him to Budapest and the Royal Academy of Music, where, during the four-year course, he distinguished himself for a scholarly mastering of the art of piano playing and music in general rather than for an inspirational and intuitive mastering which so often is the hallmark of musical genius.

None thought he had either inspiration or intuition. No one thought him a genius, since he was so self-contained and so much a young man of mind rather than emotion. During his teens he had given up composing altogether. His scholastic involvements with compositional technicalities were accompanied by fits of illness. Circumstances were twisting and dovetailing in ways unknown to us. Rather suddenly he reacquired the ability to compose. At the same time he became healthy in body. And he was finding something to live by. "Resignation I am striving for," he wrote to a friend. "We must attain to a level from which everything can be viewed with sober calmness, with complete indifference."

When graduated, he was the author of several compositions decidedly superior to the better conservatory-student compositions, but they were heartless. He played the piano on the virtuoso level. So he made a number of tours and undertook the usual business of polishing apples for established musicians in the hope they'd reciprocate and further his career. For that, with his stiff spine, he was ludicrously without talent. Nor did he have any real drive to exhibit himself, as pianist or composer or anything else. When the opportunity came for a sheltered life, he seized it eagerly.

In 1907, when he was twenty-six, he succeeded his own teacher as professor of piano at the academy. That was his shelter for thirty years and would have been for life if the machinations of Hitler and Mussolini hadn't interfered. Then and always he refused to teach composition. He said he was afraid teaching might contaminate his own composing, which certainly was a good reason. But his own composing was tentative and groping still. You may call it "experimental," if you wish; or you may take it as a demonstration that he was most unsure of himself.

What he felt about himself was part of what he called his "private life" and even the slightest notice of his private life made him furious. For instance, there was his love for Márta Ziegler, who was fourteen when she became a member of his first piano class at the academy. A year later he composed a little piano piece which he called **Portrait of a Girl** and which he enscribed "For Márta." Yet no one realized he was interested in her in a "serious way." He gave no indication—except, of course, to Márta.

As she progressed musically, she became a private pupil and so went to his home, where his mother was mistress, for her morning lessons. One day he told his mother that Márta would stay for lunch. Just before dinner, he emerged from his studio and announced Márta would stay for dinner. Mother must have shown surprise. At any rate, he added an explanation he evidently wouldn't have offered if it hadn't been required—he told mother he and Márta were married.

Mother knew better than to circulate the news. It got around slowly. Other students coming to the professor's home encountered Márta there and heard her refer to their teacher as "my husband." Bartók came to realize people were talking about his marriage—well-wishing, felicitating talk. Yet he was irked. One friend who dared to write him a letter of congratulation was all but bowled over by his fury, and was given no choice but to apologize for an affront.

Their only child, Béla, was born a year later. Through the wall of reserve which concealed his "private life" there seeped only indications of marital closeness. So the intimates of his other life as teacher, pianist, composer, and musicologist were entirely unprepared for what happened fourteen years after he married Márta. He asked her to divorce him. It was a "sacrifice" he asked of her, he knew, but there was a "human reason" which he considered a "commandment." That reason was Ditta Pásztory, a girl in her middle teens and a member of his piano class at the academy.

Márta took it with good grace. We may assume she found it hard to understand because we know his mother and his sister did. He and Ditta were married in 1923, when he was forty-two and she was seventeen. Their only child, Peter, was born a year later. She was his wife for twenty-two years, until his death. Under his tutelage she developed into a first-class pianist and musician.

When he married her he had already acquired an international reputation in music, but as a scholar rather than as a performer or composer. In early manhood he had discovered a little-known musical language in ancient music of the Hungarian peasants. Franz Liszt, that other Hungarian composer, had given the world its idea of native Hungarian music in the **Hungarian Rhapsodies** and other such pieces. All that was gypsy music, actually. Bartók dug out and gave to the world the genuine article.

No scientist ever pursued and captured insects (or other items of fauna or flora) more enthusiastically, more tirelessly, or more single-mindedly than Bartók ran down hundreds upon hundreds of songs and dances of unknown origin which had been transmitted through the generations by example and imitation, but which were dying out because the peasants were getting their music and musical ideas from the modern world. And no scholar ever dissected the grammar and vocabulary of an obscure language with more scrupulous care than Bartók analyzed the specimens he collected.

For years he spent his summers and other holidays in the remote regions of the eastern European countryside, first in Hungary, but later in Roumania and European Turkey, lugging recording equipment and persuading bashful peasants to sing and play the music their parents had taught. He learned their dialects and, as much as it was possible for a sophisticated Magyar of the educated upper classes, became one of them.

His love for this adventuring life was intense, as though he felt himself free to let himself go among simple people. Whatever were its values in his "private life," he was acquiring mastery over timbres and rhythms and harmonies of barbaric force, with spine-shivering colorations of primitive appeal. This peasant music was as close to basic humanity as the peasants were. However crude and rough, it made much "art music" seem limp and bloodless.

Having the command of this language, Bartók began using it in his own compositions, not imitatively, but originally, to express his own inner feelings. That is why the music upon which his great and rising reputation as a composer is based is likely to repel on first hearing—its grammar is more than strange; it is utterly foreign to ears trained to the refinement and general niceness of the main musical language. But that is also why it sticks. The language grew and developed out of human emotions in order to meet human needs.

This Bartók music was making its way, though slowly, during the thirties. In the years immediately before the outbreak of World War II, he was in growing demand in Europe as pianist and conductor for his own works. The Hitler cataclysm was spreading over Eastern Europe. How Bartók hated all that nazism and fascism stood for! Its exponents were "bandits" and "murderers" to him, and he said so. He would have gone into exile if his mother had been able to go. She died in the autumn of 1939, after the war started. In the spring of 1940 Bartók came to the United States for professional appearances. He returned to Hungary only to close out his affairs, and was back in the fall, a refugee.

America treated him kindly but not well. Columbia University conferred an honorary degree and a one-year $3,000 music research grant. Musicians honored him and arranged concerts for him and his wife, but the public wasn't very interested and the returns were meager. Anyway, his health was failing slowly. As his life ebbed, the life of his music blossomed. In the fall of 1944 he received a tremendous ovation in New York after a program of his works. A week or so later he was given another one in Boston. Less than a year later, on September 26, 1945, he died in New York.

As examples of the music which may make Bartók the greatest composer of the century, the following are cited: **Concerto for Orchestra;** **Music for Strings, Percussion and Celesta;** any one of the last five of his string quartets; **Concerto for Violin and Orchestra,** the **Third Piano Concerto;** and **Mikrokosmos,** which is a collection of muchly variegated and absorbing pieces for the piano.

44

Stravinsky

THE unanswered big question of modern music has to do with what happened inside Igor Stravinsky in 1913. That was the year of his masterpiece, **The Rite of Spring (Le Sacre du Printemps)**, which is no less emotionally overwhelming to a listener in its highly original way than Beethoven's Ninth Symphony (or any other towering masterpiece).

The Rite's way is a savage way. Brutes stomp the earth to awaken and then to appease their animalistic gods and, in climax, a maiden is chosen for sacrifice and required to dance herself to death. That is a shocking idea to civilized people. Yet the music has the force and persuasion with which to imprint it upon their emotions and to evoke dim memories of the remotest beginnings of the race.

This wasn't the young Stravinsky's first creative use of such material, although it was the last. The Rite was the culmination of a sustained striving. First, there had been **The Fire Bird (L'Oiseau de Feu)** with one burning episode of ferocity. Then came **Petrouchka**, in which emotions are raw and brutal but are made palatable by a guise of puppetry. These made the musical world keenly aware of Stravinsky, of his genius, and of his direction.

Even so, it was unprepared for The Rite that May night in 1913 in Paris when it was first played and danced. The effect was a riot in the theater. Men and women shrieked and screamed. Strangers mauled strangers. The French called it a *scandale*. The composer whose music had set off this chaos watched from the wings for a while, greatly agitated, and then fled by way of an open window.

He fell ill, with high fever. For several weeks there was some doubt he would recover. This illness was diagnosed as typhoid. Nevertheless, it is relevant to remember that he is and always has been a person preoccupied with the ills of the flesh. Whether the illness and the *scandal* of The Rite were coincidental or had a deep, hidden connection, something profound happened inside Igor Stravinsky.

From that time on he was in full retreat from The Rite and its predecessors. There was never again a suggestion of savagery or any other fierce emotion in his music. He devoted himself with grim single-mindedness to keeping emotion of any sort out of his music, to keeping everything out which was not, by his rigorous definitions, strictly musical. Creatively, he has lived all this time in self-imposed shackles—and maintained the paradox that the more he restrained himself the greater was his freedom.

Upon absorbing the shock of The Rite in 1913, the music world came under the spell of its force and originality. Musical people proclaimed him "the greatest composer of the twentieth century." They anticipated an evergrowing body of works comparable in power although not necessarily in nature to The Rite. However, the music world was disappointed in Stravinsky and he in turn was disappointed in the majority of the performers and followers of music. To himself, the rightness of his course—the rightness of anything he does—is a matter of dogma and so beyond any questioning. From his viewpoint, he would be justified in impatience and bitterness. But he allows himself no bitterness. That would be emotional.

Music for its own sake is his dogma. He reasons that music which appeals to the emotions and to the senses is music which no longer is pure. There we have another of the many Stravinskian paradoxes—because music depends entirely upon the sense of hearing, it is a sensuous art. In essence, his ideas are that music should be all mind and whatever heart there is in it should be under the most rigid "subjugation," and music appreciation should be an act of the intellect only.

Now deep in his seventies and living in Hollywood, he has the serenity of a zealot who is beyond even the temptation of making concessions. He admits to being saddened that he no longer has "communion" with the large public, since he feels any creative artist needs such communion. Yet he has his unalterable principles, and one is, in his words: "The artist who consciously aims at success with the masses succeeds only in lowering his own level."

He is now an American citizen. For a while he was a French citizen. He was born a Russian, in Oranienbaum on the Gulf of Finland, where his parents had a summer home, on June 17, 1882. His father was a leading bass singer in the St. Petersburg Imperial Opera; his mother was a learned musical amateur. It was an upper-class, moneyed, large and very busy family, and there's wasn't a great deal of time for detailed attention to one child. Everything was eminently correct, of course; everything was provided, including a piano teacher when the boy was nine.

From this somewhat cold childhood he emerged as a cold adult,

self-disciplined in correctness, especially the correctness of containing
his emotions tightly within his being. He was in the St. Petersburg
University studying law before he showed any real interest in music
and in getting himself muscally educated. He made a friend of one
of the children of Nicholas Rimsky-Korsakoff and by that avenue
became a private pupil of that master. He had had previous instruction in harmony, but he was largely self-taught, the reason being his
marked distaste for the conventional—in music.

Not in living, mind. In living, his taste was for the conventional.
Whereas he was correct in living, he began almost at once to be in-
correct in composing music—that is, he did more than just defy the
"rules"; he composed as though the rules had never existed. Characteristic Stravinskian harmonies began appearing very early. He shocked
ears trained in nineteenth-century romanticism with dissonances which
sounded weird to those ears, with rhythms which sounded weirder.
In short, he was acting the way geniuses act—inventing "rules" as
he went along. That is most interesting because a latter-day Stravinsky
was going to hold, as "dogma," that music has immutable laws.

His fame began with the performance of his ballet score, **The Fire
Bird**, by the Ballet Russe in Paris in 1910, when he was twenty-eight
years old. Save for a single section, **Dance of Kateschei**, which con-
veys in Stravinsky's original musical language, emotions of sheer
savagery, its basic content is Rimsky-Korsakoff conventionalities in
Stravinskian dress. It was followed a year later by another ballet score
for the Ballet Russe, **Petrouchka**, which has, among many violations
of the "rules," counterpoint in two unrelated keys—in 1911 just about
the ultimate in musical revolution.

For the purpose of conveying a brutal story, acted out by dancers,
which reflects no credit whatever on human emotions and sensibilities, this musical language was—and remains—extremely effective.
With **Petrouchka** there could remain no question that a mighty
genius was rising to his creative zenith. **The Rite of Spring** confirmed
this general feeling abundantly, and Stravinsky became the idolized
mentor who could do no wrong for hosts of budding composers and
musicians and musical people the world over. That idolatry has been
a long time in dying. Indeed, remnants of it still hang on.

What happened inside Stravinsky after The Rite no one knows.
We can't know the cause; we can only see the effect and puzzle over
it. First, there was a period of experimentation with rhythms and
timbres with small instrumental ensembles, sometimes with voices
added but voices treated as instruments. **A Soldier's Tale (L'Histoire
du Soldat)** is the outstanding example.

Then came a period of clothing the melodic substances of other composers in Stravinskian harmonies and timbres: **Pulcinella**, which uses the substances of Pergolesi; **The Fairy's Kiss** (**Le Baiser de la Fée**), "inspired by the muse of Tchaikovsky," and **Oedipus Rex**, in which Handelian materials are most evident, for instance. After that there was a striving for the pure abstractions which Bach achieved, and here you think of the **Symphony of Psalms** and the **Dumbarton Oaks Concerto**. Finally, there is his last major work, the opera **The Rake's Progress**, and here the reminders of Mozart are numerous.

All these works have the air of experimentation, as though the composer were groping—searching for something which had been lost. There is hardly one without its fleeting moments of brilliant effectiveness, to remind you that this man may be "the greatest composer of the twentieth century," even though the judgment has to be based upon what he composed during the century's first thirteen years. But there isn't one which doesn't deaden the senses with its small resources expressed by small means. Repetition begets only monotony.

The once-flourishing Stravinskian school of composers has just about disintegrated. Imitative composers have taken up fresher ideas and more glittering mentors. Although he is only too aware of having lost many of his followers and much of his audience, he is resolute about it. His assumption always is that his critics want him to return to The Rite, and in that, he says, his critics are "blind" because "they are not even aware that they are inviting me to go backward. Let it be well understood. What they want is obsolete for me, and to follow them would be to do violence to myself."

Having practiced calisthenics all his life, he is well muscled although small—his height being five feet four inches. Fears of illness, even of death, have haunted him always; yet he is healthy in his old age, which he fills with work. His mind has been phenomenally developed, too—no major composer has been more adept at explaining and justifying himself musically and artistically, with technical illustrations so involved they baffle technicians and a faith in himself which has fantastic intensity.

He is a formidable man in an argument, taking his ammunition from learning in four languages, Russian, French, German, and English. In a discussion, it is understanding he seems to seek, understanding which is thorough and complete to the tiniest detail, but with emotional content and coloring eliminated. That doesn't interest him.

In an argument, he seems barely able to endure the opposition, despite his rigid self-control. He speaks dogmatically out of his certainty of his own rightness, and it is an impertinence, the way he looks at it, when he is challenged. In little things like this, he shows he has an emotional life which otherwise has to be assumed on the grounds that everyone has one, and he must also. It is remarkable how well he has always concealed it behind an extreme orderliness and neatness in everything he does, from being a husband and the father of three living children to fulfilling schedules of personal appearances and composing just as a railroad train runs—on a timetable.

His first wife was his cousin, Nadejda Soulima, meek, self-effacing, and always frail, whom he married before he left Russia for the last time, in 1914. She was his constant companion and protector from disturbances and annoyances; he was devoted to her. Yet the warmest thing he ever said about her to outsiders was that she was his "oldest friend." As cousins, they had been acquainted since the age of two. They became parents of four children.

She died in Paris in 1938. Within one year their daughter and his aged mother (who had come out of Soviet Russia to live with him only a couple of years before) also died. Those were blows to him— no one can doubt it even a little bit. But his comment was characteristic of his self-control—after **The Rite of Spring**. "There were three coffins in my apartment that year," he said. "It became quite impossible for me."

Then there is his attitude toward country. When attacked by Communist Russia as a "renegade," he replied briefly and tartly that he was an "émigré from Czarist Russia." He seldom showed any strong interest in Russian events after his departure from home, one way or the other, and in time became a French citizen. For a couple of decades he was so much a part of the Parisian scene, so closely involved in French artistic endeavors, that it came as a shock to many of the French when he became an American citizen in 1945.

He had been coming to this country periodically for some years, to conduct his own work and make personal appearances. He left France for good at the start of World War II. In 1940, while giving a series of lectures at Harvard, he married Vera de Bossett Sudeikine, widow of a Russian painter, and it is she who is the major-domo of his Hollywood home, seeing to it that he is not interrupted while he is at work, that his food and drink are prepared in strict accordance with his very exacting tastes, that the people he likes or might like are admitted and the people he might not like are excluded.

His observances of the rituals and dogma of the Greek Orthodox Church are no less strict than his observances of what he considers the dogma of music. He is a deeply religious man, involved in a mysticism so much a part of his being that he cannot put it into words. In this connection, his comment on his **Mass** is, perhaps, significant. He wanted this music to "appeal directly to the spirit." For that reason, "I sought very cold music, absolutely cold. No women's voices could be used. They are by their very nature warm. They appeal to the senses."

45

Gershwin

IN addition to Stephen Foster, another composer touches the hearts of more Americans more deeply and frequently than Beethoven or Mozart or any other of the supreme masters. He was George Gershwin and he was neither a master (in the sense of exercising mastery) nor typically American—nor typical of anything other than his own unique self.

Amazing, unexplained phenomena are everywhere among human beings but none is more amazing than a Foster or a Gershwin somehow using music, in ways not at all clear even to himself, as a key to emotions common to masses of people entirely unlike him, and without its making any difference whether these people are musically inclined or not musical at all.

Gershwin was a child of the sidewalks of New York, having been born in a poor, crowded neighborhood of Brooklyn on September 26, 1898, and having his boyhood in at least twenty-five other poor, crwded neighborhoods, mainly in Manhattan's Lower East Side. His parents were Russian Jewish immigrants, Morris and Rose, who were unmusical and uncultivated. George was the second of their four children.

Whatever there was of disadvantage in all this, there was decided advantage within a family of unbreakable unity. The family was governed by love, uncritical sympathy, instant understanding, loyalty approaching fanaticism, and also by an affectionate mother of much strength of mind and character. Yet all was not serene within this family—it was continually beset with changes and uncertainties rising from the restless unease of Father Gershwin.

He obsessively believed there is safety and security in money, and so it was up to him as a family head to make a lot of it. This goal he pursued in quixotic ways with little success. He was forever selling a small business and buying another with the optimistic hope he would do better with it, such as a bakery or a Turkish bath or a poolroom or a cigar store. A new business meant for the family a new tenement flat in the new neighborhood.

For the children this meant a constant jumping from one teeming caldron of polyglot humanity into another. These neighborhoods were the "melting pots" of immigrants from which have emerged incalculable multitudes of Americans, some exceedingly fine, some extremely bad, but mostly solid and respectable citizens. In no way beyond that of geography were they representative of American life as a whole. And certainly there was nothing quiet, relaxed, or easy about life for the children who lived in them.

Each had to handle life's unceasing turmoils in his own way. The eldest of the Gershwin children, Ira, began early to develop the superior mentality which observes and appraises turmoils more than it participates in them. He, too, was destined for fame and fortune. But George was no bookish youth, no student in school or in life. He flung himself into turmoils, played the street games with overwhelming intensity, and when the fists began flying, he was right in there, bloodying noses and getting his own bloodied. There is no reason to think he had any real taste for this. He was concerned that an impression might get around that he was a sissy.

So as small children the brilliant Gershwin brothers were in characteristic attitudes. Ira watched people and he watched over them, especially George and his other brother and sister, with affection and tolerance. George used life as a kind of mirror in which he kept an engrossed watch upon his own reflections. One could believe he was watching lest some blemish appeared which would offend him. He was fastidious about his self-image.

Only he knew when he was first attracted to music. He hid his interest because to him, at the time, music stood for sissiness. In the flat of one of his street pals was a piano. Very privately he explored its possibilities. Meanwhile, Ira had become curious about music. Always eager to encourage anything they considered elevating, Mama and Papa got a piano.

Imagine their astonishment when Georgie, twelve years old, sat right down and played a tune on that upright. What had happened within the lad, we can never know. Quite suddenly he no longer concealed. Now he wanted to display his passion for music, and from then on and for as long as he lived he was an incessant, even a blatant displayer of himself. He was enraptured by music, especially music of his own devising.

Mama and Papa were delighted. Lessons were provided at once. Within four years he was a fluent piano player but not a pianist, nor was he ever going to be one in the full meaning of the word. He knew the keys and their chords. He had a sense of harmony. His fingers were agile and strong. He could translate printed music down through his fingers facilely, provided it wasn't too complicated. But his knowledge of the whole subject of music, which is large and complex, was slight.

You can't blame his teachers for that. One made very earnest efforts to lead him from musical shallows. Nor can you blame his having been a boy from a crowded neighborhood. One of his boyhood pals became a distinguished and learned musician. The choice was his, and he chose the superficial.

What he wanted to play on the piano were the la-de-da tunes which people sing or hum and listen to with pleasure for a week or so and then, having worn them to a frazzle with little usage, throw away. After learning to play them, he wanted to compose them. By now he was in the second year of high school and doing poorly because he was not interested. What he wanted to learn was not taught there. With his always strong sense of the practical, he knew where it could be learned.

Despite his parents' objections—they believed with all their hearts that "a man without education is nothing"—but with Mama's reluctantly given consent, he quit school and got a $15-a-week job as a piano thumper in Tin-Pan Alley. He worked for a publisher who operated a sort of factory which issued songs as other factories issue cans of vegetables. The idea was that a few of the many would become popular and keep business going with handsome profits.

But the publisher had to get his wares before the public. The only means then, before radio, was to get them performed by professionals wherever the public was likely to hear them. The boy's job was to sit in a cubicle all day, six days a week, displaying the wares by banging them out on an upright for the benefit of the shoppers: these were song-and-dance men or songs-only and dances-only men (the publisher was as pleased to have an item tap-danced as to have it sung) and music-hall band leaders. That put him into the groove where he stayed for life—and most happily, too.

No objective observer, with musical and artistic standards in mind, would have given a dime for this child's chances of rising above his limitations. There he was in the midst of turmoil. His wits were sharp and quick. The observer would have known for sure that he was going to learn Tin-Pan Alley's rhythmic and melodic stereotypes. In show biz there is cheap glamour and pseudo fame for many, but genuine attainment only for those who know it when they see it. At sixteen there was nothing whatever to indicate Gershwin knew it, or would ever.

Two years later his first stereotype was published. He had learned so well, he was turning them out as easily as he put on a shirt. At first his songs were frankly imitative. But quite soon he was departing from the models—not very far and not very much, but enough to attract attention in a business so extremely competitive that the least mark of distinction is noticed at once. At twenty he wrote all the music for a Broadway revue, which was a flop. The next year he had another musical show, which was a success. The following year his first hit song, **Swanee**, swept the country and sold in the millions.

At twenty-two he had arrived—he was a successful composer of "popular" music. If he knew it couldn't and wouldn't endure, he didn't care. Money was pouring in—he was rich. And he was famous in the way a young man of poor education and experienced only in melting pots and a music factory understands the meaning and quality of fame. His first move was to take over the support of the whole family. He moved Mama and Papa and brothers and sister out of the Lower East Side into a neighborhood which then was affluent and fashionable.

Were it not that he was always an engrossed watcher of his own reflections this would be the end of his story because everything else would be a repetition. He liked his success and fame and bubbled with pleasure. Yet, evidently, the reflections were not altogether pleasing. We can surmise that deep within himself he suspected himself of being unreal, not genuine. At least there is a veering in his songs of that time, away from the blatant and trite, toward the sincere and manifestly true. It may be that Ira had something to do with it. Ira worshiped George. He thought him the embodiment of everything wonderful and Ira always was George's favorite mirror. Now Ira was commenting on life professionally, in lyrics for songs, in verses for magazines.

George began setting those lyrics to music and soon he was setting only Ira's. He couldn't have had a more helpful lyricist from the standpoint of his lasting reputation. Ira's strength was in directness, correctness, and ultimate simplicity as regards human feelings. He had made the fundamental discovery that for all the seeming differences among human beings, whether of New York's Lower East Side or of Cherryville, Kansas, or of the Tennessee Smokies, they have innumerable samenesses—and certain ideals, sentiments, and aspirations when correctly expressed get an emotional response from all.

Some of their first collaborations in this vein were recognized immediately as works of art by the musically discerning. In 1923, when George was only twenty-five, Eva Gauthier, one of the most musicianly singers of the day, included four of his songs in a program of songs by masters, old and new, who hadn't composed and never would compose a "popular" song. A few months before, a well-known concert pianist shocked the pedants by saying in public that in his opinion Gershwin was a "great" composer.

These musical high-hats were a mirror in which Gershwin hadn't before seen himself reflected. He reacted. Within a year he astonished the musical and the unmusical alike with one of the outstanding musical masterpieces of this century, **Rhapsody in Blue**. It was his first work for orchestra, his first work longer and more complex than a song. He couldn't orchestrate it himself. He didn't know how. It had faults which no master would have tolerated. Yet back there in 1924, when it was first performed, everyone knew it was a masterpiece.

No person who cherishes the art of music can argue about the creator of such a work as that, and Gershwin was admitted instantly to the ranks of serious composers. He was up to his ears in works for the musical comedy theater, grinding out at least one complete score a year, some years two. What the **Rhapsody** meant practically was that thereafter he carried a double load, "serious" music for the hoity-toity, "popular" music for the razzle-dazzle trade. Did he complain? He did not. He loved it.

He loved anything which involved George Gershwin and music in close embrace. By choice, most of his creating was done in the midst of turmoil, with lots of people around who would reflect George Gershwin back to himself. In his large apartment there was almost perpetual open house. Scattered through the rooms were people laughing, gossiping, joking—musical people and theatrical people and their hangers-on, hero-worshipers who hadn't met the host but wanted to, assorted Gershwin relatives, and, of course, Mama and Papa beaming with pride. In one room the composer was at work at the piano, the door open, people coming and going and saying, "How's it going, Georgie?" and finding out from him in no few words and with suitable keyboard examples.

For relaxation he went to large parties and sat at the piano throughout the evening playing tirelessly and endlessly the works of George Gershwin, surrounded by admirers (and sometimes a few hecklers) three and four deep. Practically any hostess who wanted one of the most famous of living composers for a party could have him. Occasionally some well-meaning intimate would tell him he ought to be more reticent about displaying his musical wares—people might think he was egotistical. "But if I don't play, I don't have a good time," he said.

As a matter of fact, he was not egotistical. There was no sense in him that he was without flaw. His nature was modest and sweet, his generosity unbounded. Like a child, he desired to please. One of his intimates said he was "blessed with the joy of playing the piano. George at the piano was George happy."

With him, music substituted for many emotions which, in practically all people, are not only essential but automatic. For instance, he never married, and the vast literature on Gershwin contains no suggestion that he was ever in love—except with his mother. When someone said, "When are you going to get married, Georgie?" he'd reply, "As soon as I find a girl as wonderful as my mother." He loved people—and women were people to him, as men were. But he expected more of women than he did of men. For instance, in the knee-length-skirts era of the twenties, he expected women to manage those skirts with unfailing correctness. Of men he was never critical.

Thus, he lived out his tumultuous span, dying at the height of his popularity, from a brain tumor, in Hollywood on July 11, 1937, not yet thirty-nine years old. In the eighteen years of his active career he composed scores of twenty-seven musical comedies and revues and four movie musicals and contributed songs to eighteen other musicals. In "serious" music, he turned out an opera **Porgy and Bess**, a **Second Rhapsody** in addition to **Rhapsody in Blue**, the **Piano Concerto in F**, an extended work for orchestra, **An American in Paris**, the **Cuban Overture**, and three **Preludes** for piano. Among the heaps of dross in his "popular" works are heart-warming little masterpieces—for instance, **The Man I Love, Do Do Do, Someone to Watch Over Me, Love Walked In,** and **Embraceable You.** The chances are good that some of these songs will live indefinitely.

Set in Linotype Electra
Format by Marguerite Swanton
Manufactured by The Haddon Craftsmen, Inc.
Published by HARPER & BROTHERS, New York